God Doesn't Come In My Office

Struggling With Bitterness When We Are Victims of Injustice

Alberto I. González Muñoz

God Doesn't Come In My Office
Copyright © 2012 by Alberto I. González Muñoz

All Rights Reserved. No part of this publication may be reproduced, stored in a retrieval system, or transmitted in any form by any means, electronic, mechanical, photocopy, recording, or otherwise, without the prior permission of the Publisher, except as provided for by USA copyright law.

Published by ABG Ministries
Frisco, Texas 75034
521cor@gmail.com

Cover Design: Ron Adair
ronadair.com

All Scripture quotations are from The Holy Bible, English Standard Version, copyright © 2001 by Crossway Bibles, a division of Good News Publishers. Used by permission. All rights reserved.

ISBN13: 978-1479195848

Dedication

To my wife, Miriam, the true heroine of this story. The happy ending is credited to God, but humanly speaking, it belongs to her.

To all who have been victims of injustice for any reason, I have walked that path; I know how it feels.

Acknowledgements

- My wife, Miriam, saved all the letters that I wrote her during my interment for all these years, which allowed me to reconstruct the story.

- Eduardo Díaz put into my hands valuable materials, including newspaper clippings from the time of this story.

- The following people offered valuable suggestions and assisted in revising the manuscript: Dr. Leoncio Veguilla, Luciano Márquez, Antonio Rodríguez, Magaly Francisco, Mapy Martínez, Teresita Díaz, Marta Hurtado, Violeta Gener, Frank Padrón Nodarse, and Dr. Caridad Morales.

- My Christian brothers Ernesto Ruano and Julio Bajuelo facilitated the journey that allowed me to write the final chapter.

- There are many others whose names it is impossible to recount, who read the articles published in *La Voz Bautista* and encouraged me, giving me the energy to complete this work. Many others insisted that I revise the Spanish, and later translate this book into English.

- I especially want to mention José A. Leyva Mestres, now deceased. He gave the book its most thorough revision, and detailed the original manuscript. He also put at my disposal his time, his knowledge, his library, and his deep experience as a historian.

Table of Contents

	Prologue	9
	Introduction	13
1	We are Now Social Scum	21
2	Christmas in Camagüey	37
3	Farewell to Hope	55
4	God's Unfathomable Ways	69
5	The Hour of Love	93
6	Unexpected Resources	117
7	Depression Arrives	135
8	If Faith Abandons Me	159
9	Peace Returns	177
10	I Also Was a Baptist	199
11	God Doesn't Come In My Office	227
12	In the Final Stretch	241
13	The Happy Ending	269
14	Thirty Years Later	279
	Epilogue - What Cannot Happen?	303
	Afterward 2010	313

Prologue

The story that you have in your hands has been long in the making.

These events took place more than forty years ago. The first sketches were written at that time as personal letters and documents. Thirty years later, they were published as articles in *La Voz Bautista* (*The Baptist Voice*) and eight years after that they were compiled and checked over for a very limited edition and publication. As the author, I personally donated these books to Christian institutions, churches and my relatives. They were neither promoted nor sold. Why was the distribution of this work so limited? I was greatly concerned that my message would be misunderstood in some way, or perceived to be an allegation. Although it openly speaks of past events and emotions, it is mainly the spiritual pilgrimage of a young Christian man. The story leads us through all of his feelings, doubts, contradictions, and hopes, while he struggles with a tumultuous and unjust situation, without hiding from us his crisis of faith.

Although the first edition was so restricted by the author, *God Doesn't Come In My Office* went beyond its limited frontiers. I frequently receive letters from people who have read a borrowed copy of the book. They tell me that they would like to own a copy to lend to others, and they demonstrate the spiritual benefit that they have received through reading the story. Seldom has a day passed without someone speaking to me about *God Doesn't Come In My Office* and the blessing that it has been for his life. I constantly hear from people who wish they could meet me because they have read the book. There are so many of them, and they have become to me both a great reward and a reason for daily gratitude to the Lord. Not only have Baptist pastors insisted on its publication, but so also have those from other denominations. For this reason, we decided to edit the original manuscript, which had been written in 1994 and 1995. We proofread, updated, extended, and checked all the material completely. We believe that it has been spiritually deepened, and that those who read the previous edition will appreciate the changes.

It would be a grievous error to view this book as an indictment or an imputation of ill intent. This was never my purpose, and I beseech those who read it to always bear in mind this warning as they move forward in the reading. If it is true that UMAP was dissolved because of its history of misapplied goals and regrettable events, it is also true that situations of injustice and oppression similar to the ones narrated here have occurred, and continue to occur, in many places in the world in even greater magnitude. Therefore, it would be absurd to use this work as some sort of accusation, when its purpose is actually pointed in exactly the opposite direction. As the truth of these stories comes to light, what becomes evident is that all of us have gained maturity.

The constant stories of disappearances, kidnappings, crimes, tortures, molestations, police abuse, discrimination, homophobia, xenophobia, arbitrary detentions, and cruel wars with all their consequences, violence, and human injustices are the daily bread in all the newscasts of the world. The most tragic thing is that almost no country escapes from them. Compared to the atrocities that fill our television screens, the events narrated in this book seem inconsequential. This does not justify them, but it reminds us that it is pointless to continue to condemn something that has been recognized as unjust, and has therefore been remedied.

However, from the ethical standpoint it is also foolish to deny or hide the events of history. To suggest that an honest discussion of distasteful historical events is out of bounds and even harmful is to ignore the reality of what occurred. Historical events can be seen from multiple perspectives and be interpreted in different ways. It is through this amalgam of multiple opinions generated by any event that we can open up towards the understanding of reality in an objective way. In this case, thousands of people endured an experience that deeply affected their lives and those of their families. How can they cheerfully acquiesce to an historical omission of these events?

The dismantling of the Military Units to Aid Production was a triumph of good judgment, and the official decision to do so implied not only that there had been instances of excessive use of force, but beyond that, the entire program was irredeemable. That determination in itself was an act of social justice and as such should be recognized historically. However, *God Doesn't Come In My Office* does not pretend to be a history book. I think that it rather fits the genre of testimonial.

It actually is a book about the way that the truths of Christianity are to be put into practice, how real historical experiences and events in the lives of people (many still live and can confirm the truth and accuracy of what is written here) call men to reflect on human mistakes, the sufferings that they produce and the Christian's possible attitudes when faced with unthinkable events in life. After all, it is our response to any personal or social event that can make the difference between the harm and benefit that such an event may bestow on us.

Havana City, September 1, 2010

Introduction

The woman, deeply upset with the lieutenant, who had refused to tell her the whereabouts of her son, told the lieutenant, "God will let me know about my son, I assure you!"

The officer, proudly and arrogantly answered her, "I don't know how! Because God doesn't come in my office...citizen!"

"What did you say?" inquired the woman, confused about what she had heard.

Then he straightened up even more, raised his voice and repeated emphatically: "God doesn't come in my office, citizen! So, I don't know how you will know where your son is."

What a huge mistake by the officer! Although he was not capable of realizing it, God did come into his office and was working in a way that he could hardly imagine.

It is true that sometimes we think that God is absent when adverse, unjust, or unhappy circumstances surprise us. Usually, one must travel a long path to realize at the end that He has always known everything. In November of 1965, the lives of many young Christians in Cuba were altered by the decisions of others, and it seemed that God was unaware of or uninvolved in the situation. The ensuing events gave a shocking and demolishing blow to my dreams and aspirations. In a wink, my entire world collapsed. What followed was the most traumatic and anguishing experience of my life. It shook my faith and made me question my convictions.

The Military Units for Aid of Production (UMAP) were created in November of 1965, and thousands of young people, among them many young Christians, were congregated in camps created for this purpose. The organization, known by the acronym UMAP, was dissolved within three years. It had a sordid history, full of injustice and contradictions from its beginning.

The majority of the young people who were taken to UMAP were summoned to an interview for the Obligatory Military Service (SMO) and recruited at a later date. When we reported on the day of recruitment, we were not informed that we would be part of a completely different organization. We thought that we had been recruited for the regular units of the military. Others had a worse situation: they had been summoned just to be interviewed, and were sent immediately, without any preparations, to the units, all located in the Province of Camagüey, about six hundred kilometers east of the City of Havana. Some individuals were picked up from their places of employment and sent to the camps, without even having been allowed to inform their families. Later, individuals who were not of the age of military recruitment were also taken to UMAP. Some of the leaders from Cubana de Aviación (Cuban Airways) were taken to UMAP supposedly as a punishment for past behavior.

Most of the events narrated in this book took place between November 26, 1965 and June 30, 1968, the day on which the Military Units to Aid Production were dissolved. This meant that every person who had been enlisted was then discharged. In the place of UMAP there was a new organization: The Juvenile Column of the Centennial, which had a very different design. It is also true that many months after the creation of UMAP, some of the procedures were changed, and those men who were taken at the second and last call to UMAP, in June of 1966, found very different conditions from those of the first group of recruits.

Nevertheless, our experiences must not be forgotten.

They are a part of the Christian history in Cuba. The new generations of believers who are unaware of these events will continue in their ignorance unless those who experienced them are willing to discuss them.

Although it did not destroy our faith and trust in our Lord, the experience of being considered "social scum" on the same level as the criminals and others, marked our lives and caused us, our families, and our churches much suffering. Most of the young Christians who suffered in UMAP left with a much stronger and deeper faith, and have continued in the faith; only a few succumbed to the test. Almost every seminary student returned to the seminary and became a pastor.

This book, written as objectively as possible, should be read as a testimony of a time gladly left behind: so far behind that to many it is totally unknown. Many people when reading former versions protested that this book was spurious and that the events like those reported here have never occurred in our country since the Revolution. Therefore, for those who are somewhat concerned or doubtful when reading these pages, I have copied the following quotation from the Granma Newspaper, official organ of the Cuban Communist Party, from the edition of Thursday, April 14, 1966, the following paragraph, signed by Journalist Luis Baez.

"UMAP is not a place for punishment. The young people who go in there are not looked down upon; on the contrary, they are well received. They are subject to a military discipline. They are well treated and a way is found to help them improve their attitude, to change, and to learn. It is about transforming them into useful men for society. *When the first groups, in which there was nothing good, began to arrive, some of the officers did not have the necessary patience or the required experience and they gave full vent to their frustration and rage. For that reason they were court-martialed, in some cases they were demoted, and in others they were discharged from the armed forces.*"[1] (emphasis added by the author.)

---

[1] *Periódico Granma*, April 14, 1966, Havana, Cuba

I concur with this view of the absence of the necessary patience or the required experience and the venting of frustration and rage. I quote from this article as a proof from the national press, which managed to reflecte the blunders committed in UMAP. I was part of these *"first groups, in which there was nothing good,"* and was a witness and a victim of the absence of patience, experience, and venting of the frustration and rage of some officers. These regrettable events caused a great number of Cubans to be scarred forever.

Mr. Baez continues, *"Every young man must go through the military service as an honorable duty, as a modest contribution to the defense of the homeland; some will do it in the regular units, others, while studying... and others in the aid of production through UMAP. Thus, those studying any kind of religion in special schools with a professional character must not be exempt either. The objective of UMAP is not to punish anyone... the main objective of this organization is for these young people to change their attitudes, to educate them, to shape them, to redeem them, to prevent them from becoming parasites who are incapable of producing anything, or counterrevolutionary delinquents, or common delinquents, useless beings for society."* [2]

How does a young Christian feel if, after having spent all his boyhood and youth in church, upholding ethical principles at all costs, is about to complete his studies in a Christian seminary, he suddenly finds himself included in the list of those that have to be reformed in order to keep from becoming parasites, delinquents, or useless to society? And how did the large number of young people feel who did not even study religion professionally, but either studied at the university or were outstanding workers when taken to UMAP to "educate them, shape them, and redeem them"? And of the pastors of the many denominations that were there, few would have refused to enlist in a regular military unit to comply with Law of the Obligatory Military Service. Later other Christians were summoned and fulfilled the required period in the regular

---

[2] *Periódico Granma*, April 14, 1966, Havana, Cuba

units of the SMO. In the case of UMAP, everyone was placed in the same category of criminality and delinquency without any of the necessary distinctions.

From the very first moment of my involvement in the UMAP experience, I thought that one day I would write about it, but the demands of life and my ministry hindered it. In October, 1993, almost thirty years after the events, an illness forced me to withdraw into my home for four months. I tried to get relief from the boredom of this confinement by dedicating myself to reading. It was then that I opened the box where my wife kept all our correspondence from our courtship and the time in UMAP, and I decided to read our love letters. I immediately understood that if I compiled and organized the detailed information found there, I would have my book on UMAP ready for publication very quickly. In the same box I found a couple of notebooks and poems that I had written at that time (who has not tried to be a poet at some time?) which provided many details and triggered the memories of experiences that time had apparently erased. I began to write the book as soon as the doctor gave me permission to work. My only purpose was to narrate my personal story to the younger generations of Cuban Christians who were unaware of what had happened during that time.

The apostle Paul told the Christians of his time about the possibility of being wrongly accused and of suffering as a result.[3] All of those who embrace the Christian faith, in Cuba and any other country in the world, should know that this can happen at any time, and can cost them dearly. The narrow path of which Jesus Christ spoke[4] may become dangerous and difficult occasionally. This has been so since the beginning and will be until the end. He who decides to be a Christian should be aware of this possibility, because this understanding will help him overcome the temptation of abandoning the Christian way when he first encounters difficult terrain.

---

[3] 1 Peter 2:11-17; 3:8-17

[4] Matthew 7:13-14

It should not be possible for events like the ones narrated in this book to take place again, because the current constitution in our country ensures that the discrimination against and persecution of believers of any creed is illegal and punishable. We also believe that there were regrettable differences between the original purposes of UMAP and what actually took place in some of the camps. Therefore, it is good for people to know this story, of which we were eyewitnesses, because society should never ignore its own errors. Recognizing them and grieving over them is the only way to avoid repeating them. Are we amazed that a cloak of silence and forgetfulness has been spread over the organization even though approximately 20,000 Cubans suffered the injustices for nearly three years? Such a cloak of silence is a telltale sign of the kinds of injustice that occurred, of which no country could be proud. Nonetheless, the history of any nation, to be credible, should record its errors and failures, in the same way in which it does the victories and glorious events.

All of the people and places that appear in this account are real, and are designated by their proper names. Some of the names are omitted, because after thirty years it is impossible to remember them. I have decided not to mention others because I maintain above all that this is a Christian book and not an accusation. I understand that it is very possible that some of the individuals whose names I have omitted may still be living and may regret their past behavior. If any of them reads these pages, his pain in recognizing himself will be enough.

Should that happen, I would eagerly remind any reader of the truth that that is written in the Bible very clearly, and that I have experienced in my own life: The Lord does not despise a repentant and humble heart. The forgiveness of God and the spiritual peace are the primary result of repentance. In the same way, if a person mentioned in the book believes that I have been unjust in judging his character or misrepresented an event, I apologize with all my heart. I can confess that, thanks to God, I harbor no bitterness, because I believe that many were placed in difficult circumstances, and were compelled to perform difficult tasks.

I hope that these experiences will be an inspiration and a help to those who read them. I thank God for my having been in UMAP, because by means of that experience I learned more about God, about human nature, and more about myself. I also know the blessing that belongs to those who have suffered for the cause of the Lord. It is a privilege to suffer for Christ and so we must teach it to the new generations of Christians in Cuba, who, thanks to a new social approach towards religion (with a few exceptions) have been able to fill the churches.

This story is based on my personal experience of having suffered in UMAP, as a young man in his twenties. I had the privilege of being a part of UMAP from its inception, part of "the first groups in which there was nothing good." I was there the entire time of the existence of UMAP: two years, seven months, and four days; I was not one who was discharged prior to UMAP's dissolution.

By the grace of God, I have written this book, which I planned to write after realizing that I would remain in Cuba to live and to work. I was taken to UMAP because I was a Christian; however, I went back to the seminary and have been a preacher of the Gospel of Jesus Christ to the very society that considered me part of the social scum that needed to be re-educated. I became for five years, by the grace of God, president of one of the largest denominations of the country, from February, 2002 to February, 2007. It is interesting that a great number of young people who were in UMAP later became national or international leaders of their denominations. I have been invited as a preacher and a lecturer for more than twenty years to a number of countries, leaving and returning to my country, where I have lived with my family while joyfully serving the Lord.

I hope that the narration of my experiences inspire

many who, wounded by the injustices of life without understanding the reason, suffer the pain of the total loss of their most cherished dreams. I beg the Lord that the story of my journey to peace will provide them with faith and hope, by freeing them of the roots of bitterness. Such resentment can only increase the frustration and inability to live a satisfying life. Therefore, the wisest and healthiest decision is to entirely relinquish all bitterness.

1

We Are Now Social Scum

The seminary students had Wednesday nights free, so on November 24, 1965, Pablo Urbay[1] and I had gone to eat ice cream at El Carmelo and to take a walk in La Rampa, the famous stretch on 23rd Street in Havana, between the sea and L Street in the Vedado neighborhood. Afterward, we walked as far as the seawall, and sat down on it to talk about our plans following our upcoming graduation. Late that night as we returned the Theological Baptist Seminary in Havana, at the corner of Rabí and General Lee Streets (Santos Suarez neighborhood), we saw the entire building full of light. The abundance of light at that time of the night was an ominous sign.

The previous Monday, upon returning from the churches where we worked on weekends, we had learned that two seminarians had been picked up and taken to the military service. With this on our minds, we climbed up the steep hill to the seminary, that night steeper and longer than ever, afraid that something abnormal was happening. When we arrived,

---

[1] **Pablo Urbay Sánchez.** Even though he received a citation from the SMO (Spanish acronym for Obligatory Military Service), like the other serminary students, he ultimately was not recruited. He finished his studies and was pastor for the Baptist churches in Artemisa, Lãs Cañas, Mariel, Quiebra Hacha, Santo Domingo, Jicotea, and Villa Rosa. He was Vice President of the Western Baptist Convention of Cuba and held other positions. In 1980 he immigrated to the United States and settled in the City of Tampa, Florida where he still works as a pastor.

Isabel Morales[2], administrator of the seminary, told us that a dozen students had been summoned to make official their recruitment into the military service on Friday, November 26.

I was one of them. I have to confess that when I was given the summons my heart froze. The others who had been summoned had already gone to say farewell to their families. Because there was just one day before we had to report, I secluded myself in my room in order to have time to think and understand what was happening.

"What is going on, Lord?" I prayed. "How is this possible, now that I am a senior, about to graduate?" I decided not to travel to say farewell to my parents or my fiancée because it would use up the time that I needed to look to the Lord and face the reality of the situation. I only phoned them to tell them about the news. I just called them.

The Obligatory Military Service Law had been issued a couple of years earlier. The seminarians had to enroll at a recruiting station on Cocos Street, a couple of blocks from the seminary. We never thought that we would be summoned.

At the beginning of 1965, some of us were summoned to an interview in El Castillo de la Fuerza, in Old Havana. We actually joked about it. Those of us who had been summoned marched along the halls of the seminary and saluted each other in the military style. We naively thought that the usual procedure was such that we would not be recruited. When that day came and we arrived for the interview, a soldier at the door informed us that we were summoned because we were *social scum*. Did he understand the meaning of those words? We did not know that such an organism existed, but when we took a look around to see the others who were summoned, we realized exactly what it was.

---

[2] **Isabel Morales.** She worked as a librarian and administrator at the seminary. Upon retirement, she returned to her hometown of Cienfuegos where she was an active member of Nazareth Baptist Church. In 2007, at the age of 92 she went to live at the Home for Elderly Baptists – "Gaspar de Cárdenas," in Villa Rosa, Havana City, where she passed away en October of the same year.

Hermes Soto[3] became indignant. "What are these people thinking of? How can they attach this label to us?"

"There must be a mistake," I answered, "When they realize that we are students of the seminary, they will surely take us off the lists and there will be no problems."

We answered the questions with a bit of pride when our turn came for the interview. We made it clear that we had been studying at the Baptist Seminary with the ultimate goal of becoming pastors. How were we to be labeled as social scum? The contrast between our behavior and that of the rest of the other people gathered there was quite obvious. We went back to the seminary and so thoroughly forgot the incident that when I received the summons to the Obligatory Military Service, I in no way connected it to that earlier interview.

A New Kind of Military Service

The Military Units to Aid Production were formed in November of 1965, as a means of re-education and centralization of young people considered unfit to be part of the Obligatory Military Service (SMO) like every other Cuban. Delinquents, pre-delinquents, tramps, junkies, homosexuals, and all kinds of people joined the ranks of the newly created UMAP. The same horror was granted to us, the students of the Baptist Theological Seminary in Havana, and many young Christians of other denominations, especially those who held positions as leaders in the churches. Other young men under the age of 27 years whose families had immigrated to the United States were taken as well. They had not been allowed to emigrate with their families.

In the dawn of November 26, 1965, after a sleepless night, I arose before dawn, and went out to the hall on the

---

[3] **Hermes Soto Lugo.** He studied the second year in the seminary when he was taken to UMAP on November, 1965. He was discharged after four months because of health problems. He returned to the seminary and finished his studies. He was a pastor in the Baptist Church in Güines. He is currently pastor of the Baptist Church "M. N. McCall" in Havana City. Currently retired, he is rector of the seminary, where he is also professor of Christian Ethics.

second floor of the seminary, which is situated on the Chapel Mountain and offers a fantastic northward view of the City of Havana. I stayed there for a long time staring at the landscape, which I hardly noticed since it had become so common to me. I remembered the Bible passage of the transfiguration of the Lord, when Peter asked to make three tents.[4] How I wished at that moment everything had been a nightmare and I did not have to go down the hill of the seminary to face something I detested! When the Military Service Law was passed, my heart trembled at the possibility that I would have to go. I never wanted to go into the military. I went to enroll because it was required, but I always hoped that the Lord would free me from it. Because of the Marxist-Leninist ideology that the Revolution was establishing in Cuba, it was obvious that the government did not want to have any religious people in the Armed Forces. My hope of avoiding the call into the military service was bolstered because of the ideological turn of the nation. Now, in spite of all of my hopes and expectations, I was required to report that day to comply with the Obligatory Military Service Law.

With the paper in my hands, and fear and anguish in my heart because I would have to leave the seminary and with it my hopes of serving as a pastor, I looked at the illumined city for the last time. In the seminary chapel we were asked to attend a farewell prayer service. Half an hour later, all the seminarians who had been summoned were led to the place where we had to report.

The Way to Hell

We took a bus on the 10 de Octubre Road before daybreak. We had no idea that we were beginning a longer and more horrible trip than we could possibly imagine. About ten minutes later, we got off the bus and crossed the road to head to the address to which we had been summoned.

---

[4] Matthew 17:1-4

It was a small white house, 67 María Auxiliadora Street. The young people who had been summoned began to gather. When we saw them, we realized that we truly were considered social scum, just as had been stated in that interview at El Castillo de la Fuerza earlier in the year. At the appointed hour, we started to congregate in the yard on the right side of the house. An officer seated at a table beside the gate received the subpoenas and checked the names against a big book that he had in front of him. When it was my turn, I approached and handed him my subpoena. I watched as he checked my name, and with a quick look I could also see that in the next column the reason for which the person had been recruited was indicated. Next to my name, it said, "Baptist." Because the seminarians reported together I noticed that we had the same reason for being recruited. That discovery was some consolation. At least, the motive of our being taken was clear.

We did not have the slightest idea of what would happen next. We did not know where we were going or what we would suffer there, but if we were taken simply because we were Christians, that we could face. The Lord said: *"Blessed are you when others revile you and persecute you and utter all kinds of evil against you falsely on my account. Rejoice and be glad, for your reward is great in heaven, for so they persecuted the prophets who were before you."* [5] If that was what was happening, we could accept and comprehend it. We had been joined with the marginalized and delinquents, but we were there for being Christians.

Something was becoming evident: in spite of the fact that our subpoenas were the same as the ones received by the young people summoned to the Obligatory Military Service, we were led to different places. We could not understand it, but it was clear to us that this was no ordinary recruitment. We were gathered in the yard and fell in. They kept us standing for almost three hours without giving us any kind of information. We were not allowed to sit down on the ground to wait. Nobody answered the questions that we asked constantly.

---

[5] Matthew 5:11

"The trucks will be coming soon," an officer kept repeating as the only answer.

"I don't like this at all!" I commented. All of us were becoming very tense and increasingly worried.

At about ten in the morning the trucks arrived; we were ordered to get on them. We expected to be taken to the military units in the Province of Havana, but instead, after driving further into the city of Havana, were taken to the Central Railroad Station. Young people in the same "category" from other areas of the city arrived by various means of transportation. The trucks entered the yard of the station, going through the gates that are on the left of the beautiful, historic building of the train station on Egido Street. Hurriedly, we got off the trucks and boarded the train. Soldiers carrying long weapons watched over the whole operation.

We were never offered any explanation of what was happening. The only information given to us was that we could not get off the train nor open the windows as long as it was not moving. At the doors of the cars, soldiers with their long weapons watched over the exits. Others kept guard from outside.

The Long Train Ride
With an Unknown Destination

A little after ten in the morning, the whistles of the locomotive announced the departure of the train and very slowly its march began. We were not told of our destination, and were forced to shut the windows when the train stopped or went through towns along the way. Every time the train had to switch to let other trains pass, which occurred several times, we had to shut the windows and nobody could move from his seat. When the train was stopped we were not even allowed to go to the bathroom. Two soldiers with long weapons stood guard at every door of the train throughout the entire trip. Nobody would give us an explanation as to why we were treated this way, nor tell us our destination, insisting that it was a military secret.

Those who had been recruited while at the seminary (some had been recruited in their neighborhoods or towns) sat together and hardly spoke at the beginning of the trip. We could not comprehend what was happening, nor envision what plan God might have by allowing a dozen students of the seminary to be removed at the very moment when the Baptist work was undergoing a terrible crisis. More than fifty pastors of the Western[6] Baptist Convention of Cuba had been arrested, tried, and sentenced.[7] I was the leader of four churches at the time. Our course of study was to be accelerated so that we could graduate early, because of a lack of workers. But now everything had changed. I did not utter a word for hours.

At about three in the afternoon, the train of more than twenty cars arrived at the station in Santa Clara. We had taken advantage of the curves along the way to count the cars, because due to the confusion and secrecy at the train station, we had no idea how long the train was. In Santa Clara we were given a little food box for lunch, the only food that we had all day, and we continued the trip.

After eleven o'clock at night, the train passed through Ciego de Ávila. The rail crossed the city about a hundred meters from my fiancée's house, from where the train could be heard clearly as it passed by. The last thing she would have imagined that night was that I was passing by so close. I could

---

[6] In Cuba there were at that time three conventions: the Eastern, the Western, and the Free Baptist Convention.
[7] In April 1965, more than fifty pastors, among them, Dr. Herbert Caudill, superintendent in Cuba from the Home Mission Board of the Baptist Southern Convention of the United Sates, and his son in-law, Dr. David Fite, were arrested. Some were accused of membership in counterrevolutionary organizations; others of being agents of the CIA and implementing an illegal currency traffic. Some of the leaders of the so-called Mission Board, who done neither one nor the other, were accused of concealment. All of them were convictd and sentenced to terms that ranged from two to thirty years in prison. Caudill and his son in-law were permitted to leave the county together with their families at the beginning of 1969. Caudill was in prison for sixteen months. Because of an illness, he served home detention until his departure from the country. Dr. Fite was discharged a short time before the return of the whole family to the United States. The rest of the pastors were freed after plea bargaining, which resulted in reduced sentences. After being freed, some immigrated to the United States, but many returned as pastors and once again occupied the leadership positions in the Cuban work until they migrated afterwards or retired. Presently, many of the group have passed away and there are some who live abroad.

see her street when the train crossed it. She surely thought that I was starting my military life in some unit in the province of Havana. She had no idea that I was on the long, obscure train

passing by at midnight, demonstrating my status as social scum for the first time.

It was a long and exhausting trip that seemed endless. The train stopped constantly to let others pass. The anxiety of not knowing our destination, the armed soldiers, and the absolute prohibition of opening the windows after dark, even when the train was moving, assured us that nothing good awaited us at the end of the line.

We were being treated like prisoners, not like military recruits.

At about three o'clock in the morning, at last, the train stopped and it was rumored that we had arrived. We had realized that in the City of Camagüey, the train had turned north. It was still dark when we had to disembark in turmoil at the little railroad station in Central Lugareño (now called "Sierra de Cubitas"), and were ordered to get on several trucks that had been waiting for us on the dirt road next to the station. From there we were transferred to the baseball stadium near the sugar mill, which is four kilometers from the train stop, where we were all crowded together again.

The seminarians tried not to split up, hoping that we could stay together. Confusion and disorder reigned. The stadium was heavily guarded, and soldiers were posted in the center of the field; they read the lists of those who had just arrived on the train while they tried to keep us in order and gather us in groups of 120. Everything was chaotic because there was no coherent plan. As soon as we settled in one place, we were moved to another. Everything was done in a haphazard and arbitrary manner, and we were treated violently with no consideration of any kind. It was evident that they wanted to get past the distribution of the personnel as quickly as possible, and were having some difficulty.

Shouting and orders to step aside were abundant. Finally, when they succeeded in organizing the crowd into groups of 120 men, they began to usher us onto trucks, of which, apparently, there were not enough. The officers protested and argued among themselves, increasing the general disorder. We were packed together on the trucks.

Thus we began our long, cold trip along paths and dirt roads. None of us had taken a coat. The instructions we received for recruitment forced us to go with only the clothes that we were wearing, and a few other personal items. Since we had expected to be taken to the military units close to Havana, none of us had brought a sweater or jacket. We realized what a mistake that had been as soon as it was dark and everybody became cold. And now, traveling on dirt roads in the middle of the night in November, the temperature was much lower, and we were becoming desperate. Being packed on the truck helped a bit. Warming ourselves as we stood close together, we withstood the harsh conditions of the trip until we arrived at what would be our camp.

"Nobody Knows If You Will Ever Get Out"

Today I know that on that trip of about two hours through rough and twisting terrain, we only traveled thirty kilometers. But that night was so intensely cold, and after the trip on the train of almost thirty hours, the torture seemed endless to me. The situation was magnified by the fact that we had not eaten anything since the meager lunch in Santa Clara. Hunger, bewilderment, fatigue, mistreatment, and now cold temperatures made the trip a miserable experience. Because I was not ready to face reality, and was still entertaining a naïve hope that if they knew who we were we would not be left there, I initiated a discussion with an officer as we got off the truck.

"There is a mistake somewhere!" I almost shouted.

"Why?" He answered, looking at me with disdain in his eyes.

"Because not everyone here is the same!" I shouted at him again, much more upset.

"Well, I believe that everyone here is the same. Walk on and don't hold up the line anymore" he answered me angrily.

"We are Christians and we have been labeled as delinquents. That is an injustice!" I told him as I looked backwards while he forced me to go on to enter the unit. He looked at me from head to toe and burst out laughing.

"Come on, get in and stop spewing garbage!" He said, and gave me a push that almost knocked me down. Julio Cornelio[8], who was coming behind me, caught me and set me back on my feet.

"What are they thinking about us?" I protested, yelling to nobody in particular. "We have been living all our lives honestly and look how we are treated. That is not fair!"

"Be quiet, Alberto," Julio told me. "Control yourself! It could be worse."

---

[8] **Julio Cornelio Díaz**. He was a student in the third year in the seminary, and was recruited to UMAP in November 1965. He was discharged eighteen months later because of an illness. He was a pastor of the Baptist Churches in Buenavista (VC), Trinidad and Santa Clara. He immigrated to Canada where he worked as a church planter, pastor and missionary Afterwards he moved to the United States. He is presently retired and lives in Florida.

I was hardly twenty-two years old. I must confess that I suffered a certain pharisaic complacency because I was a devout young man and had lived in the church all my life without being contaminated with worldly habits and manners. My eyes were not capable of seeing then that while the situation was unfair to us, it was also unfair to the others, although some of them had different lifestyles from ours. How does one pretend to re-educate a human being if he does not respect him and understand his ways? Even if he is a delinquent, being treated with contempt, discrimination, threats, or unjust attacks cannot help a person. But I still had much to learn, and was concerned only about the injustice demonstrated toward Christians.

The 120 men who would become that company were gathered, and the "welcome" was overwhelming; an officer shouted with disdain at the whole troop, "You are here for engaging in socially unacceptable behavior within our society." And threateningly he added, "Today you have entered this unit, but nobody knows if you will ever get out!"

There we were told about the honorable duty of serving the homeland in the Obligatory Military Service. They insisted that it was our own deviated behavior that led to our being unworthy of enlistment in the regular units. We were threatened repeatedly with indefinite extension of our internment unless we amended our behavior by hard work and military discipline. The officer added that they could give us neither the name nor the address of our location because it was a military secret. He stated that from that moment on we would not have any communication with our families. After that harsh welcome, at about nine in the morning each of us was given a piece of black bread and a can of sardines. It was the first food that we had received in eighteen hours.

We discovered later that the farmers of the area were warned neither to talk to nor to approach any of us, because we were dangerous delinquents and enemies of the revolution.

Each of us was given one set of clothes, a pair of boots, one pair of underwear and an undershirt, a bar of soap and a towel. Each man received a hammock and a blanket. But no one was given a rope, and there was nothing with which to tie up the hammocks in the barracks, so that when it was night everyone spread his on the dirt floor. We Christians decided to place them outside on a small porch, because we did not like the immoral and promiscuous undercurrent that was immediately created in the barracks.

That is how our first night in UMAP began. When I lay down on the edge of the porch, I contemplated the starry sky in the darkness of the country: a wonderful spectacle, as if God were sending to us a message of comfort. But I decided to cover my head and to cry like a coward on the saddest and most desperate night of my life.

My enrollment in the seminary and all my relationships had come to an end so abruptly and unexpectedly that I could not decide whether the past or the present was real. Besides, ringing in my ears were those menacing words from the welcome: *"Nobody knows if you will ever get out of here."* All that was taking place seemed incredible to me.

It was too cruel, too unjust and painful to be true.

I do not remember when I was overcome by sleep. It was Saturday night, November 27, 1965, and although we did not know it, our company was in the *Batey* (small settlement close to a sugar mill) in Las Marías, Minas municipality, some seventeen kilometers from the Senado Sugar Mill (present day Noel Fernández), in the province of Camagüey.

When I awoke at dawn, lying in the hammock on the dirt floor of the porch of the barracks, I ached all over and was even more confused. We gathered to read the New Testament, pray and sing a few hymns.

Eight of the seminarians were together there: Julio Cornelio, David Figueredo[9], Israel García[10], José Ferrer[11], Rafael Hernández[12], Israel Cordovés[13], Ernesto Ruano[14] and I. There was also another young Baptist with us. We did not know where Hermes Soto was nor the other Christians who had been on the same train. Ernesto Alfonso[15] and Esteban Estrada[16] had been recruited a few days earlier. We supposed that they had been led to units like ours and probably were also in Camagüey.

The Horrible Shock of Reality

The mistreatment of the Jehovah's Witnesses began immediately because they refused to wear the military uniform:

---

[9] **David Figueredo Tamayo.** Third year student in the seminary. He was discharged after a year because he was an asthmatic. He finished his studies and became a pastor of the Baptist Church in Placetas. He was the director of the Music Department of the Convention and a member of the Directive Board. He was pastor of the BETHEL Baptist Church in Miramar, Havana for many years. He is presently retired and lives in Havana.
[10] **Israel García Bello.** Third year student in the seminary. He was in UMAP until its dissolution. He was pastor of the Second Baptist Church in Santa Clara. He later immigrated to the United States where he worked as a pastor. He presently lives in Miami.
[11] **José Ferrer.** Third year student in the seminary. He was in UMAP until its dissolution. He was a pastor of the Baptist Churches in La Esperanza and Guira. Years later he worked with Fraternity of Baptist Churches until he immigrated to the United States. He is currently living in Miami.
[12] **Rafael Hernández Bermudez.** Third year student in the seminary. He was discharged in April 1967. He was a pastor of the Baptist Church in Las Delicias and el Cotorro. He is presently retired and is currently living in Miami.
[13] **Israel Cordovés González.** Second year student in the seminary. He was in UMAP until its dissolution. He was pastor of the churches in San Cristóbal, Santa Clara and Guanabacoa. He immigrated to the United States where he Works as a pastor in Kissimmee, Florida
[14] **Ernesto Ruano Pruneda.** Third year student in the seminary. He was in UMAP until it was dissolved, but he did not return to finish his studies at the seminary. He married and continues to live in the City of Camagüey. Years later, he returned to the faith and joined the Second Baptist Church of Camagüey. He currently lives near the beach in Varadero, Matanzas province.
[15] **Ernesto Alfonso Díaz.** Second year student in the seminary. He was discharged in March, 1967. He finished his studies and was pastor in Güira de Melena, Alturas de Luyanó, II de San Antonio de los Baños and San José de las Lajas. He was director of the Department for Evangelism in the Convention and held other conventional offices. He immigrated in the year 2001 and was a pastor in Miami. He passed away in 2011.
[16] **Esteban Estrada.** Third year student of the seminary. He left in April 1967. He finished his studies and was pastor of Baptist churches in Sagua La Grande, and Catalina de Guines. He is currently retired and lives in Miami Florida.

a pair of denim slacks and a light denim shirt and cap. It looked more a uniform for inmates than a military uniform, but still the Witnesses refused to wear it. The techniques used in Las Marías to compel them to cooperate were terrifying. While we were allowed to wear our civilian clothes while in the unit, the Witnesses were allowed to wear only their underwear; they were forced to stand exposed to the elements day and night, deprived of sufficient clothing, as well as food and water. "You will stay there until you decide to put on your uniform or die! You must learn to respect the Revolution!" an officer shouted.

Thus, the Jehovah's Witnesses were ordered to stand outside until they collapsed from exhaustion. Armed soldiers ensured that nobody attempted to feed them. Where they were taken after they collapsed, we were never told. That first day in Las Marías, one of them was tied up by his feet and was dipped head down in a covered sanitary pit so as to convince him to wear his uniform. The officer in charge of the company constantly wore a mocking and cynical expression on his face, and oh, how he enjoyed it every time that unfortunate man was lifted up, covered with human waste!

Everything seemed surreal. Where had we been taken? In whose hands were we? What actually were the Military Units to Aid Production? The high wire fences, the numbers of soldiers with long weapons that guarded us, the threats of never leaving there, the subhuman life conditions with the 120 men sleeping stacked up on the dirt floor in the barracks, and the procedures we had seen in practice to that moment, and especially the long train ride with the unknown destination, reminded us of the stories of the German concentration camps.

Upon our arrival, we lost our names and each one of us received a number instead. My first one in UMAP was 93. In that incomprehensible re-educative machinery in which we had fallen, I came to know what a person feels who ceases to have a name and becomes only a number. I learned how to respond to 93 very soon. Not only when the chiefs called, "Hey, 93, stand fast!" but when talking to the mates: "Hey 93, let's talk for a while." Later, I became 41. This may seem odd to those who have never had this experience, but one becomes fond of his number and suffers every time it is changed.

How can I describe the impressions of that first day? It was impossible for me to have imagined anything like UMAP. I frequently looked at the place where the Jehovah's Witnesses suffered (without giving in!) from the lashes of the sun and the forced hunger. What other things were we to see there? What would we suffer?

"My God!" I prayed many times during that first day, "how is it possible that You have permitted us to be brought here?" I thought about Romans 8:28 *"And we know that for those who love God all things work together for good."* But to read the verse at home or at church in normal situations is one thing; it is quite another to explain it when the earth has opened and swallowed all of our dreams. Could it somehow be for any good that a few months before finishing my studies in the seminary, I was sent to a corner in Camagüey to work as an agriculture worker earning seven pesos a month for God knew how long? Could it be for any good that the churches for which I was responsible at the moment continued without a pastor? And the missionary fields that were under the responsibility of other brothers who had been recruited, was it for any good for them to remain alone?

I had learned this hymn a long time before, and had enjoyed for years:

> *From the divine love, who will draw me aside?*
> *I am hidden in Christ, who will ever touch me?*
> *If God justifies, who will condemn me?*
> *With Christ as my advocate, who will accuse me?*
>
> *Refrain: To those who love God all things*
> *work together for good*
>
> *This is my comfort, this is my support.*

Whatever happens in my life here,
God prepares for my good.
In my trials God is always faithful to me,
Then, why the doubts? I rest in Him.

There are plagues and death around me,
He ordered my destiny, He who is my God of love.
Not even an arrow can harm me,
If He does not permit it, it shall not reach me.

What a difference I now felt in my heart when I tried to sing it, searching for the promised support and comfort! I repeated the second stanza, I do not remember how many times. I wanted to be saturated with its message. Until that moment, I had never in my life faced a problem or situation of this magnitude. I tried to rest in Him with all my heart, as the hymn says. But it was not easy.

On the verge of achieving my aspiration of being a pastor, just a few months from graduation time, as I started to plan to marry the woman I loved so that we could go and serve the Lord together in a church, I suddenly was living in an inferno beyond description. Overnight, my entire world had been changed in the most unexpected and confusing way. What would become of my life from this point forward?

I was no longer a seminary student.

I would not be a pastor.

I was not even a young man in love who knew when he could get married.

I was not even an ordinary Cuban, who was required by law to comply with the Obligatory Military Service.

I had been robbed of my dreams and my social standing.

I was simply SOCIAL SCUM!

2

Christmas in Camagüey

"I cannot believe that this is really happening!" Ernesto Ruano told me with an enormous sadness in his eyes. He had been my best friend for very many years. Natives of the same city, we were students of the same school during our childhood, attended the same church during our adolescence and were peers in the same academic year as well as roommates in the seminary. In the afternoon of that first Sunday, we sat down by the tree close to the kitchen, waiting to get a crew cut. The recruitment was so sudden and strange that it was difficult for us to grasp its reality. The previous Sunday we had prayed in our respective churches without the slightest hint of what awaited us a few days later.

As we talked, we looked around to become familiar with that place that would be our home for how long? Only God knew. The unit was 100 meters wide by 150 long and was only partially constructed. It was made of two buildings separated by a level area approximately forty meters wide. One of them, which was partially made of masonry with an asbestos cement roof, was the dining hall and the kitchen. The other, of wood and still lacking a floor, would become the infirmary and the barracks. Behind them there was a small room for latrines, and beyond them, the new showers and latrines were being built. Everything was surrounded by a barbed-wire fence more than ten meters high. At the front of the unit stood a white masonry house with a concrete roof surrounded by thick square columns. It was a large, two-story house on a small hill, and everything that happened in the surrounding area could be observed from there. On the right side of the house, about ten or fifteen meters away, stood another wooden house and porch, where there was a grocery store.

From our unit, one could see two or three more huts behind the grocery store, which composed the little village near the sugar mill. Behind them and about 100 meters from the unit and to the right was a wooded area. To the left of the painted house there was another pair of huts.

In every direction, all we could see were sugar cane fields, and far in the distance we knew that there was a river because we could see long lines of bamboos.[1] Except for the sign, *Lugareño,* where we got off the train, there was no other point of reference. We knew that we were somewhere in the northern part of the province of Camagüey, but nothing more.

In spite of everything we heard upon our arrival, we knew that since the Obligatory Military Service had summoned us, we could be legally kept there for no more than three years.

"Then we will be here 1095 days," I said.

"Do you think that we will be able to endure 1095 days like the one yesterday?" wondered Ernesto.

That day had been relatively calm, spent working on several little jobs in the camp, picking up stones, painting the barracks with lime, and transferring different materials. Again and again we returned to the same topic:

"We were brought here for military service and even though everything is terrible, it cannot last more than what the

---

[1] **Río Máximo**, which flows into La Gloria Bay in the northern coast of the province of Camagüey. It is famous for its rocky smooth formations on its banks, called "canjilones", which provide a peculiar landscape.

law dictates. So we will need to have patience until the three years pass."

"The Lord can also take us out of here at any moment," added my friend.

Thus began what would be a constant throughout the time that we stayed there: the hope that a miracle would take place and that someday we would get out of that terrible place. We trusted that if the Western Baptist Convention or the Baptist World Alliance made any negotiations, at any moment all of us could be released. And how was it even possible for students of the Baptist seminary to have been picked up and treated as social scum? That same day I began to write a letter to my fiancée, preparing for the day I could mail it. As I read it after so many years, I marvel at the things that I said. *"Don't worry! Everyone in the group is fine and of very good cheer. God knows what He is doing. The treatment is excellent and the food is better than in the seminary."* All of us wrote things such as this because we were told that the letters would be checked; besides, we did not want our loved ones to know the truth of what we were suffering. I reiterated that lie so often that my fiancée did not write to me as frequently as I needed and expected.

One day, in a moment of weakness I wrote to her, "When I tell you not to worry and that everything is going smoothly, it is because I don't want to alarm you...I don't know...but here you are: there are things that are never said because they just can't be. Have you seen Ocaña[2] or Nemesio García[3]?" She could not see them because they were two of the many pastors who were in prison. "If you see them," I continued writing, "tell them that we are very much identified

---

[2] **Rafael A. Ocaña.** He was a pastor of "El Calvario" Baptist Church in Havana when he was sent to prison. He was the rector of the Baptist Seminary when the students who went to UMAP returned and finished their studies. He passed away in November 1976.
[3] **Nemesio García Iglesias.** Deceased. He was the pastor of the McCall Baptist Church in Havana City, professor of the seminary and secretary to the Board of Directors of the Convention, when in 1965 he was imprisoned together with the group of pastors. Later he returned to his pastorate in the same church and was again professor of the seminary until he retired.

with their sorrow and we are feeling like them, so much so that I think that we are sharing the same experience. So I yearn for you to write to me a little more frequently; letters are all we have to encourage us to persevere."

We were allowed to send correspondence after the second week, although nobody received news from his family until after the third or fourth week. However, in spite of the warning that we were dangerous delinquents who should be avoided, some of the farmers did approach us secretly. They aided us by sending telegrams or letters that outmaneuvered our communication blackout with the outside. Thus, we also learned of our location two weeks before we were officially informed.

A Black Angel from Haiti

One day, while we were transferring construction materials for the new bathrooms, we saw a Haitian man pass by the fence. Several recruits called him. At the beginning he acted as if he did not hear, but then he approached us. He was looking around fearfully.

"They told us that we must not talk to you."

"We only want to know where we are," somebody said.

"This is called "Las Marías," he answered, obviously nervous.

"But where are we, in what area?" another one insisted.

By now various recruits had approached the barbed wire fence, and although we had been warned not to do so, an opportunity like this one could not be wasted.

"That way," he said by pointing to the bamboos that were seen from the distance, "is the Senado Sugar Mill, and that way," he said by signaling the other way, "is Sola."

"But which one is the closest, my old man?" asked another one.

"Sola is the closest, about four kilometers; Senado is about fifteen or twenty."

"Is there a post office in Sola? Could you mail a letter for us?"

He agreed to come the following day at the same time to mail the letters that we would give him. The Haitian lived in one of the huts behind the grocery store, and he called himself Tiempo. Later we discovered that he was a Christian. The conversation with him ended abruptly when a guard came to intimidate us and shouted,

"Hey, old man! Don't you know that you can't talk to these people?"

The Haitian left and apologized to the soldier, but the following day he kept his word. He left the sugar cane plantation smiling, approached the fence and took the letters. The little dialogue held with the old man the day before and the relationship that we kept with him constituted the first joy that we savored in Las Marías. God knows how to send angels to comfort his own. Tiempo approached the fence almost every afternoon, and represented a contact with freedom and a hope of communication with our families. The old man developed a ministry of consolation and help with very few words, but it turned out to be a blessing to all of us. We did not know how he managed to get our letters to Sola, a round trip of more than ten kilometers, but he collected the letters and then mailed them. Afterwards we learned that our families received every letter that was handed to him.

The Infantry Classes

On Monday, November 29, the routine of our new life began. We awoke at five in the morning and were ordered to fall in wearing only our underwear to do exercises, suffering the intense cold of the dawn. We shivered all over until the exercise warmed us. After that was breakfast, and at seven, the infantry classes began.

It was a tremendous surprise to me that such classes were endless journeys of marching and double time, something that is now known as jogging. During infantry class, we left the unit, always guarded by armed soldiers, and ran along the riverbank. Sometimes, as we exited the unit we turned left and we passed by the side of a dam of reeds near the wooded area behind the grocery store and ran on along the bank, from which only vacant lots and some huts could be seen. About two kilometers from the unit were the railroad tracks. A small sign identified the intersection of the railroad with the dirt road as Truffín. We always returned from the railroad. If we exited the unit and turned right, then we marched on as far as a curve in an S-shape which was before the bamboos, and what we saw were sugarcane fields on both sides. Either way it was good to get out of the unit, and we felt better since exercising never did us any harm, although it was sometimes exhausting.

After the classes were over, we returned to the camp to work. The floor of the barracks where we slept was still bare earth. We now had ropes for the hammocks, and in a few days we got used to sleeping in them. The building of the showers and the latrines was under way, and would complete the construction of the unit. At one in the afternoon, we had classes on military discipline, and at four we spent another hour of work in the camp. We showered at five and dinner was at six. We spent all of December this way. For us the most difficult part was becoming accustomed to the immoral atmosphere of the barracks and in those bathrooms, so different from our normal lifestyle. When we lacked water, we were taken to the river to bathe. Very quickly and being very well guarded, the 120 men took a shower naked, almost tripping over each other in the spillway of a dam. As acquainted as we were to a Christian atmosphere in which privacy was respected, it was trying when we were forced to abandon some of our customary social graces due to the direct contact with the diverse group of which we had become a part.

There was no electric light in the camp, and during the night there was hardly anything to do. There were a few diesel lamps. After dinner and until it was time for bed count, we spent time talking. Sometimes we were ordered to read the official newspapers in groups and comment on them. At the end, we gathered to sing. Since we were all in the choir of the seminary, we sang in harmony. We sat very close together to stay warm, because we did not have coats, and sang all the hymns that we knew by heart. That helped us to endure the cold of the night until we were allowed to go to bed under our blankets. Many times as we sang, I lay down on the grass to look at the starry sky, so beautiful in the midst of the countryside where there is no light. That time of worship and inspiration gave us strength. We sang Christmas carols, hymns, and other Christian songs until we were tired. Others sat and listened to our group; nobody disturbed us.

A Christmas Eve in Style

During that first Christmas season in the Military Units to Aid Production, Christmas Eve was celebrated in all the camps. In Las Marías, the Christians gathered and sang the hymns, *Silent Night, The First Noel, Holy Night,* and *Birth of the Great King.* We finished by singing Handel's *Hallelujah Chorus* as long as we could. We sat and sang without being disturbed. A large group gathered to hear our concert. It was a beautiful time and then we were called to fall in for dinner. When we entered the dining hall we found that every plate had *congrí* (rice and black beans), a good quantity of roasted pork, two tamales, yucca, lettuce, and a piece of alicante nougat and another one of almond nougat. The food was abundant and we were allowed to refill our plates without limit. There was also wine for those who drank.

Afterwards there was a party, music with rumba everywhere. Any box became a conga drum. When those who celebrated became tired, we Christians sang all the Christmas hymns again.

After a while, one of the most troublesome recruits approached to listen to the hymns. A lieutenant who also approached saw the recruit and said; "Don't tell me that you are of the same religion as these boys, because they are different from you!"

He burst out laughing and answered, "I don't waste my time with that."

"Well, I wish everyone here were like them," said the lieutenant.

Recruits Were Not the Only Ones Punished

Among the officers, as among the recruits, there were all sorts of people. Some treated us respectfully and with consideration. Others certainly respected us and did not hesitate to show it; we forged friendships with a few of them. In certain circumstances, we had officers who helped us and acted with principle. There were others who simply fulfilled their duty without harming anyone, but there were still others who acted without any sensitivity, making it difficult for us to find any human decency in them. They did such things that even now I do not believe were orders from their superiors. I believe that these acts were of their own initiative and that the others could not or did not dare stop them. It was not to the recruits alone that the designation of social scum was applicable.

Among us, there was a rumor that the officer corps was made of military men whom the army had punished for one reason or another. I can neither prove nor disprove this. Nevertheless, a man who was visiting our church in Pinar Del Río many years later told me, "When I was a kid we lived across from a UMAP unit where my father was a lieutenant, and you couldn't imagine the things that I saw."

His face froze when I explained that I did know what kind of things happened.

"My father was a military man in Ciego de Ávila and due to some problems unknown to me, he was sent to work as a boss in UMAP. That was a true tragedy for our whole family," he added.

After the articles from which this book originated were published in our magazine, other people, also family members of military men who worked in UMAP, said the same thing to me. This makes me think that although not all of the military men there were being punished, it is possible that a few had been. Maybe that is the explanation for all the barbarity that was carried out. Some of them were not, in fact, military men with outstanding careers who were chosen for a special work, but were men being punished for falling short of what the military honor requires and therefore, were more inclined to commit abusive acts. The temptation was increased since most of the recruits were of a lower moral quality. Of course, I am expressing a personal opinion according to what was discussed among us then, and based on the lower intellectual and moral level of some of those men, with whom without exception we shared the Gospel.

The Farm Work Begins

The new year of 1966 arrived with our first taste of work in the country. It also brought bunk beds and mattresses for the barracks, whose cement floor had been poured in the last few days of the previous year. We spent all day Sunday, January 2 assembling the bunks that allowed us to sleep in beds for the first time since we had been recruited on November 26.

Then the training for the agricultural labors began. The great majority of the recruits had never done agricultural work. A little later the sugar cane harvest began, and we were trained in the cutting of sugar cane. We learned the same hard labor that thousands and thousands of Cubans have done throughout the history of the nation, many times earning a beggar's salary. After the time of initiation, which means blisters in the hands and aches all over the body, I learned that I liked to cut cane more than to work with smaller crops. It was an almost rhythmic labor, which we did in pairs; and there was great satisfaction in seeing how each pile of cut cane grew and how the cutting advanced. Afterward, it was necessary for us to go back and arrange the piles so that the machine lifter could pick them up. Sometimes we had to pick them up by hand, which to me was the worst part of all.

The burned cane was easier to cut. After a cane plantation is burned, it is left with no leaves, and the work goes faster, although the ashes get imbedded in the clothes and all over the body. Time is gained in cutting, but the crop is less useful. Cutting green sugarcane is a slower process; the harvesters have to hack a path through the leaves, cut the cane, and clean it, but it is more efficient. The plantations were always burned when the quality was not good. The best fields in which the sugarcane grew straight and strong were not burned to be cut.

The harvest was always tough work. During the three harvests that we worked, there was no leave of absence and the hours of labor sometimes extended far beyond the accustomed limit. In Las Marías we dreaded the nights of a full moon. During harvest time we got up very early in the morning, sometimes at four or four-thirty, and arrived at the field before dawn. The time of the cry of "on your feet!" with which we were awakened every morning depended on the distance to the field in which we were cutting cane.

We worked non-stop until time for lunch, which was eaten right in the field. A few minutes of break and we went back to cutting until dusk. When it was too dark to cut anymore, we quit. We got to the camp at night, after seven or sometimes even later, which made the workday more than twelve hours long.

The nights of the full moon were simply unbearable. Dinner was given to us in the field late in the afternoon. Later, because the moonlight was insufficient for us to see well enough to cut the cane, we worked to arrange the piles of the cane cut earlier, so that the machine cutters could hoist them. On ordinary days, we would cut cane and then throw it behind us. When we had enough quantity on the ground, we stopped and piled it neatly. When we finished that, we went back to cutting. This provided some variation in the rhythm of work, which made the labor more bearable. But the nights of a full moon we were not allowed to stop cutting to go back and pile the canes during daylight. The order was to cut during the day and then, after eating in the field, we were to pile the cane that we had cut earlier in the day. We did not leave the field until all the cut cane had been piled. Quite often, we were not finished until after midnight. Then we returned to the unit and slept as long as we could. At four in the morning, we were again given the on-your-feet order.

There were days when we worked more than eighteen hours. The weariness and exhaustion were such that we looked for a way of self-preservation. Because the cutting was done in pairs, each one working three furrows of cane, one man worked while the other one hid away in the inner part of the field and slept a little. If an officer passed by and asked, he was told that the missing man was answering nature's call. That provided us a little time to rest. Other times, if we arrived at the field before dawn, we would lie down over the piles of cane and fall asleep until some officer discovered us and wakened us. Sometimes we slept deeply for an hour or more. Since we were 120 men spread out in the dark in a large sugar cane field, this was possible. A comfortable bed is not necessary when the body is worn out, and we were! The dreams that I had while lying on a pile of cane in that first harvest! Even the officers, although they did not cut cane, showed signs of fatigue and complained of the schedule that was demanded of us all. The rhythm of life and work that we carried out was unbearable.

Another Angel, Now In Olive Green

Rafael Rosabal Viera[4] was the Chief Lieutenant of our camp. He was from Oriente and seemed to be in his thirties. He always treated the Christians well and showed himself to be just and amiable. Sometimes he hummed some of the hymns he said he had learned when he visited some church chasing after some girl. He was also immersed in that cesspool, but many times he helped us. During one of those phases of a full moon, he was left in charge of the whole company. Whereas the others had forced us to eat our lunch in the field where we were cutting cane, Rosabal let the company walk to the river nearby. He ordered us to sit in the shade under the bamboos, and to eat our lunch. In contrast to other chiefs, he permitted us to lie down and rest when we had finished eating. The shade, the breeze, and the weariness made us fall asleep.

David Figueredo, who just the day before had received the news that his brother was in prison, withdrew because he wanted to compose a hymn. About three in the afternoon he realized what time it was and went to speak with the lieutenant, who was always willing to talk with anyone of us. "Lieutenant, have you noticed what time it is?"

"Yes," answered Rosabal "but you need to sleep a little more so that you can work until late, because tonight there will be a full moon." And he let everyone sleep for as long as he wanted. It was a kind gesture that all of us appreciated. That afternoon we worked more enthusiastically and probably produced more in less time. Rosabal was, without question, a good, sensitive, and intelligent man. It was obvious that he

---

[4] **Lieutenant Rafael Rosabal Viera.** Officer of FAR who was outstanding in his behavior in the Military Unit 2237 in "Las Marías" for several months. Later, he was in other units. He is currently older than 80 years; he lives in the City of Camagüey together with his family.

sympathized with us and enjoyed our company. He frequently looked for the opportunity to approach the group of seminarians to talk with us.

One night when we were sleeping, the lieutenant came to my bed and wakened me. At that time he lived with his family in the white house that was across from the unit. In a very low voice he said to me, "There will be a requisition to take the Bibles from you. So, get up and ask the others for them; I will keep them in my house. I'll be back in ten minutes."

I got up and went to the beds of the seminarians, but some of them did not believe it. "Couldn't it be a trick to easily take our Bibles from us?" Julio Cornelio said. We decided to trust the lieutenant because it was impossible to hide our Bibles at that time. Either way, we would lose them. Only Israel Cordovéz refused to hand his over convinced that it was a trick by the lieutenant.

Rosabal returned as he promised and took away our Bibles. Two hours later, at midnight, the company was awakened and they made us fall-in in the yard wearing only our underwear, and leaving all our belongings inside. They sent several soldiers to check. We looked at each other very excitedly because God had sent an angel, dressed in olive green and ranked, to save our Bibles that we so needed. The brother who did not give his Bible to Rosabal was the only one who lost his.

Although they looked persistently, the chiefs could not understand how there could possibly be only one Bible in the camp. The following night Rosabal returned the Bibles he had kept at home. "It's an injustice," he said, "You don't deserve that. I am going to help you as much as I can."

And in fact, he did just that. The greatest help that he gave us was his friendship and his understanding by offering the Christians a preferential treatment, which was more evident by the day. Favoring the Christians discredited him and caused him problems. One day we watched as his few pieces of furniture and belongings were hauled away on a cart. We also saw his wife and children leaving. The group of Christians saw him leaving the unit, and we approached the fence to say farewell. When he saw us, he waved his hand, and lifted it up signaling the heavens, keeping it like that until he got out of our sight. We were surprised. What did he mean? Never did he confess to be a believer. Nevertheless, it was significant that he whistled hymns when he approached us. As a matter of fact, when he approached the group, we all felt his support, familiarity, and security. Only God knows. He was different from all the others, upright, honorable and very affectionate.

We never knew where he was transferred and none of us ever saw him again. When we asked why he was gone, we were told in cryptic, military terminology, *"By higher order."* Rosabal was an instrument of blessing. I have always wished to find him and thank him with a hug. If he is still living, he must be a man of nearly eighty.[5]

The Lieutenant Who Wanted to Help

God had other means of making the trials more bearable, and He used them. In my case, at first, I had been working as a sign writer. I also worked in the unit as a typist

---

[5] On February of 2011, before making the fourth edition, I was able to realize the wish expressed in this paragraph, which I had written in 1994. A reader of the book sent me Lieutenant Rosabal's address assuring me that he still lived in the city of Camagüey, and there we went to visit him. Very excitedly I gave him the hug that I promised and expressed my gratitude. I was welcomed by Rosabal and his family and shared with them some unforgettable moments. I gave him the book as a gift and read for the lieutenant, who is totally blind, that entire paragraph in the presence of his wife and children, which was very overpowering for all. He corroborated that just as we supposed, he faced problems for having helped us and was transferred from Las Marías for that reason. The most exciting moment for me was when Rosabal, very old and blind, but strong and healthy, perfectly sang for me the old song *Ye Must Be Born Again*, whose lyrics I transcribe: *A ruler once came to Jesus by night, to ask Him the way of salvation and light. The Master made answer in words true and plain, "Ye must be born again!"* Together, he and I, sang the refrain: *"Ye must be born again! Ye must be born again! I verily, verily say unto thee, "Ye must be born again!"* I hugged Rosabal again and said good-bye to him, convinced that at last I knew the reasons why he helped us so much and why his behavior was so different from that of the other officers in Las Marías. God's grace can work in unexpected ways and is sometimes incomprehensible to us. (Author's note.)

and organized the lists and documents for Lieutenant Francisco Concepción[6]. I am sure that he sympathized with me.

After I had been at the camp for a while, my father,[7] a member of the Communist Party, paid me a visit. We argued bitterly during that visit, because he tried to convince me that what was happening in UMAP was a normal situation. He believed that the things I was telling him were distortions of the truth, which my Christian faith hindered me from recognizing. Regardless of our dispute, I must say that his presence helped me. I do not know what influence he used in his conversation with the officers, but I noticed more respect towards me after his visit. Young as I was, that emboldened me. Lieutenant Concepción, who was second in command, used to call me frequently to speak with him or to help him in the office work.

Although we were not yet allowed to receive visits, Sundays had been regarded as a day of rest. One Saturday they gathered the company. The chief of the unit said that on Sundays they would start volunteer work and asked the company to have a vote in favor or against. Maybe because they thought that they would be taken to work anyway (we were recruits and obeyed orders) everyone else raised his hand in favor. Sitting right in front of the lieutenant, I did not raise my hand. Sunday was our only resting day, when we could wash, read, or write. I was determined not to go to work voluntarily.

At five in the morning, they called us on our feet. Everyone began to get up but I decided to stay in bed. In a minute the chief of the unit was standing next to the bunk bed

---

[6] **Lieutenent Francisco Concepción.** Officer of FAR. He was second in command in the Military Unit 2237 in Las Marías from November 1965 to June de 1967. He is presently retired, and lives in, Havana City.

[7] **José Alberto González Salserio.** He lived in Cárdenas together with my mother, my youngest brother, and my two grandmothers. He was a member of the Communist Party and worked as an administrator in a store of the city. He passed away in November, 1995.

telling me, "Come on Albertico," as he used to call me, a little tongue-in-cheek, after my father's visit, "today there is volunteer work."

"Precisely," I answered, "you said it was voluntary and took a vote. You must have seen that I voted against it. So, I am not going to do volunteer work. Maybe some other Sunday, I will, but not today."

The lieutenant turned red in his anger, and as he went through the door he called the second in command, "Concepción, go and see your buddy who says he is not going to the field!" and left for the room where the officers slept.

All my mates advised me to reconsider. Since we were under military discipline, my response to the lieutenant might cause me to be reported and taken to disciplinary court. They could write a report, an issue with which we were constantly threatened, which would result in an extension of the time in UMAP. One day longer would be a sentence that terrified us all. But I was determined, and stayed in bed. I heard, without getting up, when the company fell in for work after breakfast.

Shortly after, Lieutenant Concepción came in. He sat on the edge of my bed and patting me on my back told me, "Come on, get up and get dressed; we are going to have breakfast together. I'll see you in the dining hall in two minutes." His tone was kind and conciliatory, which is why I obeyed without any objection. When I arrived at the dining hall he was waiting for me. The lieutenant's breakfast was special. I cannot say that it was so every day, but it was on that occasion. Besides the milk and bread that the recruits ate, on the table there was fruit, a nice egg omelet, and ripe bananas. We had breakfast and talked for a long time about many topics.

When we finished he told me, "Come on; go for your backpack because today you and I are going to cut cane together."

Now, as I write this story, I realize that the man was helping me and doing it with goodwill. But that day I was not in a good frame of mind. So I responded to him with what he must have least expected. "Do you think that you can buy a man with an omelet and ripe bananas?"

He became visibly upset, but did not lose his composure. He bit his lip and told me, "OK, go read the Bible, which is what you obviously want to do."

He stood up, put on his cap and suddenly shouted striking his fist on the table, "But figure out a way to find a corner in the unit where I don't see you!" He uttered a curse word and quickly left the dining hall.

I gladly obeyed his order. When the others returned I told them the story and they could not believe it! I felt like a hero and was proud. My mates had been working all morning very much worried about the consequences which I might undergo for having refused to work on Sunday.

"Nothing happened," I told them. "They offered me a huge omelet with bananas, and ordered me to hide and read the Bible." However, although it was the last thing I wanted to do, the following Sunday I got up and went to do volunteer work without objecting. I knew that the outcome would not be the same if I tried that again.

While Lieutenant Concepción was good and generous with me, I do not condone the methods that he used to operate the unit. He was the instigator of the arduous hours of work during the full moon and for that he was not liked by the troops. Still, I was thankful for his favors that were incalculable blessings for my life.

Even before recruits were permitted to receive visitors, Concepción allowed my fiancée and her mother to come and see me. On Sunday January 23, 1966, pretending that I was to do some work for him, Concepción took me to La Gabriela, to the house of the head of the state farm, about seven kilometers from Las Marías. Behind his superiors' back, he arranged visits for me when it was not permitted. Within the first two months of having been recruited, I was allowed to meet with Miriam[8] and her mother.[9] That same day, Concepción invited Miriam to return the following week with my mother.[10]

Therefore, the following weekend my mother traveled from Cárdenas to Ciego de Ávila to join my fiancée. On Saturday they proceeded to Camagüey and thence to Minas and Senado Sugar Mill, where they arrived after midnight. They marched on to La Gabriela and then to Las Marías, where they arrived early on Sunday morning, January 30, and amazingly enough, appeared right in front of the UMAP unit. My mother was exhausted, not having slept at all, and thought that she had finally arrived at the end of the world after traveling a punishing 600 kilometers.

Lieutenant Concepción took me to the porch of the grocery store so that I could visit with them for two hours. There was a complete view of the camp from there. The women were horrified at the high barbed wire fences. Many of the recruits from the unit watched us, probably wondering how it was possible for me to have been accorded that visit. The families of other recruits, who had recently arrived for a visit, had been sent away without even having laid eyes on their loved ones. My friends from the seminary approached the fence to send messages to their respective families. These were privileges that Lieutenant Concepción granted to me that the other recruits did not enjoy.

---

[8] **Miriam Daniel Daniel.** Member of the Baptist Church in Ciego de Ávila was engaged to the author from October, 1963. At the time she was twenty years old and worked as an office worker in the Flour Enterprise Consolidated in that same city, which was then in the Province of Camaguey.

[9] **Clara Luz Daniel García.** Member of the Baptist Church in Ciego de Ávila, where she was a deaconess and a teacher of adults in Sunday School. She passed away in October 10, 1987.

[10] **Enna Muñoz De Bergue.** She lived in the City of Cárdenas. She was a member of the "Juan G. Hall" Presbyterian Church, although she was could not participate actively for family reasons. She passed away on October 10, 2002.

3

Farewell to Hope

The first family visits allowed in Las Marías took place on Sunday, February 23, 1966, after almost ninety days of our having been there. For a long time we were told that we could not receive visitors because there was not an appropriate venue. At last, we cleared the grove that was about one hundred meters from the camp, so that we could welcome our families.

That first visit had an enormous emotional impact. To reach Las Marías the families had to travel a long distance, because the majority of the recruits were from Havana. Moreover, the transportation situation in Cuba had already reached a crisis. The exhausting journey was 533 kilometers from Havana to the City of Camagüey, and then thirty-seven kilometers more to Las Minas. From Las Minas it was another six kilometers to the Senado Sugar Mill, and then twelve kilometers further to La Gabriela. After that it was still a seven-kilometer walk to the camp, or if luck should have it, a ride on a passing cart or truck.

Before that first official visit everyone was on edge. Would our families arrive on time? Could they make all the necessary transportation connections? After three months living of in that hell, seeing a loved one was like a gift from heaven. We could hardly sleep the night before.

Some of them arrived before dawn, but they had to wait far from the unit, in the area designated for the visitors. It was impossible for them to see the camp, and if they tried to approach it, they were stopped and sent back. When the morning arrived, and we were told exactly how to receive the visitors, all of us became upset, especially because we had to wait until ten in the morning to see them!

The recruits were to fall in with the unit and to march out as a demonstration to our family members of what we had learned in the infantry classes and military discipline. We despised having to do all that! We thought that it was irritating for our families to watch an act organized by the leaders as a welcome that, in actuality, did not interest them at all.

"We want your families to feel welcome," said the chief with his ever-present ironic smile. And he added, "We are going to explain to them the reasons you are here and the efforts that the revolution is putting forth on your behalf, so that you will be able to be contributing members of society."

Do I need to explain the humiliating effect that these words had on the troops?

The program consisted of a couple of speeches, which nobody cared to hear, and which the speakers were not well prepared to deliver. The explanation that they offered about life in the unit was greatly humiliating, and they emphasized repeatedly the dignity with which we were being treated. They stated what a wonderful privilege it was for us to be there and the immense opportunities that were being offered to us to serve the homeland and to help the revolution. Thus, they said, we were becoming true men, useful to society.

When the speech was over we were allowed to be with our families for nearly three hours. They brought food, clothing, and a lot of love and understanding, which were the greatest needs. They left shortly after noon. There were many tears during the meeting and even more tears when they left.

The Visit: Good and Bad

The experience of the visit is difficult to comprehend by those who have not undergone something similar. We waited for it with great enthusiasm and euphoria. But when the loved ones arrived, our hearts were always torn. We enjoyed the visit, but at the same time suffered with every minute that passed, conscious that every moment that went by made the time of departure closer. There was a sort of simulation game that exhausted everyone. We put on an appearance of strength to cheer up the others, both the outsiders and the recruits. The family encouraged us so that our days spent in UMAP would be more positive. We comforted them by reassuring them that they did not have any reason to worry or be concerned. But each deceived the other, and everyone knew it; at the same time we were aware that we had not succeeded in convincing the other.

It was a silly pious game to see who told the biggest and most convincing lie in exchange for offering a little comfort and hope. Only the glistening of the eyes, the knot in the throat and indescribable anxiety dared to reveal the truth. Time passed quickly; every minute had the drama of a countdown. Then the worst would come. When the families left, then came the loneliest hours. Nobody spoke. We returned to the unit and each one of us tossed in his bed in silence, listless and spiritless. In one of those incredible contradictions of life, those who had not received any visitors were, at that time, in better shape. They were free of the depression that overwhelmed those who had been visited by their families.

Visiting turned out to be a trap. The following day the work was tougher because the emotional and physical strength for everyone was down. We only began to cheer up when the countdown for the next visit started and our hopes began to build up once again.

During the visits Miriam and I talked, sang, and ate, and rejoiced; we also cried with a profound sadness. During that first official visit we tried to sing a hymn that had meant a lot to us.

> *What Christ demands is always best,*
> *Although I understand neither sorrows nor pain.*
> *He always seeks my gold to refine,*
> *In Him I trust, then, for He will surely care for me.*
>
> *Chorus:*
>
> *He keeps me and guards me day by day,*
> *His path is mine: He knows best.*
>
> *My steps always lead where He chose*
> *With Him as my guide, sure I am.*
> *In light or in shadow, I will always have Him,*
> *He knows the way; I shall never be afraid.*

We sang it many times afterwards and it became an anthem for our lives. In Las Marías, the message of that hymn moved our hearts, we who were part of the social scum that had to be re-educated, with a depth that we had never experienced before. We could not finish singing it and for a while we sat in silence, asking the Lord what plan He had with all of this. We did not understand the purpose of this painful experience.

The visit was the motivating factor for living, until it arrived. Then it became a hurricane of emotions that left the soul devastated and exhausted. The post-visit depression attacked both the recruits and their families, who usually departed emotionally torn. Although I do not have the precise data, I think that there were about 20,000 people in UMAP. According to the newspapers of the time, and the publication *Sin Tregua (Without Truce)*, the informative bulletin of the Political Section of UMAP, there were thirty-five battalions at some point, and I think I remember that each battalion had either three or four companies of 120 men, at least. You can easily imagine the number of families that were involved and affected by the UMAP experience and how many more people were moving from all the provinces all along the country

toward Camagüey in order to visit the recruits in their camps.

Still, when the visits began, our daily situation improved. We had endured the winter without having any coats to wear; they had been promised from the beginning but had never arrived. Had it not been for the sweatshirts, socks, and some other winter underwear that the families provided in February to wear under the uniform, everything would have been more difficult. Incredibly, even though UMAP did not provide any coats when we needed them, the recruits were not allowed to wear any other coat over the uniform, and the cold was unbearable. Finally, in May, when winter was long gone, the regulation coats arrived.

When Hunger Strikes

Since the only pieces of furniture in the barracks were the beds, our families also provided us with wooden boxes to store our belongings and some food that they brought us when they were able to visit.

We learned that muffins, if kept dry with no syrup, could be edible for days. So, we would first eat the other goodies and leave the muffins for later. During one of the visits, Miriam gave me a round package well wrapped, and said to me, "My mom made this for you."

By the shape I imagined it was a muffin. Miriam continued giving me the other food that she had brought and did not explain what her mother had made. I kept the package in the wooden box. It was winter, and since the area where we were staying was very cold, it was not until the following Saturday that I took the supposed muffin, sent by my future mother in-law, with me to the country.

After several hours of cutting cane, I invited several brothers to join us to open the package and eat it together. We sat among the cut cane eager to enjoy a few minutes of rest and eat the muffin. We were already very hungry and we were ready to devour it. Carefully and expectantly, I opened the package. As I did, we noticed an odd and unpleasant smell. The supposed muffin turned out to be bread pudding. But it had fermented… and was green!

"And now what do we do?" said Israel García. "Couldn't we try it?"

All of us looked at the pudding with great frustration. We were hungry and were quite excited with the idea of having a snack.

Israel Cordovés was the instigator: he cut a piece and tasted it. "It smells bad, but it tastes like wine. We can't waste this!" was his only comment.

It does not take much imagination to know what we

would do in such circumstances. We all dug in and began to eat the green and fermented bread pudding until it was gone. God was merciful and nobody was harmed.

Making Our Lives Miserable

One good day, citing concerns of sanitation and the health of the recruits, they banned food from being brought into the unit after the family visit. We had to consume all the food that they had brought in the presence of our families. Nobody was happy with this announcement. Normally, the families brought food not only to eat during their visits, but also snacks such as crackers, sweets, caramels, condensed milk, powdered chocolate, brown sugar to be mixed with water and to be drunk—a recipe very much used at bedtime to take the edge off our hunger—or goodies that we kept very well wrapped in the wooden boxes. We took these things with us for snacks during the workday, or to supplement our inadequate amount of daily food.

The food was important to us and improved our lives. We were not allowed to leave the unit to go to the grocery store of a nearby town to buy something to eat. Although the families did not bring much because of the difficult situation all over Cuba, we needed that bit of help, and we were grateful for it. We knew what they brought to us was a true sacrifice, and that they wanted to help us when we were in the midst of such a trial. Why would those in authority prohibit our families from improving our living conditions?

That was exactly the type of decision that turned UMAP into a contradictory and irritating experience. The storeroom was no better for food storage than our barracks. We had kept the food in our personal wooden boxes tightly shut and well taken care of. The officers were able to come and go from the unit to buy food and meet other needs, but the recruits spent months without ever being allowed to leave the unit. Why, then, forbid what would be advantageous for everyone, all things considered? We did everything possible to work around the order and keep the food items that had been brought to us. The result of these absurd prohibitions was an increase in the creativity and motivation to outmaneuver them. Eventually, it became evident that the men did indeed have food, and they took it with them to the fields for snacks.

Then there came another announcement that annoyed us even more. After the new bathrooms were finished, the old latrines behind the barracks were no longer needed, and were then used as detention cells. It was decided that all the wooden boxes in which we kept our few belongings—everyone had one next to or under his bunk bed—would henceforth be stored there. Thus, the food that we had hidden in our boxes inside the barracks, which had not attracted mice or insects, was now to be kept in the old latrines, where the upper hole was only slightly sealed. Obviously, this decision was made without any regard for our health.

This storage arrangement made the early mornings and evenings a trying time for everyone. All 120 wooden boxes, each the size of a small suitcase, were kept in a tight, disorganized space of approximately a meter and a half wide by five meters long, with all of our few personal belongings absorbing the characteristic stench. Every time one of us needed something, he had to rummage through the storage space to find his own box among so many that looked almost exactly alike. Since everyone was on the same schedule, we had to line up and wait for our turn to go into that cursed room morning and evening, often in the dark. The only other option was to leave our belongings in the barracks on our beds, which meant quickly losing them to inevitable theft. The slightest need to look for anything in the wooden boxes was turned into a major ordeal. This order seemed to have been conceived with the sole purpose of making everyone's life more difficult, exasperating, and unpleasant.

The former latrines had been used thus far as a lock-up for those who defied military discipline. The most troublesome recruits were confined there; their clothes were confiscated, leaving them in underwear, or sometimes completely naked.

They had to sleep on the floor, which was even worse than it sounds, because the latrines remained in place; only the upper hole was sealed. In the morning the men were taken out to work; rarely was the cell empty at night.

The only positive development of the former outhouses being used to store the boxes was that this kept the latrines from being used for such nightly physical torture. At least nobody slept there, nor would one particular guard any longer get his kicks out of dumping buckets of water on the confined men at midnight. However, now every recruit, without exception, faced a disgusting ordeal every time he needed any of his personal belongings.

An Unexpected Comfort

One of the benefits of receiving visits was that the recruits were allowed to have portable transistor radios. My mother had sent one to me through Miriam. Frequently, when we worked at night, I took the radio to the field and there we listened to the famous *"Nocturno"* Program, which was romantic music of the 1960s. Listening to the program made me feel close to Miriam. I knew that she listened to it, and we had our favorite songs that spoke to both of us in a very special way.

The radio also offered us a certain degree of freedom. We were able to avoid listening to the sanctioned programs that were piped in on the radio of the unit, and instead we listened to the news, the programs of our choice and foreign stations. We had to be very careful not to be caught, because listening to these programs was forbidden.

The arrival of the radio gave us another special surprise. One night while a group of Christians was sitting upon a pile of cut cane, trying to tune in the program mentioned above, we were surprised to hear Trans World Radio from Bonaire, Netherlands Antilles, in Spanish. It was heard as clearly and as loudly as any national station. It was the first time that I had heard such a radio station. Listening to biblical messages and to Christian music in the midst of such circumstances was an unexpected and valuable comfort. The Bible studies and messages filled our hearts and renewed our strength. Shortly afterwards, an officer arrived and when he realized that we were listening to a Christian program we were ordered to turn it off at once.

"You can't listen to subversive radio stations!" he protested angrily, clarifying, "You have been allowed to have a radio but you can only listen to national radio stations. If you do it again we shall confiscate the device. You already know this!"

Nevertheless, Trans World Radio continued to be a source of comfort. Sometimes when we were in the unit, several Christians got together in remote places during the night, and while one kept guard, the others listened to the programs at a very low volume. When we worked at night during the harvest, we took turns going deeper into the furrows of cane, hiding and listening for a few minutes. If there was no work and we went to bed early, I would cover my head with the sheet, and pressing the radio to my ear, listen to the broadcasts. The voice of the speaker announcing: *"This is Trans World Radio from Bonaire, Netherlands Antilles,"* evoked warm feelings in our hearts. Every night there was a message of faith and hope that helped us to face our difficulties.

The Baptist Work Continues Without Us

While these things were taking place in Camagüey, the Baptist work, in spite of everything, continued on. In February of 1966, the Annual Assembly of the Western Baptist Convention took place, and Pastors Humberto Domínguez Castillo[1] and Raúl Suárez Ramos[2] were elected President and

---

[1] **Humberto Domínguez Castillo.** Baptist pastor. He was elected President of the Convention in February, 1966. He was pastor of the Baptist churches in Guayos, Consolación del Sur and the Nazareth Baptist Church in la Víbora in Havana. He was a professor at the seminary for forty years and a member of the Directive Board of the Convention during the same time. He is currently retired and lives in Havana City.

[2] **Raúl Suárez Ramos.** Baptist pastor. He was Vice President of the Convention

Vice President respectively.

In April, we Baptist recruits received a visit from Ronald Goulding[3] of the Baptist World Alliance. Making the most of the opportunity of his presence, we requested an interview with Dr. José Felipe Carneado,[4] who was in charge of religious affairs in the Central Committee of the Communist Party of Cuba. The newly elected President and the Treasurer of the Convention, Manuel Salóm Estopara,[5] attended, along with the visitor. We knew the Baptist administration, and our hopes were lifted. We thought that perhaps the nightmare would end, and we would be able to go back to our churches and the seminary. The interview was cordial until Dr. Goulding asked Dr. Carneado, "Why are young Baptists and students of the seminary being taken to forced labor camps?"

Dr. Carneado concealed his enormous displeasure at the question, and diplomatically explained that they were not forced labor camps, but a new plan to help production. He insisted that the young people were complying with the Obligatory Military Service. The brothers expressed their views to Dr. Carneado, in an attempt to do something for us. However, we later learned that change advanced in the opposite direction. It was decided that every year, one pastor from each province would be required to go to UMAP.[6] This

---

when he was taken to UMAP. He was recruited by the end of June 1966 and was discharged in April 1967 because he was over 27 years of age. He continued his pastorate until he moved to EBENEZER Church in Marianao in Havana City. He was a professor in the seminary, the President of the Ecumenical Counsel of Cuba, (currently Council of Churches) and has retired as a pastor. He is the Director of the *Martin Luther King Memorial Center* in Marianao. He is a deputy to the National Assembly (The Cuban Parliament).

[3] **Dr. Ronald Goulding**. Canadian Baptist Pastor. At that time, he was Secretary Adjunct to Europe and the Socialist countries for the World Baptist Alliance. He visited Cuba many times.

[4] **Dr. José Felipe Carneado. Deceased**. He was a Member of the Central Committee of the Communist Party of Cuba, and Director of the Office for Religious Affairs, a post at which he served for more than 20 years.

[5] **Manuel Salom Estopara**. Deceased. He was treasurer of the convention and worked in its office at that time. He was also a member of the Directive Board. He immigrated to the United States in the 1970s.

[6] A short time later, the same **Pastor Raúl Suarez Ramos**, Vice President of the

news left us bewildered and shattered all of our hopes of getting out of there any time soon. The theory that we had been labeled *social scum* by mistake completely faded away. If pastors were to continue being recruited to UMAP every year, could we harbor any hope for this nightmare to end as abruptly as it had begun?

"Then, not even the Chinese Doctor will save us," said Israel García with his characteristic humor. "So, start getting used to this, kiddos. You're in the military service and you are going to spend three whole years here earning seven pesos a month. What do you think of that?"

Cordovés burst out laughing, as usual, but the glow in his eyes did not match his laugh. Julio Cornelio, sitting in the bottom bunk bed sank his head in his arms, unable to articulate a word. I do not remember if the others dared to look into each other's eyes, but I do know that from that moment on I began to see that place in a different way. Until

---

Convention and pastor of the church in Colón was recruited into UMAP. He was thirty-one years old, had two young children, and a wife who had been suffering from a pulmonary disease. There were three others as well:

Obed Millán Márquez was a pastor when taken to UMAP in June 1966. He was there until April 1967. He was discharged because he was over 27 years of age. He was the pastor of the churches in El Cotorro and Arroyo Apolo in Havana City, a professor at the seminary, and a member of the Directive Board. He later immigrated to the United States where he continues as a pastor. He is currently living in Miami, Florida.

Manuel Morales Mustelier was a pastor when he was taken to UMAP in June 1966. In April, 1967 he was discharged because he was over 27 years of age. He was a pastor of the Baptist Churches in Madruga, and in the Almendares neighborhood in Havana City. He is currently living in Nicaragua.

Lázaro Cuesta Rodríguez was a pastor in Arriete when he was taken to UMAP in June, 1966. He was discharged in April, 1967, because he was over 27 years of age. He was a pastor of the churches in San Felipe, Batabanó, El Cotorro, and Yaguajay. He is deceased.

Actually, although the recruitment of these pastors is mentioned in this part of the narration, it did not take place until three months later, because they were recruited in the second and last call for UMAP, and were in the organization for only ten months. What caused dismay and convinced us that we would stay in UMAP was the news that they would continue calling pastors every year and not the specific recruitment of these brothers, such as this narration might seem to be understood; such recruitment took place later. Since those pastors were recruited in June 1966 and demobilized in April, 1967, they were there only a little longer than nine months, a much shorter time than the seminarians, who stayed almost three years.

then, the barracks had been something alien to me, a transitory place, something I expected to vanish from my life any day. How we dreamed of the return to the seminary! But that night I started to see it as something that would be a part of my life for a long time.

At that moment I bid farewell to the hope of a prompt release. Abandoning hope is always a devastating blow. I went outside and prayed to God for some time: *"God, you have to give me strength if this is to last for a long time."* I returned to the barracks and as I stood next to my bunk bed, I started to write a letter to Miriam. I remembered and copied a poem that I had read for the first time in the newsletter of the Presbyterian Church in Cárdenas where I grew up and of which I was a member until I became a Baptist in 1962:

> *Life has its sad and bitter moments,*
> *It has its days of sufferings, days so long!*
> *But life also has happy hours.*
> *Things are not always as they seem;*
> *Enjoy your charming hours,*
> *And when the bitterness comes,*
> *Tell your soul: Why do you hurry?*
> *Don't you know that behind the clouds is the sun?*

Yes, the clouds had become thick and had completely covered the sky. The storm was strong and threatened to last for some time. Although the miracle of getting us out shortly would apparently not occur, the sun would come out again. It was all a matter of time. The clouds can only keep the sun from being seen, but they are incapable of preventing its energy and warmth from reaching us. Besides, they all pass. The clouds cover a space of the sky for a period of time, but they always dissipate.

I realized as I wrote that UMAP was a passing cloud. It was a low, dark, evil, cruel, and dangerous cloud, but it was temporary.

Nevertheless, in the face of our hopes and wishes, this cloud was to darken our sky for a long time.

4

God's Unfathomable Ways

Although it was the end of April, the normal spring rains had not yet begun. The regimen of strenuous work continued, and after having been recruited, we had spent five months without a leave of absence. The only contact with the outside world had been the visits by the families once a month and the letters that came in the mail a couple of times each week. When someone needed to be taken to the doctor, the others looked upon him with envy. If the illness required hospitalization it was considered even a greater blessing. Sickness was the least of our problems!

One morning, due to my lack of experience, I wounded one of my legs with a machete. The small wound only needed a couple of stitches. So I was rewarded with a trip to the Senado Sugar Mill to be sutured. When he saw that I was sent to the mill, Nene, a UMAP recruit who kept guard, said, "Gosh, 13, you are a lucky guy! One of these days, I'm going to take a chop and rip off half a leg. You'll see!"

Thus began the new norm: the recruits would intentionally wound themselves on their hands, their legs, or their tendons, in order to get some time off. This scheme even succeeded in getting a few men demobilized. But my wound had not been intentional and it was small enough not to prevent me from working. So, I visited the Senado Sugar Mill for the first time at the end of April, accompanied by a sergeant who not only took me to see the doctor to take care of my wound, but he also allowed me to make a telephone call to my family.

Another Friend from the Officers' Corps

We spent almost the entire day passing the time by visiting with some of his friends. The sergeant was not in a hurry to return to the unit, so we sat under the shade of a tree near the entrance of the mill. He was only a few years older than I, had a pleasant personality, and did his job without taking advantage of any of the recruits. A communication link had been created between us.

"It's an utter disgrace to be working in Las Marías, 13; the leaders are crazy! They shouldn't treat people like that." He said this as he took off his cap and moved his hands through his hair.

I just looked at him without saying anything.

"We studied in a school to be UMAP officers. We graduated on October 16 and the commencement speech was delivered by the Commander in Chief. I assure you that the things that he said then have nothing to do with what is going on here."

"Then what Granma published isn't true!" I blurted out. I was referring to the coverage about UMAP published in the newspaper a few weeks before.

"Oh, you know that reporters write whatever they want to", he said.

"The newspaper says that the idea for UMAP came up one day last November in a meeting of the General Staff officers while they discussed what to do with all of the young people that couldn't be called to active military service. According to the reporter, the officers spoke with Fidel and proposed that they create UMAP. And now you tell me that you went to a school to come here?"

"It wasn't like that. We graduated as intermediary officers for UMAP on October 16."

For me it was a terrible discovery to learn that UMAP was a project that had been devised and prepared carefully beforehand. It would have been far easier to swallow the idea that it had been hastily arranged, because the errors and abuse then would have been more understandable. The sergeant, without meaning to, had hit a raw nerve.

"And why were the Christians brought here?" I asked.

"Well, you were unwilling to go to military service and you could not be exempted. After all, every young man must fulfill his duty to his homeland. So, you must serve the time of your service here."

"Yeah, we serve the time of our service being thrown together with junkies, homosexuals, and delinquents, closed us up in camps surrounded by tall barb-wired fences and armed guards, even when we are working in the country. What a great idea!" I responded.

"Come on 13, everybody knows that you're a different kind of people. Had you been called to the regular military service, it would have been a problem because your religion doesn't allow you to serve."

"There you are mistaken, sergeant!" I said. "We were willing to go through the Obligatory Military Service like any other Cuban. So, what are we doing here? And besides, if we had known about this place, do you think we would have refused to enlist?"

We talked like two friends about our respective families and our interests in life until the day had become night. He asked me about the Baptists, our doctrines and customs. At the end of the evening, as we stood up to go back, he told me, "Bringing all of you here has been a huge blunder!"

We went back to the unit very late that night.

The Purpose of UMAP

Today, I have in my hands the speech delivered by Dr. Fidel Castro at the graduation of the intermediate UMAP officers on October 16, 1965. It was a speech that gave very precise instructions. He explained that the re-education of the moral character of the men was the main objective of UMAP. He insisted that UMAP units should not be viewed as places for punishment. The officers were urged to combine military discipline with a fair and humane treatment of the recruits. The document came to be in my hands because some officer had forgotten it and left it somewhere, and a UMAP recruit had found it.

How could there be such a huge difference between the original conception of UMAP and its reality? After the reiterated warnings of not allowing the units to become places of punishment, why had they become such?

In the following months, there were others who were recruited to UMAP, including lawyers, various officials, workers of Cuban Airways, and others; even some elderly who were punished, either for mistakes, or for living "the sweet life."[1] Here I will not address the process through which these people were recruited and sent to UMAP. Were such camps being operated in order to circumvent the legal process and allow for the punishment and incarceration of a man for a lengthy period of time, without the accused being able to exercise his right to go to court? In practice, it seemed that they were. In Las Marías—as far as I can remember—there were at least three people who suffered under such circumstances. They neither spoke of nor clearly explained their individual situations, but they were totally out of place in those units.

With what reasoning could those who had been

---

[1] **The sweet life.** From the 1960 Italian movie, *La Dolce Vita*. In Cuba, the saying referred to officials or workers who profited from the privileges of their offices, were self-indulgent, or led unrestrained lives.

instructed to treat even the most troublesome recruits humanely and respectfully have allowed themselves to engage in abuses of power that resulted in the organization's dissolution within less than three years of its inception? According to Dr. Fidel Castro's speech, it is evident that there was a concern for certain sectors of society that needed a renewed focus. The recruiting of certain people to a military service with special components might have been beneficial in some respects if the program had been conducted in a positive direction. But the procedures employed by UMAP were not what were intended by Castro's speech; the indifference to the differing backgrounds and needs of the recruits exacerbated the fallout which UMAP certainly caused.

Sadly, UMAP left a deep scars on a large majority of the recruits who were forced to spend time there, and on their families as well. I would suggest that with few exceptions, it also was a negative and baffling experience for many of the officers.

Another Friend in the Underworld

"Hi 13! How many days will you be allowed to miss work?" Nene asked me when I entered the barracks.

"None," I told him. "It was just two stitches and it doesn't even hurt."

"Boy, you're scr--ed! If only you had cut yourself a little deeper, you could have had a few days off work.[2] If you want, I know how to make it so that your wound gets infected. Then, you will be able to lie down for a few days and escape working in the fields."

I smiled and said no. Actually, I would rather have worked in the fields than stayed in the unit, and I did not at all like the idea of intentionally infecting the wound.

"Your loss, Man, but Nene is here to serve you if you

---

[2] **Curralo**. Slang for *work*.

want." And he left. Nene was a real big shot. He had been recruited because he was a junkie and was cocky on the street. In the unit it was rumored that he was a petty thief.

On the day of the first visit, when he saw his mother, he went running and crying, "Here comes mi *pura.*"[3] And he cried like a little baby for a long time. "Mi *pura* doesn't deserve to be here. She has already suffered enough in her life," he said over and over again while he caressed and kissed her.

Nene suffered from epileptic seizures. For that reason, he did not have to go work in the country, but had been named the guard-keeper and was put in charge of the cleaning and up-keep of the barracks. One day, when I returned from the country, I found that the padlock of my box had been forced open and some of my belongings had been stolen. I started to complain loudly and I must have said something obnoxious. I became very upset and did not stop complaining. Nene listened to my emotional outburst and observed me with a solemn expression. A few others came to see what had been stolen. Because of what we were suffering and the exhausting work, the theft of my few belongings became a major tragedy.

Shortly after, Nene came over to my bunk and said in a serious tone, "Hey 13, come with me behind the bathrooms."

The area behind the bathrooms was a dangerous place because all sorts of things would happen there. The fights took place there because it was out of the officers' sight. It was also the place where the homosexuals met. Since I had nothing fear from Nene, I went with him. There he gave me the surprise of my life.

He returned everything that had been stolen, and said, "Look 13, forgive me; I didn't know it was your box. I don't steal from people like you, because God helps you. I want you to show me which of these boxes is yours. From now on, nobody is going to steal from you. And don't worry about your

---

[3] **Mi pura.** Slang for *my mother.*

broken padlock, because even though your box is without a padlock, no one will touch it. I guarantee it!"

Moved by Nene's gesture, I was ashamed of the words that I had spoken. I hugged him, apologized and tried to speak to him again about the Gospel. I told him that the Lord could make him a new creature.

"Yes, that sounds nice when you say it, but I am already a worthless man. Besides, look where God has put us, you and me," and he began to cry. Nene cried about anything, in the same way that he loved to start a fight in no time.

Nobody touched my box again, although it had no padlock for a long time. Despite his constant boasting as a delinquent and a bully, Nene was a decent guy, and he always respected us, although he constantly offended everyone else. Perhaps deep inside, he wanted to be like us.

Nene was a special person, and had the virtue of gaining the goodwill of people. In spite of the hard outer shell that he exhibited in front of everyone, he could also be very sensitive and was capable of showing affection and loyalty. If he had accepted the Lord, everything would have changed in his life. But sin enslaves a man and binds him with strong chains. Nene also was in his own environment there, and some of Satan's servants had him well bound. Finally, one day he was released from UMAP due to his sickness. A few years later I heard that he had died in a street fight.

The Plans for the First Leave

Another Baptist was transferred to Las Marías. Ruben Deulofeu[4] had been a student of medicine at the University of Havana until he was forced to discontinue his studies when the university was "purified" by the expelling of the Christian

---

[4] **Rubén Deulofeu.** Member of the Baptist Church in San Luis (currently Santiago de Cuba Province). He studied medicine at the University of Havana, from which he was expelled for being religious. He was recruited in November 1965. He was discharged in April 1967 because he was over twenty-seven years of age. He later immigrated to Spain and finished his education. He now lives in Miami, Florida, where he practices medicine.

students. A short time afterward he was sent to UMAP, at the same time as we. He served as a health worker in another unit and one fine day he was transferred to Las Marías. They intended that he work in the country in spite of the fact that he suffered from an illness in his knees for which he had surgery a short time later. He was very talkative and he loved to read. His presence was good for the group. From him, we learned how to play chess and he increased our appreciation for our cultural literature. We developed a good friendship that has survived the years and distance.

Little by little, the time for the leave drew near. We had been promised that we would receive our leaves by the end of the harvest. The showers of May arrived very late, but their arrival put an end to the cutting of cane. Some of us had been making plans to get married during that leave, which seemed that it would never come. Miriam and I, with her parents' consent, had decided to marry during the first visit. Also José Ferrer and Estrellita[5] decided to get married, as well as Rafael Hernández and his fiancée Glide.[6] Rubén Deulofeu was also planning to marry María.[7] For a long time we just spoke of weddings; it seemed odd to plan a wedding that would take place without any advanced notice, but we were unable to set dates.

"I am going to write to the seminary asking for permission to get married," Rafael Hernández told me. Circumspect and restrained as always, he wanted to do things methodically.

"Why write?" I said. "Has the seminary written us, by any chance, to see how we are doing?"

---

[5] **Estrella Ruiz. Native of Placetas.** She was a member of the Baptist Church of that city. She passed away in the 1980's in Güara, Havana Province, when her husband José Ferrer was a pastor.

[6] **Glide Alonso.** She was a member of the "Aposento Alto" Baptist Church, in Havana City. She currently lives with her husband, Pastor Rafael Hernández, who is retired in Miami, Florida.

[7] **María Ponchete.** She was a native of Guantánamo and a member of the Baptist Church of that city. She currently lives with her husband in Miami, Florida.

God's Unfathomable Ways

The seminarians and pastors of the Eastern Baptist Convention were visited officially by their leaders, as were those from the other denominations. But nobody visited us. It is true that the work was in a crisis, but if the administration of the seminary had sent a letter encouraging us, it would have been very good. Instead, we received word of some criticism from some of the professors because we were thinking about getting married.

Pastor Francisco Rodés[8], who was my personal friend, visited me several times and wrote to me frequently. But, from the seminary, or from the leadership of the Convention, we received nothing and we felt completely abandoned. Since there was an agreement that seminarians could not marry while they were studying in the institution, I did not want to write asking their permission. I reasoned that since we were in the military service, there was no reason to request permission, especially since they were ignoring us completely. Ferrer did not write to them either. But Rafael insisted and wrote a letter explaining the reasons for which he needed to get married and requested the authorization from the faculty of the seminary. The response did not take long. Rafael received a disheartening letter that stated emphatically: *"You are not students of the seminary. Therefore, you do not have to ask for permission."*

That was the first and only letter that we received from the seminary while we were in UMAP. Did they consider us to be social scum also?

"That's why I didn't write!" I said when Rafael, very dismayed, read the letter to me. We knew about their comments and about the judgment that they made in their last meeting of the faculty about our wishes to get married.

Such judgment, which consisted of considering our

---

[8] **Francisco Rodés González.** Baptist Pastor. He was pastor of the First Baptist Church in Matanzas for almost thirty years, and was the President of the Baptist Fraternity of Cuba. At present, he is chairperson of the Kairós Center in Matanzas, and is a professor of the Evangelical Seminary of Theology. He is retired as pastor and lives with his wife in Matanzas City.

decision as being hasty and carnal, came primarily from a female professor. It was false and unfair. Those who planned to get married were senior students and all of us had spent years in our courtship. Marrying was a necessity. Our fiancées had to travel constantly to visit us, and we would have to wait three more years to fulfill our term of service. Marriage would make many things easier, and would create for us a tangible benefit within the difficult situation in which we were living. We decided to continue with the plans and hopes for our weddings and ignore the unfavorable comments toward us.

Rubén Deulofeu and María planned to get married in Oriente and would travel by plane to Havana for their honeymoon. Miriam and I wanted to be married on the same day as they, but we planned to be married in Ciego de Ávila, and then we would also go to Havana. We had planned that both couples would meet at the Riviera Hotel. Rafael and Glide would marry in Havana, Ferrer and Estrellita in Placetas, and then they were going to the Mayajigua Lakes for their honeymoon. It all depended on the leave and all of us longed to be in the first group. Because we were repeatedly told that the recruits with the best behavior would leave in the first group, we always expected that this recognition would be given to us.

Christians and their Foolishness

"I can't believe that the best that we have here are the Baptists, with the pile of foolishness that they believe!" commented Lieutenant Concepción in the officers' room a few days before the first leave. He had realized that our behavior was very different from the rest of the troop.[9] I heard his comment while I was working in the office.

Because our relationship was friendly, I waited for an opportunity to tell him, "I heard your conversation with the officers. Allow me to tell you that the foolishness that we believe in is the very cause of our uncommon behavior."

---

[9] In Las Marías there were no believers from other evangelical denominations.

"Well, you all have had a different education but when you are released from the bonds of religion you are going to be more useful to society."

Then a political discourse ensued, which had apparently been memorized. He moved his hands wildly about and yelled loudly thinking that the louder he spoke the sooner he was going to convince me of all the evil that religion had brought to the world. I listened to him patiently until he finally stopped talking. Then I asked him, "And what do you think the company would be like if all of us here were Christians?"

"This place would be great, there is no doubt about that!"

"And if everybody became Christians, wouldn't the world be better?"

"No, that is not so!" He sprang to his feet, and began to speak loudly again, as if he were delivering a speech in a convention. "It's communism that will bring happiness and well-being to humanity, because all that capitalism has brought us is poverty."

"I am not talking, Lieutenant, about communism nor capitalism. I am talking about Christianity...."

Concepción turned his back on me and bolted from the office like a meteorite. He had already said all he intended to say, and was not willing to discuss anything further. Actually, the Christians had gained honor and we had good relationships with our superiors.

Life is Full of Surprises

On May 25, almost six months to the day of our initial recruitment, it was announced that, the first group of recruits would be permitted to go out on leave. When the list of lucky ones was read to the troop, not one Christian was among them. All those who were in that first group to go out had been selected to serve as corporals in other units upon their return. They would also be assigned to the new camps that would be populated by those from the second UMAP recruitment, arriving in June. The group of politicians for our unit did not consider the Christians suitable for that position. As a reward, the chosen ones obtained eleven days of leave.

The second group left on June 6. They were also selected to become corporals, but their leave was granted for ten days. In that group, the only Christian chosen was Ernesto Ruano. The others, they told us, would go out in the third group, on June 16. The fourth and final group, would be the most disobedient of the recruits.

Ernesto had also planned to marry but we already knew that this would not be possible. His fiancée's father, who was a pastor, was opposed to the wedding occurring at that time, and she had decided to obey her father. For Ernesto, her stance proved to be a devastating blow. He was my best friend. For many years, we had travelled parallel paths in life and we loved each other as true brothers. Now, the UMAP experience had brought us closer together. We slept in the same bunk, he in the lower bunk and I in the bunk above. When I knew that he was selected for that group I was puzzled. This meant that we would be separated. When he returned he would go as a corporal to another unit.

When I saw him leave the barracks to fall in with those on leave, I had a premonition that later came true, and sparked a pain that I was unable to shake for thirty years, and then, only in part. We never knew the reason her father opposed the marriage, but oppose it he did. They had been engaged for several years and appeared to be the ideal couple, but her father thought that it was better for them to wait until after he was discharged from UMAP. Ernesto wanted his fiancée to agree to marry him despite her father's opposition, but she refused. These events plunged my friend into a deep spiritual crisis. As I narrate this story, I am not blaming either his fiancée or her father; both were godly Christians who believed they were doing the will of God. It is possible that the pastor was influenced by the attitude of the seminary faculty who had discussed our weddings, and perhaps he thought that it would be wiser to wait.

Ernesto went on leave, and when he visited his fiancée they broke off their engagement. He was one of the two who did not go back to the seminary after being released.[10]

After the second group left, we were informed that the remaining Christians would be allowed to go out next, and we immediately notified our fiancées. Although we had learned that nothing was sure until it happened, all of us fixed the dates for our weddings for Sunday, June 19.

Suddenly, on June 7, there were abrupt changes in the officer corps, which proved tragic for me. I lost Lieutenant Concepción, who had helped me so much and with whom I had formed a warm friendship. I learned then that changes in the leadership always resulted in further destabilization, because the recruits had to meet new people, and, at least in the beginning, that was always unsettling. So, encouraged by the hope of the leave, we lived by counting down the days until Thursday, June 16. It seemed never to arrive.

It would finally come, but everything changed for me, one day before, on Wednesday, June 15.

Towards the Pit of Despair

Since some of the officers also went on leave, the new leaders placed a few of the UMAP recruits as corporals and chiefs of platoons. Ours was led by a man from Havana who was nicknamed "El Moro". Until that time, he had been known for being unruly and quarrelsome. Now in command, incredibly, he was being tough on all of his former mates. On Thursday morning, when we fell in for work, he began to stir us up as if he had been a shining example of discipline and work before then. It occurred to me to make a comment while falling in; "It seems incredible that El Moro, being the mess

---

[10] The other seminarian was also named Rafael Hernández, then a member of the Baptist church in Güanajay.

that he is, is being tough on us all."

A recruit with whom I was not on friendly terms, and who had been appointed corporal of my squad, went straight to the new chief of the unit, Lieutenant Raúl Marrero[11] and told him his version of my comment. According to him, I had said the following: "It seems incredible that that Negro, as degenerate as he is, is being tough on us," and then added a four-letter word that I had never expressed.

The lieutenant was black, and he assumed that my comment had been made against him. I was totally ignorant of what was taking place and was unaware that the corporal had gone to the office to talk to Marrero. Later that day, I sensed something wrong while in the country, but I only learned the details after we returned from our leave of absence from the lieutenant's own mouth.

The fall-in had been delayed that morning because the carts that took us to the fields had not arrived, so we were waiting in the yard of the unit.

"Pardon me, lieutenant, what did I do? Why did you talk to me like that?" I asked.

"What did you do? You have the nerve to ask what you did? You know better than anyone else!"

Every time that I tried to speak it infuriated him more.

"You have no right to open your mouth! And you call yourself religious! Beyond that your leave is suspended," he added, "so that you will learn not to speak disparagingly of Negroes!" The lieutenant seasoned his words with other insulting epithets that I wish not to repeat.

I cannot possibly describe what I felt. It was a total injustice and extremely cruel. The worst of all was that at that

---

[11] **Lieutenant Raúl Marrero.** Officer of the FAR. He was in Las Marías from June, 1966 until June, 1967. When the term of his service was over, he was discharged from the military in UMAP. He is currently retired, and lives with his family in Madruga, Havana Province.

moment I did not have the slightest idea of what was happening. Some of my friends tried to intercede on my behalf and were not allowed. Probably the reaction of many in my defense angered the lieutenant. Everybody knew that I was getting married on Sunday, including Marrero.

Many approached me to comfort me, assuring me that during the day everything would be cleared up, because we all suspected that some breakdown in communication had occurred. I spoke with the chief of the politicians[12] of the company so that he would intercede for me, and he assured me that he would resolve the problem. I spent the day praying, with the hope that the Lord would work for me and I would be able to go on leave. I could not conceive of it being any different. God did know what had taken place and would surely work in my favor. I went to bed really looking forward to what would happen. I slept peacefully.

But on Thursday morning, I was called to fall in with my hoe in order to go to work to the country with those who remained to leave in the fourth and final group. On the way to fall in, I found the politician. Frustrated and angry as I was, without making the usual military salute, I demanded, "Don't you see that it's all a lie? You aren't here to help anybody. Lieutenant Marrero doesn't know me, but you have been here for months and you know my behavior very well."

"Stand at attention! And shut your mouth once and for all." It was his only response.

I stood at attention and waited for him to give me some explanation. He looked at me from head to toe with an arrogant expression that I have never forgotten. He kept me in that position for some time, which seemed endless to me. Other recruits passed by and watched the scene, and a few who stopped to watch, he quickly said, "Walk on, walk on: this

---

[12] **Political instructors.** They were soldiers whose function was to teach classes of Marxism to the recruits. They were the real "re-educators". The recruits had to go to them if they had any kind of problem or needed any kind of help.

is none of your business".

I felt humiliated and ridiculous standing at attention before that man who supposedly was there to help me, but had actually done nothing for me. When he grew tired of having me in this position before him, he said, "Join the fall-in and go to the country. You deserve it!"

I got on the cart after saying farewell to my companions who would go on leave, hardly speaking, with a knot in my throat and a grievous pain in my heart. When the tractor, which was pulling the cart started, the group going on leave had already fallen in. I asked someone to tell Miriam not to expect me, and I begged all of them to pray for me.

I felt totally overwhelmed, destroyed, and outraged. I was completely unaware of the reason I was being punished, but I began to suspect that it had to do with my comment about El Moro, although I did not understand what would cause such a reaction. That morning my furrow was watered with bitter tears. My emotions went from anger to rage, from impotency to despair. I do not know how many questions I asked the Lord again and again. So many dreams and so many hopes! So many months waiting and now, in the blink of an eye, everything collapsed without a coherent explanation. As I worked in the country, another recruit let me know that it was all due to a report that the corporal of my squad had told the lieutenant in the office. But then nobody actually knew exactly what he had said. What was true was that the man in question, a UMAP recruit like all of us, had shown an aversion toward me, and toward the group of seminarians, on several occasions.

My friends believed that he wanted my job of working in the office, which frequently freed me from going to the country. His enmity was unfounded and senseless; perhaps he had some ulterior motive that I could never discover. His accusation succeeded in having my leave suspended only one day in advance, which prevented my marriage from taking place the following Sunday.

How could have that been possible? After much prayer, rage, and crying, at some point I found peace, and God gave me the strength to go on. The morning was exceedingly long, but when I returned to the unit for lunch, I remained quiet. I only asked God that the brothers would already be gone, because I did not want to say goodbye again. I also wanted to find an opportunity to ask the man for an explanation. What in the world had he said about me?

If I had already lost my leave, nothing else mattered.

God's Plans Cannot be Frustrated

When we arrived, I could see from the cart that the group had already departed. As I entered the unit, Lieutenant Marrero left his office quickly and called me. Clearly, I had earned his contempt, for he told me abruptly, "Take a bath and pick up your belongings. You are going on leave because a relative of yours has died." I was dumbfounded. I asked who had died but he did not know. A message had arrived from the battalion that I should report to go on leave because of the death of a relative. "But listen very carefully: your leave is for only four days. Your regular leave for ten days is suspended. Hurry up! We are taking you to the battalion."

I ran toward the barracks while reciting Psalm 42:7, *"All your waves and breakers have gone over me."* Because my grandmother on my father's side was sick, I thought that it was she who had died. I quickly took a bath, got dressed and reported to the office ready to go. My soul was like a erupting volcano. So I was back on the cart, this time heading to the battalion to pick up my permit for my leave.

The sergeant who accompanied me was the same one who had taken me to the Senado Sugar Mill the day of my wound, with whom I had developed a good friendship. Lieutenant Marrero sent with him a message to the battalion telling them of his decision to suspend the ten-day leave. But the sergeant had wanted to help me from the very beginning, even though he did not know the details of what had occurred that morning, either. On the way, we agreed that he would let me enter the battalion first, and that I would go on leave before he delivered the message. When we arrived, the sergeant stayed at the door and said to me, "Go and talk with the head of personnel. I'll wait until you leave; maybe you will be granted fourteen days. Later we'll see what I will say to Lieutenant Marrero, because he ordered me to tell the head of personnel his orders before you saw him."

The head of personnel confirmed that my grandmother had passed away. My father had notified them through the Military Committee. Then he explained to me, "You have the right to take a four-day leave for the death of a relative, but since you haven't had the regular ten-day leave yet, tell me what you'd rather do."

"What can I do?" I asked. My heart was beating so loudly that I am sure that the head of personnel could hear it.

"Well, you can go now with four days, and when you return you can take the other ten that pertain to you. Or you can leave for ten days now. But when you return I can't grant you the other four due to you."

"I'm going on the regular leave," I responded. He pressed, telling me that the other way I could have more days off, but I knew that if I returned after four days, I would not be able to take the ten-day leave. So I asked for my ten-day leave and got out of there as quickly as I could. The sergeant was waiting outside of the battalion by the coconut trees.

When we met he told me very happily, "Get out of here immediately! And *pray*, man, that you will not have problems when Marrero finds out!" He gave me an affectionate pat on the shoulder and told me, "Get married, man! Don't waste this opportunity!" When I got to the dirt road, he yelled, smiling, "Congratulations!" The sergeant was happy because I was on leave.

My departure was like a scene in a movie. A truck, going to the Senado Mill passed by at just the right moment, and I jumped on it while running, barely stopping, although I was very troubled and hardly knew what I was going to do. I thought that the wedding would be impossible anyway, since I had to go to Cárdenas for my grandmother's burial. I decided to call my parents' home once I got to the mill to find out what to do.

God and His Mysterious Ways

When I was able to communicate, I learned that my grandmother, who had been bedridden for some time, had died two days earlier and had already been buried. My father insisted that I go to Ciego de Ávila so that I could get married on Sunday as had been planned. It was amazing: God had delayed the news of her death so that I could go out on leave!

I thought of the recruit who had tried to harm me and I felt compassion. I never knew why he had turned into my personal enemy. He always managed to put me in difficult situations. In this case, his triumph was limited and brief. Nothing and nobody can step in the way when God wants to bless someone. How did he feel when he saw me go on leave? All my sufferings of those two days turned to radiant joy and the conviction that God was blessing our plans for marriage. Had the news arrived on time, the wedding might have been postponed. It arrived when everything was over and when I needed it to go out on leave.

My poor grandmother died at precisely the right moment, giving me the best gift that she could ever have imagined. She was not really my grandmother, but my father's godmother. When he and his younger brother were orphaned in the midst of their boyhood, she took over their care and raised them. She always lived in our home and showed a very special affection for me. I had dreamed of her two or three nights before.

In my dream, I was sleeping in the unit and I had felt some very familiar footsteps. My grandmother suffered from a huge deviation of her spinal column and her back was bent at a ninety-degree angle to the rest of her body. In the dream, when I felt my grandmother's footsteps, I recognized it was she and awoke. She walked up next to my bunk bed. "What are you doing here? Who brought you?" I asked.

She smiled and began caressing me as she used to when I was a boy. She said, "Why wouldn't I come to see you? I couldn't come before because I was very sick. I know that you are having a hard time, and came to tell you not to get desperate, but to be patient, because God is going to help you."

I leaned my head against her, feeling once again like the little boy that she had caressed and spoiled. I felt her hands play with my hair like she did so many times when I was a little boy and an adolescent. Then I awoke. It was one of those amazing events of life: I dreamed of her the very night that she died!

I had spoken with my parents over a public telephone in the post office in the Senado Sugar Mill. When I hung up the telephone, I sat on the wooden bench that was outside in order to sort out my plans and emotions. There I cried over my grandmother for the first time, and for the jumble of the events that had kept me from knowing of her death. There I thanked God for her life, for the love that she always showed, for the dream that permitted me to see her and, in a mysterious way, to tenderly bid her farewell, as she well deserved. She had been a very special woman. She took care of my father and his brother with an immense love and dedicated her life to them like a true mother, even though she had never even married. Had she known what her death meant to me, I think that she would have been very happy.

Just a few hours later than was planned, I departed on leave on the appointed day, June 16. For a while, I could not deal with the storm of emotions that had assailed me since the day before: first, the happiness over the coming leave and our wedding, then all of it frustrated with the Marrero incident, the memory of which confused me more by the day. After that had come the hope that everything would be arranged during the day before the leave, and then the utter collapse that occurred the next morning combined with the embarrassing meeting with the politician. There was my despair in the country, and upon my return to the unit, the sudden news of the death of an unidentified relative. Later came the thrill of receiving additional days to be on leave, even though Marrero had told me that I would only have four days, followed by the tentativeness of the wedding, the grieving over the death of my grandmother and the remembrance of her kindness to me. That same morning I was in anguish to the point of desperation as I worked, and tonight I was going to give Miriam the surprise of my arrival when she least expected it. How could I calm the beating of my heart?

I arrived at Ciego de Ávila after dark. I was excited to see the city lights, having been for the past seven months out in the country without any electrical lights. A few blocks from Miriam's home, I stepped off the bus. It seemed like a dream to be walking freely on the streets. Since she was not expecting me, her face froze when she saw me. She thought that her heartache was making her delusional, and she did not want to suffer from another disappointment. That same afternoon she had cancelled some of the arrangements that had been made for the wedding.

When the two of us absorbed the reality of being at last together and that we would, in fact, be married, we developed our plans quickly. We did not care if anyone discovered that we hardly had any money, because at that moment we were floating on a cloud of happiness. What we both had suffered from the suspension of the leave gave us even more joy in seeing our dreams come true.

A Strange Man in the Mirror

After being in Miriam's house for a while, I went to see my mother's cousin, who always allowed me to stay with her while I was visiting in Ciego de Ávila. After the greetings and talking a little with the family about the experiences that I was living through, I went into the bedroom to change clothes and take off that uniform that I so hated. As I undressed, I sensed another man undressing at my back and I was startled. I turned back to see, but then I realized that I was alone in the bedroom. It was my own image! I saw my full body in the mirror of the closet, but I did not recognize myself! I had not stopped to realize that during the seven months of being confined in Las Marías, I had lost more than forty pounds.

I experienced an odd feeling that I still remember vividly. I used to look at myself in a little mirror as I shaved in the unit; it was impossible to see even my full face at once. I stood in front of the mirror in order to look myself over. My naked body was skinny, and all of my ribs could be seen; it seemed like somebody else! My appearance had radically changed. I shall never forget that startling feeling as that "other-me" stared back at me from the mirror.

When I looked at my eyes, I realized that my changes were more than just physical. I found that there was an expression of hardness and some kind of darkness in my eyes. I shuttered. I found the man in the mirror, in addition to being unfamiliar, to be repulsive. Everything was different in his— my—countenance and expression. What was happening inside of me that made itself so apparent in my outer appearance?

To make matters worse, my baldness was cruelly displaying advanced symptoms. As I dressed, even my clothes seemed like someone else's. Seeing my whole body after seven months, either with or without clothes was quite unsettling. Finding that I was turning into another person proved to be both terrible and surprising. Something was painfully evident: the recent experience of my life, which in many respects was only beginning, had marked me forever. The worst thing was that nothing seemed clear to me anymore, and I knew that the path in front of me was still long, although at least at the moment, there was a happy respite.

The strange man in the mirror smiled at me with insolence and decided to enjoy the upcoming ten days, by forgetting at once everything he had suffered in the past.

5

The Hour of Love

After seven months of being confined in Las Marías, in the middle of the country and without any electrical lights, walking on the streets of Ciego de Ávila made me feel as if I was on the famous Fifth Avenue in New York City. Actually, I have done that several times in the past, without experiencing the sensation of freedom and wonder that filled me that Thursday night in June 1966.

Ciego de Ávila had about 70,000 inhabitants at that time. It is located on the Carretera Central (main highway), 110 kilometers from the City of Camagüey. The four-story Santiago Havana Hotel was the tallest building in town. It was the second most important city in the province, with a typical central park across from the Catholic Church, a large and beautiful church that had been rebuilt in the previous decade. Across from the square there was also the bus terminal, which gave movement and life to the place.

Many of the largest sugar mills in the country surrounded the city and contributed to its economic prosperity. Independence Street, the main commercial arterial of the city, made it possible for people to walk under its balconies all the time. A couple of movie theaters and the beautiful Teatro Principal (Main Theater) livened things up at night. All in all, it seemed to me quite a dazzling place after my stay in Las Marías.

I had known the city since I was a boy, because a brother and a cousin of my mother lived there. The brother[1] had lived there for many years and we visited their family during our summer vacations; I have wonderful memories of them and of that time in the city. They moved to Havana and then immigrated to the United States, but my cousin still lived there[2] with his family, in whose house I always stayed every time I went to visit Miriam. I enjoyed walking around without being constantly guarded, and I thought of how we sometimes value too little the small pleasures of life. We realize the importance of them only when we lose them. Being able to walk freely on a street, going wherever you want, without being watched after or hurried seems like something unimportant. But on that night it was a very meaningful experience.

I was heading to my fiancée's house to finalize the plans for the wedding that would take place on Sunday at six in the evening. I had forgotten very quickly about all the sufferings of the last few months, and I preferred not to dwell on having to return to the awful place ten days later. I wanted to make good use of that time and not ruin it by thinking ahead to the anguish that would follow. I certainly felt like a happy man.

What wonderful resources God has given to the human mind! I could disconnect, forgetting about UMAP and all that it had meant to my life. It was as if I had a magic psychological switch that permitted me to turn off all the unpleasant memories of the past seven months. I felt as if UMAP no longer existed.

---

[1] **José Luis Muñoz De Bergue** lived with his family on República Street between Maceo and Honorato Castillo in Ciego de Ávila. From there, they moved to Havana and immigrated to the United States in 1963. He passed away in West Palm Beach in June, 2008.

[2] **Dr. Antonio Sánchez de Bergue** lived in a beautiful two-story mansion on Maceo Street, between Independencia and Libertad. He was a dentist, and had a private office and also had a department store that had been a branch of the famous "El Encanto" in Havana. At the time of these events, the store had been confiscated by the state and no longer belonged to him. He immigrated to the United States with his family in 1967, and passed away in 2007.

It was during that time of my life that I began to really understand what the Lord wanted to teach me when He said in Matthew 6:34: *"Therefore do not be anxious about tomorrow, for tomorrow will be anxious for itself. Sufficient for the day is its own trouble."* I learned in that horrible place what it was to live one day without worrying about the next. Every day at dawn amid the bellows of: "On your feet!" and a series of four-letter words from the officers urging us to rise, as well as the protests and curses of the recruits, I asked God for strength to live that day. My goal was to make it until the night.

When we returned from the country, we took a shower and ate. After that, I was the owner of that brief period of time in which I could devote myself to reading, writing, or simply talking. When the nights of a full moon extended the work beyond midnight, I felt satisfied when at last I could lie down in my bed and be alone to pray and plan for the future. I slept peacefully and even happily. I had conquered that day!

I enjoyed that time of solitude and communion with the Lord without worrying about what I would have to face the next morning, and I slept in peace. The next day, again asking the Lord for strength to get to the night and when it arrived, I enjoyed my victory with a feeling of gratitude that nothing or nobody could take away. With God's help, Jesus' teaching, *"Tomorrow will be anxious for itself,"* came to be a reality in my life and a true blessing.

I learned that a day's burden was bearable, if not complicated by the anticipation of what difficulties might come the following day. I could now apply the same principle. Within ten days I would have to return to the same place to suffer the same cruel, unjust, and oppressive routine, but now I was simply a young man who was going to get married. I was full of dreams. I walked on the streets of a province town as if I were doing so in the capital city of the world, refusing to allow the future affliction to stop or cloud the present happiness.

Thank God I was able to do it.

A Wedding of Poor People...but Rich

"How much money do we have for the wedding?" I asked Miriam when at last we could talk alone in the living room of her house. She smiled and said, "We only have forty-five pesos (about two dollars) which I just received for my salary for the past two weeks."

I also smiled. Our plans, love, and dreams were plenty... but there was not enough money.

As a recruit I received seven pesos a month. This was not even enough to buy candy for snacks that some Haitian women sold near the unit in Las Marías. Although it was not such a big deal, they were paid as if it were. Oftentimes the food was not enough, so we waited for those women as if they were going to save our lives. They arrived carrying large baskets on their heads full of homemade candy, sometimes walking several kilometers to the cane fields where we were working. They lived in huts halfway between Las Marías and Truffín, about a kilometer away from the unit, but they managed somehow to get to any place we were working. Over the years, they also washed clothes for many of us.

Besides the seven pesos that I received as a salary, the church in San Antonio de Río Blanco, where I served as a seminarian when I was recruited, sent me monthly aid of fifteen pesos. Miriam worked, but she only earned around a hundred pesos a month. The economic situation was not good, and she spent much on the trips to Las Marías when she visited me.

"Well, that doesn't matter," I said, "God will provide what we need!"

Obviously, I was floating on a cloud of happiness from which I refused to see any problem. After seeing how God got me out of that place even though my leave of absence had been suspended, I knew He was going to open all the doors and provide what we needed.

When we went our separate ways that night, we were the two happiest people in the world, even though we neither had the money, nor knew how we were going to make all the arrangements. When I look back on our situation then, I realize the value of love and hope. We felt rich, although we had nothing, and immensely happy, even though we were experiencing a true tragedy. We were short of everything, except for love and dreams.

When Paul said, *"Love bears all things, believes all things, hopes all things, endures all things,"* [3] he knew what he was talking about. In the same way, when comparing love with faith and hope,[4] he assured us that love was the greatest of the three. He was stating a fundamental truth that men and women should remember and apply more often when facing the great problems of life. Love has the power to mitigate the effects of any tragedy and encourages people to live above their misfortunes by enjoying the true values of life, in spite of everything around them.

Only Flowers...and Much More

The next day in the morning, with the only forty-four pesos we had, we bought some flowers to decorate the church, and rented the veil that Miriam would wear. The wedding gown would be borrowed from another young woman of the church, Dania Paz[5], who had been married a few months earlier. We were penniless, but we had the flowers to decorate the church! Did it matter that we had no money two days before the wedding? I could buy absolutely nothing of what was being offered in the "House of the Bride and Groom,"[6] a store which had been owned by my mother's cousin until the day it was confiscated by the government. Miriam could only

---

[3] 1 Corinthians 13:7

[4] 1 Corinthians 13:13

[5] **Dania Paz.** She was a member of the Baptist Church in Ciego de Ávila and a very good friend of Miriam's. She is presently living in Atlanta, Georgia. USA.

[6] **House of the Bride and Groom.** State-owned store in which clothes and household items were sold for couples getting married.

buy a couple of pieces of lingerie. I looked as if I were wearing borrowed clothing, because of my recent loss of more than forty pounds. The small value of our possessions did not diminish the greatness of our dreams at all.

Who said that these are the most important things when two people really love each other and are about to get married? We were going to begin our marriage without money, possessions, a house, or even the ability to be together from that moment on.

None of this kept us from being truly happy, because true love is sufficient by itself and does not need many things for its fullness. We did not even have wedding rings. Somebody lent them to us to wear in our wedding. The reality was that after we had bought the flowers and we had run out of money, gifts started to arrive. Miriam's aunt and uncle[7] gave us eighty pesos that morning (considered a significant amount of money then) and afterwards some other gifts came.

My eldest sister called me by phone to say that she was going to pay for our reservation at the Riviera Hotel in Havana. My mother's cousin who lived in Ciego de Ávila promised to make arrangements and pay for the tickets for the train trip to the capital, which was not easy to get either. The photographer, who was a member of the church, told us that we could pay for the photos on installments as we were able to pay. It was certainly a wedding of poor people, but we felt like millionaires. At no time did the shortages that we faced manage to cloud our happiness. We had an enormous sense of gratitude to the Lord for the joy that we felt.

We were married on Sunday, June 19 at six in the evening at the Baptist Church in Ciego de Ávila. When I saw Miriam in her wedding gown, accompanied by her father[8] at

---

[7] **Daniel Gomez and Margarita Daniel.** She was Miriam's oldest sister who also lived in Ciego de Ávila. Both were members of the Baptist Church, and he was a deacon. In 1970 they immigrated to Spain, from where they immigrated to the United States and settled in Boston, Mass. She passed away in September 2003.

[8] **Camilo Daniel Mesa.** He was a deacon of the church, and his wife a deaconess. He passed away in March, 1991.

the door of the church, she was the prettiest girl in the world. For me, she certainly still is! Pastor Gilberto Prieto[9] officiated the ceremony. From my family, only my mother was able to come to serve as the matron of honor. Miriam and I sang *"Dream of Love"* by Liszt during the ceremony. Between the stanzas, I took the opportunity to tell her that I already had the tickets to Havana, which I received five minutes before the wedding. When we had parted earlier that afternoon to get ready for the wedding, we still had not known how we would be traveling. Some people in the sanctuary who knew all about our story broke down and cried when they heard us sing. We were radiant.

Our dreams, at least in part, were being fulfilled.

That night at about ten o'clock, on the special train, we left for our honeymoon in the capital. I was carrying in my pocket the largest amount of money I had ever had in my life and which was only a little more than what I now receive as my monthly salary. The satisfaction that we felt was impossible to describe. There had been so many months of suffering and tears that it seemed to us that we had reached heaven.

We arrived at Havana and at the Riviera Hotel almost at dawn. We were given Room 604. When we went in it was daybreak. We opened the curtains of the room and sat down very close together to watch the dawn. A beautiful view of the Havana skyline was seen from our room. We saw the sun come out filling everything up with light and our love found its fullness in the early hours of that morning.

For us our new life had started.

Love, Laughter, and Plenitude

I do not remember at what time I decided to call Rubén Deulofeu. Although they got married in Guantánamo,

---

[9] **Gilberto Prieto**. Baptist Pastor. He was pastor of the Baptist Church in Ciego de Ávila during the time when this story takes place. Later he was pastor of the churches in Manzanillo and Guantánamo. He presently leads a ministry for the deaf-mute.

they flew to Havana and were staying at the same hotel. He had witnessed the incident with Marrero in Las Marías, and had seen me leave devastated, to work in the country on that Thursday morning when the others had left together on leave. His silent goodbye hug and the pain that was in his eyes when he saw me on the cart to go off to work were still fresh on my mind. For that reason I wanted to find and surprise him. He could never have imagined that I had gone on leave at last, miraculously. I called the desk and I asked to be connected with his room.

"Hello?" I heard a sleepy voice on the other side of the line.

"No, it's I who am listening to a guy half asleep," I responded.

"Who is speaking?" He asked surprised and a little annoyed, trying to recognize my voice.

"It's incredible that in such a short time you have already forgotten the voice of a friend who is suffering like you are!" I added, "Everyone who gets married comes to the Riviera Hotel on his honeymoon!"

Rubén, more awake, said slowly as if not wanting to be happy before being sure. "But...it's just that...the voice that I am hearing...if I'm not mistaken...it sounds like...it's the voice of someone ... it can't be."

"Are you sure it can't be?"

Rubén definitely recognized me, "Kiddo! Where are you calling from? Where are you?"

"I think a couple of floors below you. And my wife is beside me," I notified him. "You are not the only UMAP soldier who got married yesterday. What do you think about that?"

"How did you do it?" I could feel his emotions rise as he listened to my words. "You cannot imagine how miserable we felt when we left Las Marías and left you there! Did you find out what really happened? None of us understood anything and that made us feel even worse."

In a few minutes the four of us were together in their room and I could tell them the whole story. So many times in the camp we had discussed how we would meet in Havana after we were married; it seemed like a distant and almost impossible dream. We were now sitting in the room which he and María shared, across from the sea, looking at the waves break on the Havana seawall, talking about many different topics and laughing at the times and afflictions that we went through in Camagüey.

There always comes a time when you can laugh at the hardest times. It is an ability that God has given us and I think that it helps us to maintain our emotional stability. There we talked about the things that had happened and we even mocked those who had made us suffer. The events that only a few days before had caused us to be torn up with anger and tears now were the source of laughter and joking.

Rubén mimicked Lieutenant Marrero and repeated the scene of the previous Wednesday in Las Marías, "You don't have the right to open your mouth! And he says that he is religious! Your leave of absence is suspended so that you will learn not to speak disparagingly of Negroes!"

We laughed until we were tired. We acted as if we did not have to go right back to the same place! We mocked and laughed because, after all, nobody could take away our joy at that moment. UMAP was an episode of our lives that in some way would pass. They might take three years of our time, but they could not control our thoughts or feelings.

That same night we received a visit in our room from Israel Cordovés and Alida Carrazana, who were still engaged. Almost all of the seminarians who were in UMAP had met in Havana. One night, in the recently opened and now famous ice cream parlor, "Coppelia" on L and 23rd Streets, we met by chance. José Ferrer and Estrellita, who had recently been married in Placetas, were also there.

Anticipated Visits

We all went into the heart of Havana, mainly to visit the seminary.

Miriam and I went on Tuesday morning. Despite that very discouraging letter that we received telling us, *"you are no longer students of the seminary,"* we loved the place, and the wound from being uprooted from there was still very deep. Because it was vacation time, there were no students, but we visited with Mrs. Caudill,[10] who received us with much affection and joy. This exceptional woman suffered from the experience of having her husband imprisoned and accused of being a CIA agent, but still kept a joyful spirit and remained very optimistic. It was inspiring to listen to her explain how her afflictions did not prevent her from being active in serving the Lord.

To once again walk through the halls of the building and to be able to look at the splendid view of Havana that you can see from it had been a dream that we had cherished over and over again for months. All of us who were in Las Marías visited the building during our leave. We still felt like seminarians, even though at that moment we were not.

On Wednesday we left the hotel and went to San Antonio de Río Blanco, the small town about seventy kilometers from Havana where I had worked weekends during the time I was in the seminary. The brothers and sisters from the church there prepared a feast for us. They were very affectionate and generous. How hard it was for both of us to come for only a visit, and for only a single day, to the house in which we had expected to live after finishing my seminary training and getting married! I loved that church very much

---

[10] **Marjorie J. Caudill.** Wife of Herbert Caudill, the superintendent of the Home Mission Board in Cuba that at that time was taken to prison. She lived in the seminary because her husband had been the Rector. At the time of the writing of this book she lived in Decatur, GA. She later went to live in Honduras with her missionary son and died there at an age over 90 years old.

and had dreamed of being a pastor there.

San Antonio had fewer than three thousand inhabitants. The church building was very beautiful, certainly the best and most modern in town. It had been built less than a decade earlier, and the parsonage was located above the sanctuary. As the bus approached, I had a lump in my throat and even more, a pain in my heart. But the love of the brothers and sisters, their joy at seeing us, and the multiple ways that they labored for us to be happy during those hours swept away the sadness that had come over me when we had first arrived there.

The next day we traveled to my parents' house in the city of Cárdenas. We arrived on Thursday night and on Saturday we went back to Ciego de Ávila, because on Sunday I had to report back to the unit; the leave would be over. I enjoyed the week without thinking of what would come next. I think that we were as happy as a couple could be on their honeymoon.

But when Sunday arrived, I was afraid to go.

The Return to Hell

The psychological switch with which I had been able to turn off my thinking about UMAP ten days earlier refused to work in reverse. It was neither so magical nor so effective. At times I was unable to enjoy the present happiness, and only with a great deal of effort could I keep myself from counting the remaining hours of freedom. I became less talkative and withdrawn. Although I was supposed to go back to the unit on Sunday afternoon, I decided to steal one more night. We attended the church service, though I could not enjoy it. We went back to the Santiago Hotel where we had been staying. The love of the last night that we were together was full of sadness. I was so distressed that it was impossible for me to enjoy it.

On Monday morning we said goodbye at the train station. When the train left, I saw Miriam until she stopped waving goodbye to me on the platform, appearing to have a strength and calmness that really I did not possess. I would rather not describe my feelings.

I arrived at Las Marías twenty-four hours after the official termination of my leave, but I encountered no problems. Other recruits had not returned either. A few days earlier, the officers had lowered the height of the fence by a little more than a meter, and the camp had a better appearance. At least it did not look like a German concentration camp with high barbed-wire fences.

They had made an effort to improve the unit. The barracks were repainted white and looked more pleasant, at least on the outside. Some of the officers had been replaced. There were rumors of changes in UMAP and its procedures. During our absence, new recruits from the second call[11] had arrived at the camp. I entered the barracks, which seemed dirtier and gloomier than before, without wishing to speak to anyone. I wanted the night to come so I could sleep. Most of the seminarians wanted to see and share the photos of their weddings and tell the stories of everything they saw during their leave, but my mood was different. I only wanted to be left alone. I had been able to forget about everything during the days that I had been on leave, but now the oppressive reality overwhelmed me. We did not know when our next leave would come, and although some things were changing, it continued to be the terrible place where the social scum had been taken.

Many years later, looking back, I could appreciate the lasting impact of UMAP on the Cuban Baptist Work. In addition to our group, they had recruited nine students from the Baptist Seminary in Santiago de Cuba: Samuel Entenza,[12]

---

[11] There were only two recruitments for UMAP. The first was in November, 1965 and the second in June, 1966.

[12] **Samuel Entenza**. Actually he was not a student of the seminary when he was recruited, but he registered right after he was discharged from UMAP. He was a pastor in different churches in the Eastern Baptist Convention Cuba, holding other

Melvin Puebla,[13] Eliezer Prieto,[14] Rolando Cañizares,[15] Rafael Mustelier Retilado,[16] Jesús Sayas,[17] Enoc Fumero,[18] Moisés Abella,[19] and Héctor Hernández.[20] Eight pastors from Oriente had also been taken: Luis Villalón Rubio,[21] Pedro Pérez Torres,[22] Azael Corrales Cervera,[23] Raimundo García Franco,[24] Cloduardo Malberti,[25] Elmer Lavastida Alfonso,[26] Rigoberto

---

leadership positions as well. He presently lives in Santiago de Cuba and directs a ministry of help to pastors and missionaries.

[13] **Melvin Puebla.** He was not yet a student of the seminary when he was recruited. After he was in UMAP, he joined a brigade of construction of INRA and received a salary as a civilian. After he graduated from the seminary he was the pastor of the Baptist church in Ciego de Ávila, where he retired due to an illness. He is currently living in Manzanillo, province of Granma.

[14] **Eliezer Prieto.** After he was released from UMAP, he finished his studies and was a pastor of various Baptist churches in the Eastern Convention, and later became its President. He is presently the pastor of the church in Jiguaní, Granma Province.

[15] **Rolando Cañizares Luna.** He became a Pentecostal pastor afterwards.

[16] **Rafael Mustelier Retilado.** He became a pastor of various churches. He is retired and is presently living in the City of Santa Clara.

[17] **Jesús Sayas.** He later became the pastor of various churches in the Eastern Baptist Convention of Cuba.

[18] **Enoc Fumero.** He was the pastor of different churches in the Eastern Convention. He retired due to an illness. He went to live in the City of Havana, and from there he immigrated to the United States.

[19] **Moisés Abella.** He finished his studies and was the pastor of various churches in the Eastern Baptist Convention of Cuba. He immigrated to the United States.

[20] **Hector Hernández.** He was a student in the seminary in Oriente when he was recruited. He was the pastor of various churches in the Eastern Baptist Convention of Cuba. Afterwards he moved to the Western Convention and was a pastor in Aguacate y Villa Rosa. He is presently a pastor in Union City, NJ.

[21] **Luis Villalón Rubio.** Deceased. He was a Baptist pastor when he was recruited by UMAP. Later, he was a pastor in Guaimaro until he passed away.

[22] **Pedro Pérez Torrez.** Deceased. He was a pastor when he was taken to UMAP. He belonged to the millionaire brigade of cane cutters.

[23] **Azael Corrales Severa.** Baptist pastor. He was a pastor when he was taken to UMAP. He was the Vice President of the Council of Churches of Cuba (Former Ecumenical Council of Cuba). He is retired and is currently living in Guantánamo.

[24] **Raimundo García Franco.** He was a Baptist pastor when he was taken to UMAP. Later he started working with the Presbyterian Church. He was pastor of the Presbyterian Reformed Churches in the City of Cárdenas. He is currently directing the Christian Center for Reflection and Dialogue in the City of Cárdenas.

[25] **Cloduardo Malberti.** He was a pastor when he was taken by UMAP. He is currently retired. He lives in Vertientes, Province of Camagüey.

Cervantes Pérez,[27] Joel Rosales Cortés,[28] and Orlando Colás.[29] Orlando Colás was at that time the Executive Secretary of the Eastern Baptist Convention of Cuba. From the Western Convention, twelve seminarians had been recruited in the first call, and another three were mobilized in the second one: Eleuterio Figueredo,[30] Tomás Inguanzo,[31] and Efraín Reyes.[32] There was a time when the Cuban Baptist work had thirty-six workers in UMAP. It is foolish to suppose that this was a coincidence, considering that more than fifty pastors had been imprisoned within the three-month period from April to June, 1966.

A large group of young people from the churches was also recruited. From the Church in Batabanó, they took five of the best leaders. Six were taken from the San Cristóbal Church,

---

[26] **Elmer Lavastida Alfonso.** He was a pastor when he was taken to UMAP. He has been a pastor for many years in the Baptist Church in Sueño neighborhood in Santiago de Cuba, where he also directs the B.G. Lavastida Center.

[27] **Rigoberto Cervantes Pérez.** Deceased. He was a pastor when he was taken to UMAP. He was the pastor of the Baptist Churches in Holguín, Baracoa and Baire. He was the President of the Ministerial Department of the Eastern Baptist Convention Cuba, and also occupied other directive offices. He passed away in November, 2002.

[28] **Joel Rosales Cortés.** He was a pastor of the Baptist church in Baracoa when he was taken to UMAP. Later he was a pastor in Contramaestre, and First Baptist Church in Santiago de Cuba. He is now retired and lives in that city.

[29] **Orlando Colás.** He was taken to UMAP when he was the Executive Secretary of the Eastern Baptist Convention Cuba at 38 years old. He was discharged fourteen months later and immigrated to the United States, where he ministered as a pastor. He is currently retired and lives in Miami, Florida

[30] **Eleuterio Figueredo Tamayo.** He was a first year student in the seminary when he was taken to UMAP. After he was released, he finished his studies and has worked as a pastor of the churches in San Luis and Calabazar (Havana City). He currently lives in Calabazar.

[31] **Tomás Inguanzo Tejera.** He was a student at the seminary when he was taken to UMAP. He was discharged due to an illness a few weeks afterwards. He continued his studies and worked as a pastor for the Baptist churches in Ranchuelo, Yagüajay and Buenavista. He is currently working with the Fraternity of Baptist Churches of Cuba.

[32] **Efraín C. Reyes.** He was a student in the Baptist Seminary in Havana when he was taken to UMAP in June, 1966. After being discharged he did not return to the seminary because he planned to leave Cuba. He was a member of the Baptist Church in El Cerro until he left for the USA in 1985. He is a graduate of Northwestern Theological Seminary in New Orleans, and currently lives in Miami, Florida.

and eight from the church in Cruces.³³ Other churches like San José de las Lajas, Pinar del Río, San Luis, Güira de Melena, Artemisa, Batabanó,³⁴ San Antonio de los Baños³⁵ and many others saw their most active young people disappear overnight, sent to Camagüey as social scum without any previous warning.

Some of the brothers, like Iván Delgado Marrero,³⁶ from the church in Pinar del Río, were summoned for an interview and from there were sent, just as they were, to Camagüey, without any time to prepare or say goodbye to their families. This recruitment method was preferred in that province; the youth of the church in San Cristobal suffered the same lot.³⁷ They were summoned by the Military Committee together with a large group of young people in town for an interview at eight-thirty in the evening. After ten, without any explanation, they were taken by truck to Mango Jobo, a place

---

³³ It was the church most affected by UMAP. Its young people, Jose Antonio Gil López, Rubén Sol Sardiñas, Agustín Ayo Lí, Wilfredo Suárez Consuegra, David Lema Morfi, Elpidio Pérez Martínez, Ricardo Pons Lí, and Jorge Péres de Alejo were taken. When they were taken away, the church lost two deacons, the Treasurer, the President and Vice President of the church, the director of the choir and that of the Department of Education. Of these young people, two stepped aside from the ministry: José A. Gil y Jorge Pérez de Alejo. One of them David Lema, is now a pastor in the United States. Ricardo Pons Lí passed away in 1989. He was an active member in the church and its choir director. The others live in Cruces and continue to serve as leaders of the church.

³⁴ From the Baptist Church in Batabanó Rolando Acosta Luis, Roberto and Rodolfo Luis Delgado, Moisés Echevarría Luis, and Ángel Quintana Pérez were taken. Of these, Rolando, Roberto and Moisés are currently leaders of the church. Rodolfo lives in the United States and Ángel Quintana is a pastor in Cumanayagua, Cienfuegos Province.

³⁵ From this church José N. González García, José I. Rodríguez and Alfredo Capote were taken. They are currently members of the following churches: II de San Antonio, Iglesia del Nazareno and la Sala Evangélica de San Antonio de los Baños respectively.

³⁶ **Iván Delgado Marrero** was a member of the church in Pinar del Río when he was taken to UMAP. After being released, he stayed in the same church most of his life. He was a deacon and the Vice President. He immigrated to the United States in late 1990, and lives in Miami, Florida.

³⁷ Of the Baptist church in San Cristóbal, the young men Laviña, Alberto Mena, José Antonio Sánchez, Ismael Valdés, Alberto Montalvo and Andrés Macías were taken. All of them occupied leadership offices in the church. Pablo Laviña, Alberto Mena and José A. Sánchez currently live in Miami, Florida.

nearby, where there was a military unit. At midnight, they were taken to the City of Pinar del Río, in a place known as La Loma de los Coches, and concentrated together with other young people of the province. They spent the night and part of the next day in the damp cool air, with a starry sky as their only roof. The buses began to arrive after seven the second night to transfer them to Camagüey. They did not touch any food until they arrived at their respective units where they were offered bread and sardines, almost forty hours after they had been detained!

Most of the young men taken from the church in San Cristóbal, were employed, and were exemplary workers. Some of them were apprehended while working at their jobs, and had no opportunity to return home to inform their families that they would be leaving. The recruitment occurred without any explanation, and the young men were taken without knowing where they were going.

It is probably impossible, after nearly fifty years, to develop a comprehensive list of the young Christians who went to UMAP. Although the Baptist denomination was greatly affected, UMAP also took pastors and laity from other evangelical churches, as well as priests, seminarians, and young Catholics. The current Cardinal of the Cuban Catholic Church, Monsignor Jaime Ortega Alamino,[38] was also in UMAP. I do not know the exact number, but I am sure that the group of Jehovah Witnesses recruited was numerous.

Some people, when reading the articles published in *La Voz Bautista* (The Baptist Voice), and realizing the magnitude and implications of what was written, have commented to me, "Had it been anyone but you who wrote it, I would never have believed that something like this could have happened in Cuba!"

---

[38] **Monsignor Jaime Ortega Alamino.** Catholic priest. He was a priest in the City of Cardenás, Matanzas when he was taken to UMAP. Later he was a bishop in the Pinar del Rio diocese and in Havana. In 1994, he was named by the Pope as a Cardinal of the Catholic Church in Cuba.

Cubans, like any other group of people, are neither saints nor angels. It is good for us to understand how far we are capable of sinking, for that can make us better and much more careful in the future. History is not only made up of the great feats and extraordinary events that make a nation proud. Misdeeds and failures also have a part in history. Although painful, they play an important role when they are recognized and accepted honestly. It serves no one well when we remain silent and hide these events as embarrassing stains that cannot be discussed. The victories and achievements cause pride and, at times, vanity. Wrongdoing, when recognized, reminds us of our vulnerability, and as a result, such recognition can help us to become wiser and more just.

When I returned from my first leave just married, the reality of UMAP and the path ahead became overwhelming to me. Although some things had changed, making life more bearable there, I returned much more sensitive to all the suffering that ensued from just being there. The first trial that I faced was a new change of number. Since many new recruits had arrived and some from our company had been promoted to the rank of corporal, the next day during fall-in, I received my third number while at UMAP. Now I would be 41. I had been 93 for a few days and then 13. Adapting to a new number might seem simple, but it is not. We were already conditioned to respond to the previous one. It is as if all of a sudden somebody changed our names. Maybe because I had spent a few months as 13 and I was suffering from depression after my leave, I felt the change as an attack. I had a hard time accepting my new number. The emotional shock that I suffered after I returned from that leave did not quickly dissipate. A few months later, I wrote the following letter.

I am Only 41

A fence. It is most important. It limits my radius of action. A few thousand square meters. No more. Beyond that, I ask for permission. Whether to go to the grocery store or to the laundry, I ask for permission. I cannot go out freely; I am a soldier.

A fence. Inside, two long barracks. In one, there is a kitchen, a dining hall, a room for the officers, an office and a bedroom for the chiefs of the unit. In the other, we sleep, 120 men stacked in bunk beds, barely separated a foot apart. There is also a clinic and the room where the security recruits sleep. They are the ones who guard the camp with rifles. What else? The bathroom with showers and the toilets. There are also places for washing. Three little places under the avocado trees, with rustic benches made of logs. That is all. That is my house.

My house: A long and narrow shack. On the right, sixth bunk bed from the window. I sleep there. Along with the bunk bed I have a wooden box. There is talcum powder and soap, underwear, and a few letters: my belongings. Against the wall, the hanger with the only change of clothes that I have. You do not need many clothes to work in the country. It is still night. The moon still shines in the sky above the wretched houses of the farmers. There is silence. The countryside and the animals sleep.

All of a sudden a shout. Once and again. It recurs, every time louder and more urgent. You have to get up. For us, long before the sun rises, our day starts. "There is no light!" someone protests. It doesn't matter; you have to get up anyway. The yelling goes on, nasty and coarse. Sometimes threatening. I sit up in bed. The others start to get up. Life starts in my house.

My neighbors are also getting up. Above and to my right lives 58. He is from Las Villas; a farm worker who is thirty years old. He was sent here because he decided to leave the country. All his family lives in the United States. Below him lives 33. A communist, first captain. He is thirty years old and is being punished here, although nobody knows why.

Below me lives 45. He is a young man of twenty years from Havana whose whole family left to live abroad. They gave him permission to live alone in his house in Santos Suarez until he was twenty-seven years old and then to leave the country. He is a well-bred young man and he suffers a lot. He suffers twofold, the abandonment of his family and the situation of his recruitment. Nobody comes to visit him and nobody writes to him. He is worse off than I.

To my left, below, lives 69. He is a Jehovah's Witness. He has no right to visits, nor mail, nor leave. Last week his mother and another relative arrived at Las Marías to see him. He couldn't see them because he was forced to wear the olive green pants to go outside of the unit, and he only will wear the blue denim pants. He did not yield to his mother's crying and requests to see him, but neither did the chiefs yield so that he could go out and see his mom in the same clothes that he goes out to the country to work. Above him lives 88. He is blond, and wears dark glasses. He came fat and is now skinny. So skinny that he looks sick. He hardly talks or communicates with anyone. A few beds over lives 77. He is a lawyer of about fifty years old and his hair is already grey. He works in some office of the government and is being punished in the same way as 33, but we do not know why. He is a very serious and learned man. He suffers intensely. It is sad to see a man so old living here. Next to him lives 65, a homosexual who is upset because he was not taken with the others to the unit where all others like him were concentrated. He is comforted by receiving customers at night, right there, in front of the others. 77 can hardly sleep from the indignation that he suffers from being a spectator and a listener just a foot away. Such is my house. I hope that if someone gets to read this, he does not panic. I don't any longer. Only sometimes I don't sleep so well.

All the other men also get up, although they

protest and complain, "This is just unbearable!" But they get up. So do I. I do it without thinking, and it is better this way. Thinking would be too cruel. In the darkness, I search for my clothes, dirty, ragged, and to top it all off, wet, because yesterday afternoon a heavy shower fell on us in the country, and they did not dry during the night. They are stiff from the mud, rain, and sweat. Getting up at four-thirty in the morning when it is still very cold and putting on wet clothes and shoes from the day before is a torture impossible to describe. So, I do not think. I am a machine labeled with a number that must not think.

Suddenly, another shout. Two and three times, loud, urgent. We have to fall in for the roll call to see if we are all here. I am 41. I yell: "Here" when I am called. Nay, rather, when I am counted. They never call me, for I have no name here; they count me. I am just 41. A number. Afterwards, milk and crackers, quickly. Another shout. Two, three times, loud, urgent, and full of threats and four-letter words. We have to fall in again. This time with a machete, or a hoe, or both. We get on the cart, pulled by a tractor. Two soldiers go with us armed to guard us. We leave our house and we head toward the fields. It is not dawn yet.

The country. Green and fertile. Long fields of sugar cane full of very cold dew. Work time. Incredibly, work time is a happy time. The sun rises and dries the dew. We work. I work hard to keep from being yelled at or threatened. Thus the day goes by until the afternoon. Many times we have lunch and eat in the same field.

The sun goes down, at last! It hides behind the clouds and the houses. Dusk. We go back to my house. A good bath and clean clothes. Dinner. A quiet time. Conversation with a friend. Bringing back memories. Plans and dreams for a distant and uncertain future.

At night, sometimes you can hear songs that seem full of sorrow. And they are.

Another yell is heard, two, three times, loud and urgent. We have to fall in again. There will be classes on politics, which everyone hates to hear, or "a court" where you and the undisciplined of the day will be judged and sentenced, for we are under military discipline. At ten-thirty there will be another shout for the fall in and roll call. I shall respond to my number. I am 41. That is it: a number. My duty is to be there when they count, every time they count, and make my number work, that it is not absent.

It is night again. The moon shines in the sky, above the clouds and the wretched houses of the farmers. There is silence. The countryside and the animals sleep. My neighbors also. Or so it seems. Maybe there is another one thinking or writing, lying down like me, in the light of the full moon coming through the window.

I am 41. In the long and narrow shack, on the right, sixth bed, above, by the window. I talk to God and ask Him many questions that He still does not answer. Although I do not understand the things that He is doing, I know that He loves me and I love Him too. Then, I realize that I had better try and sleep. In about five hours' time, they will start yelling again...and a new day will start exactly the same, horribly the same, uncomfortably the same.

There is much pain locked up in my house. Worst of all is having lost my name.

Being a number is... to not exist. I am only 41.

Camagüey, October 8, 1966

I also wrote other things just to vent, without the least hope of ever being published. Writing was a comfort and somehow it helped me to recognize and face my emotions and feelings. I moved away from the group or lay on my bed, and there I wrote poems or reflections like the one above. After writing them, I shared them with one or two brothers at the most. I have kept them all these years. Some embarrass me when I read them: some for being very intimate, others for being very painful, and some for being very cheesy. I can assure you that the latter category will never be published!

Some Humor Comes in Handy

One night, when I was already in bed, Israel García approached me. He came smiling, as usual, with a joke. Israel was our joke man. He always had one ready to tell. I was in the middle of writing the most horrible poem that I had ever composed in my life. At that time, I had been very careful to tear up my bad creations lest they fall into anyone's hands. He put his hand on my shoulder and told me:

"Hey, comrade 41. Do you know what the acronym for UMAP stands for?"

Being a little irritated, I answered him, "Look Israel, let me write in peace. The whole world knows what it means: Military Units to Aid Production."

"Ha! Ha! You see? You don't know anything kiddo!"

He stood at my side, looking persistently and smiling, waiting for me to ask him. Because I wanted to get rid of him so that I could continue writing, I agreed to play along. "What do they mean, Israel?" I asked him hoping not to be interrupted anymore.

He smiled again, shook his head both ways as he said, "I knew you would fall for it." He then approached me and when close to my ear, he said with a mysterious tone. "**O**nly **D**ead will we **R**each **P**eace. What do you think of that?" (**Ú**nicamente **M**uertos **A**lcanzaremos **P**az.)

I burst out laughing; Israel was a riot! Through it all, he always had a funny phrase and a smile on his lips. He suffered with a true Christian spirit. We all loved him very much and enjoyed his company.

Later, another brother who was also in UMAP told me another joke. Although it was incorrectly spelled, it showed how we were ready to laugh and eager to maintain a good sense of humor despite all the sufferings. He told me that in the unit where he was, the recruits said that UMAP meant (H)**U**miliated, **M**istreated, **A**nd **P**risoners. I am sorry for the absence of the letter H, but there is no doubt that we felt like that.

After all, it is good thing to laugh a little about our personal tragedies, because it shows that there is still hope and good cheer to keep on fighting.

6

Unexpected Resources

Despite the suffering that the UMAP experience was causing for all who were there, somehow the Christians felt a certain satisfaction. After all, it is always a privilege to suffer for our faith. The Lord said: *"Blessed are you when others revile you and persecute you and utter all kinds of evil against you falsely ON MY ACCOUNT. Rejoice and be glad...."* [1] And Peter had written: *"Yet if anyone suffers as a Christian, let him not be ashamed, but let him glorify God in that name."* [2] Not that there is ever any happiness in suffering, but there is an unspeakable joy when we are able to share the sufferings of Christ.

It is a joy unknown to those who have not had to pay a dear price for their faith and principles. Suffering for the cause of the Gospel is a privilege that is not granted to everyone. I have a good friend in the United States who tells me painfully:

"I have never had to suffer for my faith."

I know that somehow, he envies and admires me when I have told him of my experiences. UMAP was offering to us a tremendous privilege. It is not that because we suffered we were being turned into heroes and martyrs, because certainly, we were neither. If the idea was to take Christians there in order re-educate them in such a way that they would question

---

[1] Matthew 5:11

[2] 1 Peter 4:12-19

their faith and eventually abandon it, then the re-education project was an outright failure. The vast majority of believers who went there are still serving the Lord today. While the experience undoubtedly shook everyone's faith to its core, the end result was that it became much deeper and firmer.

Most of the Christians who suffered at UMAP subsequently left Cuba. Perhaps those who were not Christians also migrated, although I do not know if after so much time that this could be verified. I have met with some former recruits to try to obtain some evidence of their UMAP enlistment, but have been told that there was no way to get it. Will there be some set of records or archives somewhere that provides some evidence of all the names of those who were sent there? Unfortunately, there is not. The reality is that leaving the country turned into an obsession for most of those who spent time in UMAP. This attitude was logical not only because so many were so socially marginalized, but also because the units were concentrated with people supposedly disenchanted with the Revolution, and therefore, not politically eligible to enroll in the regular units of the SMO. Some of them found a way to leave the country illegally when they went on leave. So, the Military Units to Aid Production, although not effective in "saving" ideologically those who were confined, were successful in two outcomes that were totally contrary to its proclaimed mission. First, it projected a very negative image of the Cuban Revolution abroad, and second, it contributed to a significant increase of Cuban emigration, mainly to the United States.

A Best Friend when Least Expected

Lieutenant Marrero, the new chief of the unit, was in his thirties. He was tall and strong, sanguine and choleric, very talkative and witty, with all the virtues and failings that come with that temperament. He made a very strange pair with the second in command of the unit, who was phlegmatic, noble, and very quiet, and of peasant origin. He respected and gave respect to those who only spoke when it was necessary.

Unexpected Resources

When I returned from my leave, Lieutenant Marrero had changed his attitude towards me. I came back fearing that he would be insulted, because in a certain sense, I mocked him by taking the ten-day leave which he had suspended, instead of the four days that I was supposed to get for the death of my relative. All my fears, heightened by the fact that I returned a day late, vanished when he received me with a big smile, a very affectionate greeting, and asked how the wedding was. Marrero was a good man.

"Man, 41, I couldn't wait for you to get here," he told me. He went on, "The paper work in the office now is a mess, and you always told me that you could help with this type of work. Could you do it now? Since the scheduler is also on leave, there is a huge mess." To my surprise, my relationship with Lieutenant Marrero made a complete turnaround. The man who previously had shouted at and humiliated me, the victim of slander, became one of the people who helped me throughout my time at UMAP.

When the sergeant, who had taken me to the office of the battalion on the day of my leave, had returned, he had reported that I had been granted ten days. Marrero had had no problems with it. "Fine. I am glad for him anyway," said the lieutenant at the time, adding, "I know that 41 is a good recruit and that the other one is an envious snitch. 41 wasn't speaking about me. When he returns I am going to help him, because I was unfair to him."

Marrero was the leader with whom I spent the most time, for he stayed in Las Marías for a year. In time, he showed that he trusted me and liked to talk with me. He looked for me when he had an important job to do, and gave me passes at certain unexpected times. He did everything within his power to make my situation as comfortable as possible. He was the person whom God used during the longest period of time to help me and to allow the time to pass more easily. Working together in the office, often very late into the night, we would talk about every possible subject. Despite the differences in age and interests, we developed a genuine friendship. He was an easygoing and very personable man, with a high regard for family life. He also was suffering in UMAP due to the distance from his family. I do not remember how long it had been since I had first worked with him in the office, but one day he commented that he wanted to help the lawyer who was fifty years old, who had been held there since arriving at the beginning of the summer.

"Grillo is an old man. I don't want him to continue working in the country. Would you consider going and working as a counter, so that he can work in the office?" It was a concession that Marrero made in asking my opinion, because he could have simply ordered it, so I accepted gladly. I was twenty-two years old, so to me, the lawyer of fifty was an old man on the verge of death. I never knew the reason why this man was taken to UMAP as a recruit. He was learned, measured, and very serious. His presence commanded respect. It was very hard for him to adapt to that environment where he felt out of place due to his age, culture and character. Grillo took over my place in the office and I became the counter in the company.

The Freedom and the Pleasure of Walking

My new job did not consist in setting rules or quotas, but only in measuring and calculating the amount of work that was accomplished during the day. During these times we measured the harvest or the cleaning of the cane. I achieved this with a wooden instrument, which looked like a drawing compass, whose tips spanned about three feet. I had to walk all around the field, measuring the area of the land where people had worked and then prepare the corresponding report for the offices of the farm unit. The main advantage was that I did not have to go out early to the country with the rest of the recruits. The disadvantages were that I had to walk a lot, and did not finish my work until late at night. As the three brigades of the company sometimes worked in different places, on any given day I had to walk several miles. The other inconvenience was the responsibility of taking the report of the day's work to the battalion, which was about three miles away from the unit. I had to walk the distance on foot—both ways—so I often returned after midnight.

Neither inconvenience was a problem to me. I got up late and went to the country at noon. I worked alone all the time; nobody gave me orders or constantly watched me. I arrived at the fields where the company was working and started to measure it. Many times the recruits left and I stayed behind measuring the day's work. I enjoyed the dusk by singing hymns and worshiping God. When I finished, I went back to the unit, took a bath, ate, prepared the report, and left for my nightly six-mile walk. Now when I think of it, it horrifies me, but at that time I enjoyed walking alone at night on those dirt roads where not a soul was seen, and certainly not a vehicle. I felt free. Many times I imagined Miriam beside me, holding hands, and making plans for the future. We would speak of children that would come and of how happy we would be when we could be together. Other times, I tried to remember, and even preached, sermons that I had written. Frequently, I recited long passages from the Bible, which I knew by heart.

I really enjoyed the work as a counter. There was such beauty in walking on those moonlit nights, when all the country took on dreamlike colors. Also, on the dark nights, the sky would often become a spectacular and immense spectacle of lights. I enjoyed the peacefulness of those walks, which did me good. When the night was dark and the stars shone brightly, I sang the words of the famous hymn: "*O Lord my God, when I in awesome wonder consider all the worlds thy hands have made.*" During the day, I longed for the night to arrive so that I could go out and walk and enjoy the sensation of freedom. The greatness of the heavens made me feel my smallness and increased my dependence and need for God. When I returned to the barracks everybody was already asleep. I went to bed very tired but happy. Working as a counter isolated me and freed me not only from difficult labor in the country, but from many oppressive situations experienced in the unit.

UMAP's Attempt to Change Its Image

There had been some definite changes in UMAP. Reducing the height of the fence seemed like a small thing, but it was not. Psychologically, it is not the same to be behind a fence too high to be climbed as to be behind one that is just a symbol, whose only function is to define a space. On September 6, the company got together and Lieutenant Marrero, visibly excited, made a surprising announcement. The recruits would work only six hours a day, if they met the standard, and could walk back alone to the unit if they so wished. Also, if they preferred, they could sit in the country and wait for the cart to take them all back to the camp when the rest finished. Working hours would be no more than eight hours. He said that more improvements were to be expected and that soon there would be leaves granted on Sundays.

The new system worked for a few days. A couple of weeks later, when he saw that the recruits met the standards too quickly, they were increased so that it was not possible to complete them in less than eight hours. Anyway, during that period, we never worked for more than the announced eight hours and that constituted an unquestionable improvement for all. Those who had been there and experienced the periods of work from 4:30 in the morning until after midnight knew very well what the difference was. But the promised leaves on Sundays never materialized.

I went on leave for the second time on October 17, four months after the first one. Miriam and I had seen each other three times since then, during the allowed monthly visits in July, August, and September. I went on leave for seven days and we traveled to Cárdenas to visit my family and spent a few days in the International Hotel in Varadero. The five-star hotels were only ten pesos a night, which for me, and my monthly salary of only seven pesos, was a lot of money. For that reason, we started a tradition during our honeymoon that we observed many times thereafter. We stayed in a nice hotel but we avoided going to the restaurant. We ate inexpensively wherever we went, or we ate ice cream. The system allowed us to stay at the best hotels on several occasions. We learned how to be happy with what we could enjoy for ourselves without being resentful about that which was out of our reach. When we were together we were so happy that we did not need much.

On the second leave, Israel Cordovés and Alida Carrazanagot were married in the church in Vueltas. He was another seminarian who married despite the criticism that we received from the seminary. During that leave, Grillo, the fifty-year-old lawyer who was in our unit was notified of his release and we never saw him again.

"I'm glad you're back, 41!" Lieutenant Marrero told me the day that I returned. He added, "Next month we celebrate the day of FAR and we need you to paint some posters that we will need."

The ability to work as a sign writer had helped me from the beginning. I returned and had that paintbrush in my hands for the following two weeks. One of the weeks was spent in the office of our battalion, which had moved to Laguna Grande, right next to one of the units where the homosexuals were concentrated. I stayed there and ate with the officers, but I had to bathe in the common bathroom used by the recruits. Some situations that I witnessed in that place forced me to shower only at times when all the recruits were outside the unit and working in the country. I painted on the tables of the dining-hall, frequently surrounded by recruits and I listened to their conversations. I worked night and day in order to get out of there as soon as possible. The only nice thing was that I could spend time during those days with Ernesto Alfonso, another of the seminarians who was in UMAP but had never been with us in Las Marías. After the first leave, he had been appointed as a corporal[3] for that unit in

---

[3] Corporal. In the military organization that governed UMAP, four corporals were assigned to a sergeant, who let a platoon of forty men. Each corporal was responsible for a squad of ten men.

Laguna Grande. We had not seen each other since our time in the seminary. It was a comforting experience for both of us to be together that week.

Ernesto suffered horribly for having to work in that unit of such immoral behavior and was praying intensely, asking the Lord to allow him to be transferred. He had written asking many brothers to form a prayer chain for that. For him, although he did not despise homosexuals as human beings and took the opportunity to share the gospel with them, it was extremely difficult to co-exist in that environment. Ernesto deplored the fact that a few of the corporals of the squad, UMAP soldiers like him, and even some officers, committed sexual acts with the recruits, and he felt that they abused and took advantage of them. Ernesto was unaware then that the Lord, only a few months later, would answer his prayer in a more wonderful way than he could have expected.

The Aggression Toward the Homosexuals

When UMAP was inaugurated, the homosexuals were scattered among all the units. In Las Marías there were about twenty. A few months later there came the order to concentrate them in special units. One day, the company was gathered in an area and ordered to fall in. Someone read the list of those who were being transferred; there was a truck waiting for them. The leaders ordered those who were being called out to leave the formation and to go collect their belongings quickly. Although there was no explanation, the rest of the troop immediately understood the reason, so everyone began mocking and teasing those who were leaving. It was undoubtedly a demeaning, contemptuous and highly discriminatory show. When all those who had been ordered to go were on the truck, a young man who had not been mentioned in the list and was still in the formation, cried out sheepishly, "You have to take me also! I do not want to stay *alone* in a unit with so many men!" He ran from the formation and rushed to the barracks to collect his belongings.

It was a shameful and cruel deed that led to his

outburst and departure from the formation. In the end, his name was added to the list and he got into the truck while the entire troop mocked and shouted insults at those who were preparing to go. Although they seemed to be enjoying what was happening, that vehicle was loaded with many disgraced and humiliated homosexuals.

I do not know how many separate units of homosexuals were created. I only knew of the one in Laguna Grande because it was part of our battalion. When I went to work there to make posters, it had been in operation for several months. In Laguna Grande, I saw that some of the recruits' own relatives provided them with women's underwear and even sanitary pads for their menstrual periods that some of them said they experienced every month. I saw how they converted their work clothes into feminine garments and in an ingenious way turned the farmer's straw hat into a broad-brimmed lady's hat, by adding laces and pieces of cloth. At night, they shut themselves in the barracks and put on shows that nobody tried to stop. I also saw the pride with which most of them flaunted their homosexuality. Although there had been a group of homosexuals in Las Marías from the beginning, I could never have imagined what I saw in Laguna Grande, where everyone was a homosexual. The relationships in that unit were complex, volatile, and contradictory in many aspects.

Who came up with the idea that isolating them together would help in some way? How was it possible for somebody not to realize that such an idea would shut the door to any possibility of change or re-education, if that were the purpose? How could anyone pretend to think that by making them work hard, and mistreating them, something good might happen to people who were despised and mocked by a great part of society? Even after forty years, I cannot find any answers to these questions. Among those young men were many whom, had they not been taken there mistreated in that way might have been able to channel their lives in a different direction.

One young man who had just turned eighteen years old sat beside me many times as I painted. When I talked to him about the gospel, he told me his story. At the age of thirteen he realized that he felt attracted to men. He belonged to a very reputable and wealthy family. Because he did not like the idea of being a homosexual, he did a lot of soul-searching, and found the courage to tell his father what was happening. He asked him for help to get rid of the inclination that he felt inside. His father's reaction was violent. He beat and insulted him, and left his son locked up and humiliated in his room. The young man spent all day crying and without any food, because his mother was away from the house when the incident took place. When she returned and saw her son in such a condition, she lovingly asked him what had happened, but he refused to tell her.

"I was embarrassed to death," he told me. "I didn't want her to know of my inclinations and I couldn't understand why my father had reacted that way if I was only asking for his help."

One night, his father abruptly burst into his room. With a deep look of contempt, he ordered him, "Get dressed right away! We are going to solve your problem once and for all." He took him in his car without uttering a word, even though the trip they made took close to an hour to a nearby town.

There, in a horrible and dirty house, he locked his son in a room with himself and three women. "Take off your clothes; tonight you're going to learn how to be a man! We are going to teach you in graphic detail what life is like," he yelled at him.

Everything that took place in that room, with his father fully enjoying it all, provoked an easily understandable aversion in him toward women and heterosexuality. The young man told me the story crying, repeating once and again, "Why did he have to do that? I hated the idea of being a homosexual and wanted him to help me."

Unfortunately for him, he was now in a unit of homosexuals and everything was positioned for him to further develop his inclinations toward his own sex, tendencies he deplored. The saddest part of the story is that the young man, after that experience with his father, had avoided homosexual behavior and had longed to have a heterosexual life. He was willing to fight what he considered a weakness or deviation in his behavior. And where did he have his first homosexual relationship? It occurred in that very camp and with a corporal of the squad. His superior officer almost raped him, forcing him to please him afterwards every time that he wanted it. How many more like him were there in that unit? To concentrate all the homosexuals, and those who seemed to be, in separated units was an outrageous idea that humiliated and denigrated all of them. In many cases, like the young man of this story, it created the conditions for many of them to have their first true homosexual experience in an oppressive environment where everything favored repetition. All this was done in a promiscuous atmosphere in which it was impossible to promote and enhance human dignity.

The Shame of Being a UMAP Recruit

On November 6 we were taken to the celebration at the Senado Sugar Mill. We worked in the morning, had lunch very early, and then left for the parade. All the carts were decorated with posters, many of which I had made myself. We headed for the parade in Senado and Las Minas without knowing the number of UMAP recruits who were to participate. Also, of course, there were carts from the units of the homosexuals. While we paraded I wondered nervously what the people must think of us.

Although I had never been able to be proud of being a UMAP recruit, I felt that afternoon like a circus animal on exhibition. Everything seemed freakish, absurd, and humiliating. When UMAP was organized and they took us to Camaguey from Havana and the other provinces, the residents were warned that we, the UMAP recruits, were all dangerous delinquents, vagrants and homosexuals.

Although almost a year had passed and the recruits had more contact with the population, the people still rejected and feared the types of people that formed the ranks of UMAP. So, why a parade? We had been brought in on a train in the middle of the night, and the recruits were divided among the units before dawn, so that we would not be seen. That night, nobody had wanted any witnesses of the operation. For what reason now were they parading us in front of everybody with such great fanfare?

We were on that cart, including the parade, the celebration, and the trip back and forth to the camp, for more than seven hours. All afternoon there was shouting and incessant beating of the drums and congas; I recall that parade as one of the most unpleasant and humiliating episodes of the entire UMAP experience.

By the time we returned to Las Marías it was late at night.

The Little Harvest and the Christmas Leave

I once again cut cane during the so-called Little Harvest that began in late November and lasted less than twenty days. On that occasion, Israel Cordovez and I made a good team cutting cane together, and we averaged a large number of kilograms every day. We were an outstanding pair of cutters. Working in the country was not bad. Although the work was tough, we felt useful and the physical exercise did us good, although it proved exhausting. We got up at four in the morning when it was quite cold and we left for the country before five. We returned to the unit at night. The only bright hope in that Little Harvest was the promise that we would be granted a leave for Christmas. At least we never worked until midnight as we had in the previous harvest.

On Tuesday, December 23 we went out on leave again with seven days off to visit with our families. So, Christmas in 1966 was not as traumatic for me as the previous one, because

I could be with my wife, attend the activities at the church in Ciego de Ávila and sing in the choir, as I had done for so many years of my life. I enjoyed and treasured the Christmas activities that year more than ever, remembering how I had felt the previous year being away from the church.

It is very common to become accustomed to the things that we love, so much so that we stop appreciating their value. I always liked to celebrate Christmas. I remember as a child how we gathered as a family to decorate the tree at home and attended the activities in the church. As a teenager I started singing in the choir and enjoyed all the carols and Christmas music, but it was just normal and usual, almost routine and we did all of these things with very little emotional connection.

But after the first Christmas in UMAP, I realized the beauty of the celebration and all the happiness that it brought to my life. Maybe it was then when I decided that I would always celebrate that day in a special way, regardless of the circumstances, because I have never forgotten what the Christmas in 1965 meant in Camagüey, far from everything that I loved and that which had meant so much to me. On December 30 my leave expired, so I could not celebrate the new year of 1967 together with the church. I didn't have the strength to return that day, so I waited until early in the morning on December 31.

The unit held a party to ring in the New Year, and some of the recruits, including some of the seminarians, who had been out on leave had not yet returned. Those of us who had returned gathered in a little park outside the barracks to share our experiences as we waited for the New Year. I decided to wait until midnight to write Miriam. As I was accustomed to doing, I stood next to the bunk bed and used the higher bed as a desk. I cut myself off from the noise and the party atmosphere about midnight and began to write the following letter:

Las Marías, December 31, 1966

My love,

The New Year is approaching and I am asking God for forgiveness because I feel desperately sad. Last night, we were together and now it seems to me that you are so very far away. But, I feel so close to you that it is as if you were sitting beside me in the pew at the church, where you must be right now in your green dress that I like so much. I hope you don't cry at midnight, because I think that if you do, I will feel your tears here, and then I will cry also, which is a very dangerous weakness here.

However, neither you nor I have the right to cry tonight. We should not be selfish. God has been good to us and we were able to be together this Christmas. We have to be happy because this year is coming to an end, and if we have suffered during these twelve months, maybe we should feel more relief than sadness, more gratitude than pain. What we suffered will not return again, and it has served to unite us more so that we'd learn to be happy when we are together. When this entire nightmare is over and we are able to live our lives as a normal married couple, there will not be a happier pair than we. You can be sure of that! The tears have been so many, that even the smallest things will surely give us great times of happiness. Will a day come when I can thank God for all that I have experienced here? Undoubtedly, He has a plan, and it is surely a plan of blessing.

If only you could see how beautiful the sky is here tonight! I have spent a good time looking at the stars and remembering the first night I spent in this place when I refused to watch such a spectacle, because I felt very sad, desperate, and alone. How many things have happened, my love, since that November 26 of 1965! We could never have imagined how many *horrible experiences life had in store for us. Yes, we should be happy as we see this year come to an end. Tonight, I dare to look at the stars because above everything, I have you, and because even though we are not together, I feel you near me and our hearts are so united that it doesn't matter that we are separated, because we are feeling the same. Isn't that a reason to be happy? Some people are together and don't know how to enjoy it.*

It will be twelve soon...It is horrible not being able to give you a kiss when the New Year comes. But I know that God will let us be together for many New Year's Eves, at church, and with how many children will we wait for the New Year? I know that there will come a time when we will look back and everything will be a distant memory. Maybe we will even be able to smile when we remember these times and ask ourselves why we felt such agony, because it was not so much.

But now, yes, it is, a lot...! Only God has given us the strength so far and He will continue giving it until the end. It has been more than a year and He has sustained us. We must recognize that in the middle of this tragedy He has let us live many happy moments. That is why I was asking for forgiveness when I started writing this letter to you.

Ah... It is now twelve midnight and I already know that you are crying. I...well...I love you with all my heart! And I promise...solemnly...that I shall not allow myself to shed even a tear...that day when we will be together waiting for the New Year to come.

A new year had begun and I did not yet know how long and difficult it was going to be. In spite of all that I said, I knew that my faith was on the verge of a deep crisis, of which I was terrified. I had experienced the collapse of my dreams, but my faith and trust in the Lord had sustained me. I had even suffered the humiliation of being labeled as social scum in my country, and had endured it and felt privileged to suffer because the cause, the Christian faith, was worth it. Now, after thirteen months of suffering, I began to feel that my faith was wavering. Some of the thoughts that came to mind were not helpful. Never before had the biblical truth, *"Be watchful, your adversary the devil prowls around like a roaring lion, seeking someone to devour"* [4] been so real. In was in this mental state that the brothers found me when they returned to wish me a Happy New Year.

"May the Lord get us out of here this year!" Julio Cornelio told me as he hugged me.

His eyes were full of tears. We prayed together and our petitions had a common denominator: *"Lord, you know that we cannot stand it any longer."* After we finished praying, we stood in silence for a few minutes. We felt an immense sadness, but at the same time, we knew that the Lord was there with us. He always was there really, in spite of our doubts, sufferings, and fears.

We repeated Bible verses from memory for a long time. Afterwards we went out to share with the other recruits to wish them well also. Some of them were happy because they had been given beer. Everyone was encouraged by what was being said about UMAP for the New Year.

Would UMAP Really Change?

The rumors were predicting an imminent change.

"Don't you see how we've been given two leaves lately?" some said.

"Things are not the same as before, when we stayed for eight months without leaving," others responded.

"Don't you remember? For a long time they didn't even tell us where we were," another one pointed out.

---

[4] 1 Peter 5:8

"Bah! You're all talking garbage. This is not fixed yet, it is not even Monday," said 73.

73 was from Pogoloti, in Marianao. He was over six feet tall and was very thin. He had a deep voice and he spoke very slowly. His laziness was greater than his height, and every time that he was ordered to work or was scolded because he was doing little work, he answered with his loud voice, "Yes, I will do it on Monday." And he continued his pace as if nobody had talked to him.

With that type of attitude, he often succeeded in causing several officers to lose their tempers. He was constantly in trouble and he gained the nickname of "Monday". But this time when he said that "*it's not fixed yet and it is not even Monday*," his voice sounded as if it came from beyond the grave. A general laughter was heard, of which even the officers took part.

The second in command, one of the very officers with whom 73 had been in trouble, could not stop laughing, and went to where the recruit was. He patted him on his back and told him, "Oh man! So, it's on Monday when this will start getting better, huh?"

However, the general topic of conversation that New Year's night was the rumors about the demobilization of all the recruits older than twenty-seven years. It was rumored that there would be substantial changes and that the best recruits would be transferred to regular military units. Others would be transferred to Havana to work on military construction projects. Others might go to either Matanzas or Pinar del Río, depending on the province they came from. It was also said that those who wanted to leave the country and had made arrangements, could leave when their permit arrived, even though they were in UMAP.

There were rumors that in the next harvest they would be giving prizes and that recruits could win a car, a motorcycle, or a vacation trip to another socialist country. They talked of the possibility that after the harvest was over there would be a general demobilization. An inner voice, that was not mistaken, told me that none of these possibilities would come to me.

"This will change a lot, guys!" said Lieutenant Marrero, who sat in the dining room, also cheerful and enjoying the general feeling for the arrival of the New Year. "You all will see the way everything will change in the Military Units to Aid Production," he added, as he lifted up his bottle of beer to make a toast with everyone. It was clear that the lieutenant also wanted UMAP to change.

The truth was that the organization, more than a year after it was founded, had not gained the admiration that was expected when it was formed. Even within Cuba, UMAP's abuse of power had given it a bad reputation, and abroad this was being used to criticize and strongly question the Cuban revolution.

UMAP was already an utter failure and was headed toward its dissolution. Although serious efforts were made to change its performance and its image, in the end, for the sake of justice, it would need to be dismantled.

But there was still a long way to go.

7

Depression Arrives

"On your feet!" The shout was heard as usual at four in the morning. It was a cold January morning, and the night before it had rained heavily due to a cold front.

"Move it! On your feet! The fields to be cut are far away," one of the politicians of the company insisted.

The cane fields where we would be cutting that day were several kilometers away. Every time this happened, they wakened us earlier. This greatly annoyed the recruits because it robbed us of sleep, and everyone was always exhausted. As the recruits were waking up, many were cursing and protesting bitterly. Taking advantage of the darkness, the recruits took revenge by insulting the officers and speaking about the horrors of UMAP. That morning somebody disguised his voice to yell at the politician, "Go bother your mother and stop mistreating the men!"

"OK," said the politician, full of rage, "who said that? If he is really a man, then let him say it again to my face! Let's see if he has the guts to do it!"

Others repeated it and added to it with profane and worse insults, which made everyone laugh.

"OK. Where are the big mouths? Why don't you stand up and repeat what you are saying to my face?" The politician repeated every time angrier.

The louder he yelled the more insults they uttered. The politician yelled across the barracks and threatened the troops without achieving his goal of getting the troops to be quiet. The wake-up call that morning was turning into a rebellion.

"You're not gonna get away with this!" The politician yelled from the door of the barracks. He then left, but not before pouring out a string of profanity himself to get revenge on all those who were insulting him.

Actually the recruits often made fun of this particular politician. He was young, short, and not good looking at all, big headed with a cleft palate and resulting speech impediment. His unfortunate physical features had earned him the nickname of "the fetus". It was a nickname that the recruits used when talking about him: *"There goes the fetus,"* or, *"tonight the fetus has to teach."*

The politician was of peasant origin and he hardly had any education. He taught his night classes on political instruction with a great deal of difficulty, which was the reason they mocked him openly to his face. In order to mock him, they would often pretend that they had not understood, or that they really had an interest, just to make him repeat over and over what he was trying to teach. Due to his limited education, he simply was unable to explain things differently and always ended up repeating exactly the same thing.

"I've already explained that... Hell!" he said, adding more swear words. "You're a bunch of gross misfits. That's why you're gonna rot here. I explain it to you, and explain it to you and still, you ain't gettin' nothing. What do you have in your heads? I think what you have is what the chickens pick!"

Usually the classes would end when the politician became incensed and began to utter his lengthy exposition of obscenities, and in that he *was* an expert. His favorite insult was, *"You're gonna rot here!"* He repeated it as if it were the most powerful threat possible. Nevertheless, the politician was an obliging man. Within minutes, he'd forget everything. The recruits who exasperated him the most would later constantly ask him for cigarettes.

"Come on, politician, toss me a cabo[1], my cigarettes are gone," someone would say.

"Who do you think you are? Hell! You're gonna take all I have," he responded.

"Ah, politician. You have a salary and you can buy more cigarettes; the seven pesos that we get are good for nothing."

The politician complained, but he indulged them anyway. He frequently shared his cigarettes and then complained because they had taken them all. In spite of it all, he had good relationships with the troops. All in all, the recruits felt some sort of affection towards him. He came to Las Marías together with two others that I remember, but I'd rather not mention them because they were very different. Maybe they were alike in ineptitude. When we were told that we would be given politicians who would help us to "learn about life's truths in order for us to remedy our antisocial behavior," as had been reiterated by the former commander of the company, I felt a little fearful. I expected that well-prepared people would come and we would have truly serious discussions with them. But, when they arrived, it was embarrassing to hear them teach their lessons. I do not know if the same thing happened in the other units as what took place in Las Marías where the politicians were totally incompetent. It was cruel to even have placed them in such situations. They just made fools of themselves in front of the recruits. They did not know how to answer the questions that people devised to confuse and frustrate them. In the units, there were some recruits that had very little education while others were university graduates.

---

[1] **Toss me a cabo.** Expression used to ask for cigarettes. It means not to ask for the whole cigarette, but only the remainder of the one that the other person is smoking. The same expression can be used in the sense of "help me."

The Little Farmer Who Wouldn't Be Fooled

"This is very hard, 41," the aforementioned politician told me. "I don't like being laughed at, and I don't like waking them up for work. I don't know how I got into this."

He had come over to help me, because I was cutting a part of the field where the canes were very entangled and I had gotten behind. I saw sadness in his eyes. He told me that he got offended and swore when people made fun of him. Actually he suffered and longed for a simple life with his family, working in the country as he had done most of his life. When I heard him, I understood that even though he was a part of the re-educative machinery, he was as much a victim as any of us. The politician would have been much happier working with his father, whom he evidently missed very much, in his parcel of land in Sierra Cristal![2] He spoke to me about his dad with an admiration and a love that moved me.

"I'll tell you a secret, 41. I'd give anything to be working the land with my dad; he is a simple peasant but I'm very proud of him. He smiled as he spoke to me and I saw in his face a little peasant boy in love with the land and his crop, who God only knows how, was turned into a soldier and political instructor who was hardly able to express himself, and was not knowledgeable in the discipline that he was teaching.

"Well, then why don't you leave?" I asked him.

"Not possible! I was sworn into the army for twenty-five years," he answered, heartbroken and sad.

Twenty-five years! I thought to myself. The politician is worse off than I! I'll leave when I complete the three years, but he is going to spend the longest and most fruitful part of his life in a job that he doesn't even like. How could he have sworn in for such a long time? Why did he decide to dedicate

---

[2] **Sierra Cristal.** Mountain range, the second most important in the eastern region after the Sierra Maestra. It extends to the north from the province of Holguin to Baracoa.

his life to a profession in which, due to his personal attributes, he would never be able to succeed? I truly felt sorry for him.

From that day on, I viewed him differently, and I did not like it when the recruits made fun of his speech impediment. I realized that he was a man whose circumstances of life were counter to his real desires. He had been pulled from his environment and the place where he would have been more happy and useful. When I came to that conclusion, I discovered that we had a lot of things in common. Neither of us was in the place where he belonged. And one of the worst tragedies that can happen to a man is to be in the wrong place. Different circumstances, sometimes completely uncontrollable, can put people in places or jobs that are not fitting and in which they cannot excel. Many times men spend their entire lives in such a situation. I have met doctors that should never have been doctors, teachers who will never be educators, pastors who would have been excellent deacons, people, who, had they lived their lives in another place or another capacity, would have developed their skills in positions more aligned with their abilities, and would have had a greater opportunity to prosper.

One day I talked to the politician about Christ, because he also needed to know the gospel. When I became very excited explaining to him how putting his faith in Jesus could help him, he interrupted me and told me that a rich man invented religion in order to fool the poor. Whatever else I tried to say, I was unsuccessful in changing his opinion. He talked with me about a subject that he knew nothing about with an absurd and astounding arrogance.

"Religion in Cuba won't last five more years. Soon nobody will believe in any of that. When the exploiters are gone, religion is done!" he told me smiling, with a lofty arrogance. "The churches are going to close," he added. "Nobody will go, and you are going to shut them down yourselves."

"That's just not so, politician." I protested.

"Yes, it is so! You are being fooled! I know the Bible completely by heart, and nobody can tell me tales."

"What are you saying, politician?" I asked him a little upset, "do you know the entire Bible by heart?"

"Yes, sir! Yes, sir! That is why I know that the one who wrote it was a rich man seeking to fool the poor. Yes, sir. But, you're all being fooled and are being told something different. But not me! Nobody will come telling me tales! This little woodland peasant won't be so easily fooled!"

All of my enthusiasm to evangelize the politician vanished. He laughed as if he had made an uncontestable argument against the Bible and faith. When he said that a rich man had written the Bible in order to fool the poor, and then insisted, that he knew the *entire* Bible by heart, the politician demonstrated that he was caught in the worst and most malevolent of webs, that of the ignorant who assumes knowledge. Still, I felt sorry for him.

"Look, politician," I tried to say kindly, "the Bible is not a book that can be learned completely by heart. Besides, it was not written by only one man."

"Ha! Ha! Ha! You see how you are all fooled? Ha! Ha!" He repeated. "But nobody is gonna fool this little farmer. It's incredible that you who have studied have let yourself be fooled like this!" He continued to explain to me, with his defective speech and poorly-pronounced words seasoned with his favorite expletives, that early in ancient history, a man invented religion as an instrument of oppression. Full of pride, he loudly asserted his ultimate argument, "Man, so that you will know once and for all, just in case you have never been told: the Bible was written by a feudal lord!"

When I heard his conclusion I realized the tremendous confusion that the unfortunate woodland peasant, who would not be fooled by anybody, had in his limited religious, historical, and social knowledge. My missionary effort ended in an argument in which I lost my temper along with my compassion. I almost decided to spit out that his nickname, *Fetus,* was well earned. God had mercy on me and I held back; it would have been cruel. Because of my anger, my words failed to convey all that Christ could do for him. My evangelistic attempt with the politician was a total failure. The only thing I accomplished was that he would never again approach me to talk.

Others Cut Cane for Me

The harvest had begun and the work regimen went back to being very difficult. It was not as bad as before, when Lieutenant Concepción made us work until after midnight on moonlit nights, but we did work from dawn to dusk. After I had been cutting cane for a few days, I was summoned to Lieutenant Marrero's office.

"Listen, 41, I need you to solve a problem for me. I want you to work as an accountant. So starting tomorrow, you will put down the machete and pick up the pencil. What do you think?"

The accountant was in charge of calculating and writing down the quantity of cane that every pair of cane cutters had cut as the lifting machinery (lifters) picked it up from the field. The cane fit in the mechanical arm of the machine, called the "crab." This was part of a process by which the cane was carried by the lifters onto the carts, which in turn, would move them to the scales to be measured. The accountant wrote the number of "crabs" that the lifters picked up so that he could record how much each cutter had completed. He had to know precisely in which part of the field each recruit was cutting, because the lifters always came after the brigade had gone.

Calculating the amount of cane that each pair had cut was a job that carried a lot of responsibility. Any mistake or oversight could cause trouble for the cutters. Sometimes they disagreed and claimed to have cut more. Since, in the end, it was an approximation, it created a lot of controversy with the cutters. It was easy if a pair of cane cutters filled up a cart, but when there was a mixture of cane cut by several different pairs of cutters on a cart everything became very complicated. The cart was put on the scales and weighed, and the accountant decided how many kilograms corresponded to each pair. The important part of this was that, by higher orders, the accountant could not be a recruit, but one of the chiefs of the brigade. In Las Marías they were not doing the job well, creating tremendous confusion, and the cutters were constantly complaining.

"They are making such a mess of it that we'll never know how much cane we have cut," said the lieutenant. "I'd prefer that you work as an accountant and that they will cut cane for you."

For me it was a great deal. Three brigade chiefs, who were experienced cane cutters, would be working all day long and the cane that they cut would be counted as if I had cut it. I would do the work that should have been done by them but they were unable to accomplish because they lacked the necessary skills.

"And what will I do while the cane is being lifted?" I asked the lieutenant.

"You may stay in the unit doing whatever you please, since when the lifters come you will have to work the job is done," he answered.

I saw the skies open. The lifters came two or three days after the cutting had started in the fields because the farm did not have many of them. They waited for the unit to have cut enough cane and then they sent them. Along with the lifters came the ox carts or the trucks. When they started with a company, it was a marathon until they finished lifting up all the cane that had been cut. Many times we finished after midnight. I stayed in the country with the operators of the lifters and the drovers, and when we finished, I was taken back to the unit in one of the lifters.

Depression Arrives

Occasionally, the work extended until dawn. I arrived at the company after having worked all night long while my fellow recruits were leaving for work. Then, I had to produce the report of how much cane everyone had cut; only then could I finally retire in order to rest and then once again I would wait for the cane to stack up again on the ground and for the lifters to be sent out to the company again. While this was taking place, I spent two or three days in the unit writing, reading, or simply sleeping. That is how I started working in the harvest of 1967. I liked the work as an accountant.

During the harvest, the group of Christians in Las Marías began to diminish. Ernesto Ruano and Davis Figueredo had already gone. Now Julio Cornelio and Rafael Hernández were released because of back problems. Rubén Deulofeu left when the order was given that those older than twenty-seven years were to be demobilized. Esteban Estrada also left in this group. A few days earlier, the prayer chain that Ernesto Alfonso had begun so that he would be transferred away from his unit of homosexuals proved to have a result more powerful than expected: it caused him to be released due to his flat feet! Israel Cordovés, Israel García, José Ferrer, and I stayed. The group of Christians in the unit, which previously had been ten, was reduced to four. A few months later, brothers Rolando Acosta[3] from the church in Batabanó and Iván Delgado[4] from Pinar del Río arrived. Transfers, for whatever reason, were common.

There was another young man in Las Marías who was a member of a Baptist church in Havana. He was a leader in his church but from the beginning he did not associate with us. He became a friend of a group of homosexuals and always spent time with them. He taught them how to sing evangelical

---

[3] **Rolando Acosta Luis.** He was a member of the Baptist church in Batabanó when he was recruited as part of the first call, on November 23, 1965. He was in UMAP until its dissolution. He is currently living in Batabanó and is a member of the same church, of in which is a deacon, director of the Music Department, a Sunday School teacher as well as serving in other positions.

[4] See footnote 36 in Chapter 5.

hymns and according to him, he talked to them about the gospel in order to try to win them over to Christ. The situation was confusing with him. He suffered from asthma fits and some nights when he felt bad, he always called for some homosexual to help him. We thought that he was compromising his testimony and was creating an awkward situation. The situation was such that when Lieutenant Concepción wanted to concentrate the homosexuals into specific units, he intended to include this man on the list of those to be transferred. Since I was working in the office at the time, I strongly opposed this.

"He may appear to be a homosexual but he is not," I told Concepción, "because he is a member of a Baptist church. You can't send him to that camp."

"That guy is fooling you!" He assured me.

I succeeded in convincing the lieutenant, and he was not transferred. I believed that when the homosexuals were gone, he would associate more with our group, but that did not happen. He joined others who, while they were not known to be homosexuals and therefore had not been transferred, actually were. He separated himself from our group more and more so he could maintain a closer friendship with a few homosexuals that had also stayed behind. He was never known to have engaged in a homosexual act, but his close relationships with them made the other recruits think that he was one of them. After he left UMAP, he was married and had a son, but some years later, his church removed him from their membership for having homosexual relations. The lieutenant had been right.

Alienated from my Brothers

Since the group of Christians was reduced and I was working as an accountant, I spent far less time with the other Christians in the unit. When we happened to be together, I rarely had time to talk with them because my job was done during different hours and I spent more time with the leaders and the other workers. I did not meet with them to read the Bible or to pray.

I became an isolated believer, constantly surrounded by people who were not of the faith. Having lived my entire life in a Christian setting, suddenly I found myself immersed in the worst possible environment since I had come to UMAP, but I was not alone. The fellowship with the group of believers had been a protective shield. After a year and a few months, I lost that shield due to the type of work and my job schedule. When I had worked as a counter, I had also spent a lot of time alone, but at that time, my relationship with God had been stronger. This situation was different. My vocabulary began to change. I started to enjoy the conversations and friendships that I had deplored before. Miriam immediately realized it, and warned me.

"Don't worry, my love," I told her, "nothing and nobody is going to make me change."

"But, don't you realize that you are already changing?" She told me with her eyes full of tears.

"Bah, don't exaggerate! You're worrying about nothing." I tried to calm her down, but she knew that I was not doing well.

I formed a strong friendship with the chief of the allotment, a hard working farmer who was responsible for the cane lifters. He was about thirty years old. The chief of the brigade introduced us the day after Marrero offered me the job as an accountant.

"Look, comrade, this is 41, and he is going to work as an accountant in our place."

He got off the horse immediately, extended his hand, and with a frank and clean smile said to me, "Tell me what your name is, because I don't like men to have numbers."

From that moment on we became friends. He did not know much about me other than that I was a UMAP recruit, but he refused to call me by a number. As the days went on, we became good friends. When he arrived at the field where I was, he got off the horse very happily and greeted me. "Let me know when you want me to send you the lifters. If you are not ready for them, then just say so and I will send them somewhere else."

My friendship with the chief of the allotment also made it possible for me to go on leave on weekends. One morning when I stayed behind in the unit because there still was not enough cut cane in the field, the captain of the battalion came unexpectedly, and found me writing in the dining hall. I rose when he entered, stood at attention and saluted. The captain came over to where I was. "Why aren't you working? Are you sick?" he asked.

The company medic, another UMAP recruit, who at the time was also in the dining hall, responded immediately so to defend himself from possible blame. "No, captain. Nobody is sick in the unit. He is here because he works as an accountant."

"How is it that he is working as an accountant? The accountants are the chiefs of brigades! Where is Lieutenant Marrero?"

"Lieutenant Marrero is in the country." I responded.

The captain left like he was shot out of a cannon to go find him. I thought that my job as an accountant was probably over that day and I regretted having decided to do my writing in the dining hall, something that I never had done before. I was caught red-handed writing letters at ten in the morning. To my surprise, when Lieutenant Marrero returned from the country, he was outraged at the captain, saying, "I don't care what he thinks. I am not going to let the brigade leaders make a mess of this work. Everything will stay the same, 41. You're going to keep working as an accountant but you cannot stay in the unit. When you are not lifting the cane you either hide in the grove and rest there, or you go on leave to your wife's home."

A Particular System of Leaves

I could not believe what I had just heard: "*You go on leave to your wife's house.*" Marrero knew that Miriam lived in Ciego de Ávila and I had asked him to let me go on Sundays. I had already found out that the trains that went through Truffin went as far as Morón. From there it was slightly more than thirty kilometers. It was also an easier trip, at least the return trip was, than going through La Gabriela-Senado-Minas and Camagüey.

"Work out an agreement with the chief of the allotment so that he will tell you in advance when he is going to send the lifters. That way you can go and come back the day when you have to work; you spend the rest of the days with your wife. Does that captain think that he is going to mess with me?" he added.

When I told the chief of the allotment what happened he responded, "You know that you don't have any problem with me. I'll fix everything so that you can go to your wife's home every weekend."

The chief of the allotment would send the lifters to me every Wednesday, or at the latest by noon on Thursdays. So, I worked lifting the cane that the unit had cut since Monday. Because this took place a few days after the cutting, we would be lifting cane all day on Thursday and probably Friday too. When I finished, I wrote the report, and then went home on Saturday to my wife. I would return early Tuesday, just in case it was necessary for me to work with the lifters before Wednesday, because everything depended on how much cane that the other brigades that worked in each area had cut. Lieutenant Marrero gave me a pass that I was not to show to anyone in the battalion, because he lacked the authority to do so, but I could produce it on the streets if some military man stopped me and asked me to prove that I was not AWOL. I had to leave the unit without going through the battalion, because in reality my pass was a fake. But once in the city, it was seen as a legal pass. Thus Marrero solved his problem: I could do the job and I did not have to stay in the unit. I could go to Ciego de Ávila, be with my wife on weekends, and even go to church every Sunday!

Marrero was putting himself at risk in this situation. Miriam's home was not around the corner, but almost 150 kilometers away. I had to be sure to travel within the allotted time and never fail him, because if it should happen that the lifters came and due to transportation problems I was unable to make it on time, the entire arrangement, with all its privileges, would collapse.

We started the new system that same week. On Wednesday, the lifters came and in two work sessions all the cane that was on the ground was lifted. On Thursday, we worked until eleven at night, so that we could finish in time for me to leave for the weekend. I prepared the report and then very early on Friday morning, I took it to the battalion office at the farm in La Gabriela. From there I took a truck that was going to the Senado Sugar Mill. This was the most dangerous part of the trip because if an officer stopped me and asked for my leave permit, I would not be able to use the one that Marrero had given me. By three on that Friday afternoon I had arrived at home. The lifters would come again on Wednesday, so I did not have to return until Tuesday.

Alone at Night on the Railroad

On Tuesday, for the return trip, I explored the Morón-Truffin route by train. I had to know if that route was better, because by going that way I would avoid the dangerous part of the trip where I needed to steer clear of the battalion officers. I left Ciego de Ávila after midday, because the train left Morón at seven-thirty in the evening.

I found out that the only problem was that the train did not stop in Truffín, so I had to get off at the Sola Station and walk along the railroad tracks for the remaining five kilometers. Afterward, I walked along the road to Las Marías. I had been trained to walk long distances, but walking on the railroad tracks for five kilometers in the middle of the night was something different. Even worse, I did not know the area. I was afraid that I might not see the Truffin sign and walk straight past it. Of all the roads that the train crossed, the Truffin intersection was the only one that I knew. And what if by chance the sign, which was pretty old and in bad shape, was pulled down by someone? Or what if a strong wind had knocked it down?

I felt relieved when I finally saw it because it had seemed to me that I had walked endlessly and that I had surely passed the dirt road that I was looking for. I watched carefully and looked for good reference points for future journeys at night. It was well past midnight when I arrived at the unit. Despite my anxiety and fear of getting lost, the first trip was a success.

This same routine was repeated week after week. Sometimes I made the reverse trip by walking as far as Sola and by taking the train from there to Morón, but the schedule of the train in that direction was not always suitable. The weekly leaves were accumulating, so that some brothers from the church in Ciego de Ávila joked with me, "Are you going on leave back to the unit?"

I know that the Lord was working to help me. Suddenly the circumstances had been arranged that allowed me to spend more time with my wife and I could attend church. But the devil is crafty. Everything that had happened was feeding my own self-sufficiency. I had come to believe that I could get past every obstacle by my own ability. I began to feel that I could master every situation.

And there is nothing stupider than walking unconcerned and confident over quicksand.

The pastor in Ciego de Ávila invited me to preach several times, but I would not accept his invitation. I told him that I was too tired because I had been working a lot, and that I would rather listen to him. The truth was that I had no desire to preach at all. I knew that I would not have any message to offer.

A Downhill Slide

Paul knew very well what he was talking about in 2 Corinthians 12, where he speaks of his famous and debated thorn: *"Therefore I will boast all the more gladly of my weaknesses, so that the power of Christ may rest upon me."* Real strength resides in humility and dependence on the power of God. Arrogance, pride, and self-sufficiency can only make men weaker and more vulnerable. Proverbs 16:18 says, *"Pride goes before destruction, and a haughty spirit before a fall."* Even though I thought that I was in control of every situation, I was completely blind to the fact that I was actually at the mercy of the winds.

By mid-April, 1967, I was upset because the coordination with the lifters, which made it possible for me to go on leave, had not been working well for two weeks. Miriam sent to me, along with her own letter, one that my oldest sister had sent her, with evidence that she had taken steps for me to go on a special leave.

Traditionally, I had been the family's blood donor. My sister, who then worked as a civilian in the 1089 Military Unit in Havana as a Chief of Economy, wrote a letter requesting that I be permitted to go on leave to donate blood for my other sister who was about to give birth. There had been no response to the application, but she sent a copy of her letter to me as a proof that she had tried. When I received the letter with the stamp of the General Staff and signed by Enna González Muñoz, Economic Chief,[5] it occurred to me that I could probably use the letter to go out on leave. By then I was not doing well spiritually and I had no problems telling any lie

---

[5] **Enna González Muñoz.** Oldest sister of the author. She died in Havana on May 10, 2003.

just to escape for a few days. So I rushed to see the lieutenant. I lied, saying that my sister had sent the letter to be presented to the battalion. He picked up the letter and only saw the stamp of the General Staff.

"This is a letter from the General Staff!" He said enthusiastically, and asked me, "And who is this Enna González Muñoz that works in the 1089 Unit? Is she a relative of yours?"

"She is my sister, lieutenant," I responded, being sure that I had hit the target.

"So, you have a sister working in the 1089 Unit?" He asked.

"Yes," I answered, "and she insists that I present this letter to the battalion." It was a complete lie. My sister had not asked me to present the letter.

"Then, pick up your belongings and report immediately to the chief of personnel of the battalion!" And he gave me the letter back without bothering to finish reading it, and added, "It's just incredible, now that we are in the middle of the harvest that you have to go on leave! We'll just see how the brigade chiefs will do the work during your absence."

If Marrero had read the letter he would have realized that it was a simple request to the Military Committee in Havana and was not addressed to any battalion. Besides it was only a copy. But he was impressed by the stamp of the General Staff and by the job that my sister occupied as a civilian worker. When I arrived at the battalion, I asked to see the chief of personnel. I repeated the lie that I had told Lieutenant Marrero when I handed him the letter, expecting that the same thing would occur. He started to read the letter out loud, but as soon as he saw the stamp of the General Staff, he asked me, "Is this chief of economy of the General Staff your sister?"

"Yes," I responded. I was trembling as he examined the letter. But just like Lieutenant Marrero, the chief of personnel hardly read it.

"Officer in guard duty!" He yelled, "extend a leave for ten days to this comrade. With a sister working in the 1089 Unit he probably will not return."

I hardly dared to breathe. They gave me the permit and I left. At the door of the battalion I realized that I could not leave the letter behind. If they read the letter carefully I could have problems upon my return. I went back to the office and asked for the letter. I told the third lie. "My sister asked me to bring the letter back to her."

He took it out of his pocket, took the envelope and made a gesture as if he was going to read it again. The beating of my heart must have been as loud as a galloping horse. He pursed his lips as if to say, "And what for?" Then, he looked both ways, shrugged his shoulders, and gave it to me.

The Reign of Lies

I totally deceived them. I also made arrangements with the company planner to extend my leave beyond ten days. He, a UMAP recruit and a Jehovah's Witness who had renounced his faith, promised me that after the ten days he would count me as present in the report that he would send to the battalion, as if I had returned from my leave. He would then tell Lieutenant Marrero that I had left with fifteen days of leave and not with ten. In the middle of the harvest, I managed to take fifteen days of leave thanks to lies and other unethical arrangements. I did not even hesitate to double-cross Lieutenant Marrero who had trusted me and helped me to go home every weekend.

Are these schemes warranted from a Christian perspective? Does suffering from an unjust hell like UMAP make it acceptable to abandon one's beliefs and principles, and to engage in deceit for his own security and comfort? Some might think so, and even find some shrewdness in such an attitude. I felt just like that then. I was a "*bárbaro*"[6] to be able to go on leave by using a bogus letter, by lying, using the ignorance or lack of diligence of others to my benefit, and for allowing a friend to falsify information to cover for me. Thus I betrayed the trust of a man who relied on me because I was a Christian.

This was a consequence of an unfortunate reality: I was no longer the same person who had arrived a year and a half earlier. I was neither as innocent nor as honest. Almost without realizing what was happening, I had begun a process by which I *was* becoming social scum. We are never immune to the influence of the environment around us. Spending day and night with immoral people, especially in an oppressive and abusive atmosphere, would leave its mark on anyone. My lack of fellowship with other Christians, which is one of the ways the Lord alleviates our suffering, increased my vulnerability. I am not saying these things to justify my behavior, but to illustrate the process of Christian backsliding.

When a Christian is facing oppression and mistreatment, it is easy and natural for him to compromise his faith and conduct to protect himself. He might put on a moral mask to soothe his conscience and mute the convicting voice of the Holy Spirit. When he is willing to accept and participate in actions that he had previously avoided as a method of survival or self-defense, it is an indication of spiritual peril. When he can lie shamelessly for selfish benefit, the journey to depravity has already begun.

As I withdrew from God and began to behave in ways that I thought would help me survive there, I was really dismissing everything that was good. It would have been more honest and Christ-like to have suffered the humiliation and difficulty without giving in, whatever the cost. But I was becoming like those around me, and I had no idea what was happening. The worst thing of all is that the path to depravity

---

[6] **Bárbaro.** In vulgar language, a smart individual who has the ability to succeed in all difficult situations.

follows a parallel path to bitterness. The two are so close that they eventually merge, becoming the perfect way to sink a human soul into desperation.

I enjoyed the fifteen days of leave, refusing to acknowledge what was going on inside of me. Miriam and I traveled to Havana and stayed in the Habana Libre Hotel. I was present at the birth of my niece, and donated the blood that my sister needed. They were happy days, as long as my wife and I could be together, and I never felt a twinge of guilt for my dishonesty in obtaining my leave. In fact, I thought I was evening the score for my not having been demobilized like some of the other seminarians. I was glad for them to be released, but I was upset for not being one of them. I began to think of the irony that my bad back, which had bothered me for so many years previously, leaving me incapacitated for days and days, now gave me no problem at all. Many had been released for having back problems, but my back refused to help me with that. I was also upset because I was not old enough to be released as were those older than twenty-seven. I thought that many of those who were demobilized were less deserving of it than I. It hurt to remain confined when others were being freed.

I was involved in resistance warfare against God and was allowing a root of bitterness to spring up because I had to remain in UMAP. That root was growing secretly, but powerfully and quickly.

Hatred and Urges to Kill

When I returned to the unit I learned that the captain, who found out that I had continued working as an accountant, ordered Marrero, this time more firmly, to use the chiefs of the brigade. The lieutenant tried to salvage the situation, but this was a direct order. He tried hard to explain it, and evidently he felt bad for me; he was unhappy that he was required to do what was against his own wishes which he knew would not work well. The following day I took the machete once again to cut cane. I had instantly lost all the privileges that my position as an accountant and the friendship with the chief of the allotment had given me. I became very bitter and went to the country that day in a terrible mood and spiritual state.

It was then that the sergeant of the third platoon struck a raw nerve. He was a very stupid man; he looked like an orangutan. He was fat with a body that hardly had a neck. His lower jaw was long and he had hard and dismissive eyes. He barely knew how to speak. He mumbled the words one after the other. He growled rather than spoke. He did not like me, and I liked him even less. I was not a member of his platoon. Mine was the first one, and he led the second. He was an unjust man who was despised by everyone in the company. I had several previous altercations with him because he liked to supervise my work even though it was not his responsibility. When I worked as a supplier, a counter, and as an accountant, the sergeant would appear once in a while to check on what I had done, always questioning the quality of my work, despite the fact that he was almost illiterate.

The man had the ability to make me completely lose my patience. In the past, every time I had seen him coming to ask questions, I had prayed fervently to God. This had helped me overcome the antipathy that he evidently had for me and that I had developed toward him. But the sergeant was persistent and there was rarely a day that he did not make me feel uncomfortable. It was as if it was his mission to make my life miserable.

And he was succeeding.

When he saw me fall in that morning with my machete ready to cut cane, he came and stood directly in front me, crossed his arms, and then holding his chin with his right hand and without saying anything, he just stared at me and laughed for a long time without uttering a word. He repeated the same thing two more times in the country. He came to where I was, crossed his arms and burst out laughing. About noon, he abandoned his platoon and went into the field where I was working again. He approached the place where I was cutting cane. There he stood, laughing for a fourth time for a while, and suddenly yelled, "Well, well, well! How nice, eh, 41? The party is over for you. Ha-ha-ha! I'm so glad! You think you are mommy's little boy but here everybody has to *bite the green!*" [7]

Once again I tried to ignore him and went on working, but a feeling of hatred gradually overwhelmed me. Never had I felt anything like that before. I bit my lips and I began to cut with much stronger force, almost five canes with a single chop. The sergeant continued.

"Ha-ha-ha! I like to see you work like this. Come on, come on, cut cane like a man! Did you think that you would always get to work with a pencil? You were mistaken whitey! Hell! Who knows if you're a real man? I am so happy to finally see you cutting cane and sweat rolling down your back!" He yelled for the rest of the brigade to hear him, "Look, look at the proud whitey; how he is sweating! It makes me so happy! Ha-ha!"

I stopped cutting cane. I had the machete in my right hand and felt an enormous desire to pitch it at him. I was holding the handle of the machete with an ever-increasing anger. My whole body became tense. Inside me, there was an unknown desire that urged me to lift up the machete and charge against him. I clearly felt the desire to tear him to pieces. I stared at him with hatred as he continued mocking and laughing at me.

Then I turned my back to him so as not to look at him again. I began to tremble all over. I am afraid to say it, but I felt like killing the sergeant. I did not dare to do it but I felt it intensely.

"Come on, come on," continued the sergeant. "Don't stand there like a stake. Cut cane, whitey, that's why you're here! Ha, ha! See? It will make you into a man! I love to see these soft boys from Havana have a tough time!"

---

[7] **Bite the green.** A common expression at that time referring to someone who was forced to work in the country.

I started cutting cane frantically. I imagined that every plant was the sergeant. I was filled with rage, feeling humiliated and belittled. He went on with his rant until he got tired. I continued cutting cane the rest of the day like a machine. The work finally ended and we went back to the unit. I remained silent; I did not want to talk to anybody. Everyone irritated me. I took a shower and we were allowed to go to bed early. When I climbed into the bunk bed and being alone with my thoughts, I discovered that I still had the desire to kill the sergeant. I felt my heart harden and become as cold as a block of ice. I thought to myself, *"I'm not going to kill him because I'm not going to ruin my life. He isn't worth it."*

"My God!" I shuddered as I thought to myself, *"What is happening to me?"* If anyone had told me before that I was capable of having desires to kill a man, I would have burst out laughing. It was impossible. Now some difficult events, the evil environment, and my shallow walk with the Lord were working together to produce some responses and emotions in me that were a stark contrast to anything that I had ever experienced. How had I become like this?

I tried to pray, but everything I said seemed hollow. I tried to remember some hymns from those that I had enjoyed and inspired me in the past. I recited the lyrics of *He Knows Best*, which Miriam and I sang and had always moved me. But my heart continued to be cold and my eyes were dry—so dry that they burned. That night I twisted and turned in bed without being able to sleep. I could only doze for short intervals.

Morning came quickly and I was tired, confused, and bitter.

The worst spiritual crisis of my life had begun. I would only overcome it a few months later by the grace of God and with the patient and wise help from the woman that He gave me as a partner. Other brothers, who demonstrated mercy, also tried to help me through that time.

This will be the most difficult part of the story to tell.

8

If Faith Abandons Me

The state of spiritual exhaustion hung over me for a couple of weeks after that afternoon when I felt like killing the sergeant. I worked and lived like a robot. I felt like something I had read in a poem: *"too tired and empty for praying."* I returned to working with and socializing more with the Christians that remained in Las Marías, but I spoke very little and felt incapable of sharing my true feelings. Maybe one of the problems was that, even though I had good relationships with the brothers that were still there, still, I was much closer to those who had already left.

The harvest continued its hectic pace of work, and we were hopeful that the rains would begin. When the rains came, the cutting would be finished and then we would go on leave. There were rumors circulating that summer. One that was often heard was that each of us would be transferred to a unit in his own province. Any news was an encouragement and we clung to the smallest of these rumors with hope.

I rushed to change my mailing address in all of my documents because otherwise, if this rumor were true, I would be sent to Havana, since I had been recruited while living at the seminary. It would not be good for me to be sent to a unit near Havana; I was married and Miriam was living and working in Ciego de Ávila. Havana is even farther away, and it would be more difficult for her to visit me. Besides, when I went on leave everything would be more difficult due to the longer distance between us. Although I didn't like the idea of staying in the province of Camagüey at all, I was content knowing that for our situation, it was much more convenient. It was also rumored that some of us would be transferred to regular units of the military service, which by this time did not appeal to us either. At the end of the day, being close to Miriam was the only thing that mattered to me. Some new rumors came out almost every day and we were all clinging to any hope of change.

One night, after Julio Cornelio, Esteban Estrada, Rafael Hernández, and Ernesto Alfonso had been released, I dreamed that I also had been demobilized. Such as dreams are, I found myself arriving by surprise at the seminary, but without having stopped by my wife's home in Ciego de Ávila on the way. As I approached the seminary building on General Lee Street I was thinking that it had been unfair of me not to get off the bus in Ciego de Ávila to tell her that I had been demobilized. My hope was to get to the seminary so that they would know that I too had left UMAP and was able to return to class.

I was full of excitement when I approached the classroom that was in front of the entrance hall on the ground floor of the building. There, Dr. José Manuel Sánchez[1], who had already gone abroad by that time, was teaching all the brothers who had returned from UMAP. With them, though he was not a student of the seminary, was Rubén Deulofeu. Next to him was Ernesto Ruano who, like me, had not yet been released.

In my dream I interrupted the class with much fanfare, expecting everyone to be glad when they saw me, but they all went on as if nothing had happened. Standing in the middle of the doorway I insisted on calling for everyone's attention. Suddenly Dr. Sanchez looked at me, very annoyed and told

---

[1] **Dr. José Manuel Sánchez.** Deceased. He was the Director of Christian Education, professor in the seminary and pastor of the Baptist Church in el Cotorro then. He was appointed rector of the seminary after the imprisonment of Dr. Caudill. He was very much affected by the imprisonment of the pastors. He immigrated to the United States, where in spite of his precarious health, he was a pastor in West Palm Beach for many years.

me, "Don't bother us, please; these students are really behind and we have to make the most of our time. They came back from the military service and we want them to graduate soon."

"And what are you doing here?" I asked Dr. Sanchez because I knew that he had left for the United States, and besides it was not the classroom in which he usually taught his classes.

"I have the same question for you," he answered, and then added, "Please stop bothering us, because we have no time to waste. These students are way behind, because they were in UMAP for so long."

Dr. Sanchez treated me as if I were a stranger whom he had never met. The others acted the same way, which increased my embarrassment and frustration. How could they ignore me that way?

"But I am one of them!" I protested. And I stood at the door with a tremendous sense of frustration, noticing that nobody paid attention to me. Everybody continued to listen to the lecture, ignoring my presence. Then I looked at Ernesto Ruano, and very upset, I said to him, "You were also here and didn't tell me anything? I thought you were working as a corporal in La Reforma. How is it that you were released and didn't let me know?"

Then Ernesto got up from his seat, took me out of the classroom and said, "Don't be a fool. This is a dream. Neither you nor I are here. Calm down!"

"The last thing I need to hear is my best friend telling me that! I am coming in and I'm going to sit down to take my classes even though Dr. Sanchez doesn't want me to. I don't know what he is doing here anyway since I know that he has already left for the United States."

Instead of doing that, I left Ernesto standing in the hall and I rushed to the third floor where the telephone for student use was located. On the way to the staircase, I ran through the dining hall knocking over the tables and chairs as I went, and turning to the stairway, I climbed the stairs as fast as I could. In the meantime, I was listening to the music of the hymn *Rock of Ages* and felt that somebody was chasing me. He hit me on the shoulder even as I tried to elude him.

I wanted to get to the phone and call Miriam and tell her: "*Look, I was released and they want it to be a dream. They don't want me to call you, nor let me in for classes.*" But the person kept hitting me on my shoulder as I struggled to get hold of the phone, which always slipped out of my hands. I already knew that it was a dream, but I tried not to wake up. Then, I desperately yelled, "Leave me alone, I don't want to wake up!"

The Root of Bitterness

"Hey, hey! Wake up! Don't you hear what's on the radio?"

It was José Ferrer who was trying to wake me up, because it was almost time to be on our feet although they had not called the troops to fall in yet. The officer of the watch, who sometimes turned on the radio and played some music, had tuned into a station that was broadcasting a beautiful instrumental of the hymn, *Rock of Ages*. The entire unit was listening to its melody. "Hey, brother," he told me, "they don't know what they have turned on."

Still feeling the agony of my dream, perhaps triggered by my mood and by the music that I had recognized while asleep, I awoke in a deplorable state. I looked around, trying to figure out where I was, because hearing the hymn confused me.

"Hey, wake up!" Ferrer insisted, "Look what a surprise they are giving us this morning. They tuned in the radio for us!"

At that moment they said, "On your feet!" When the other Christians woke up, they looked at each other smiling as they recognized the tune. The usual commotion began as the other recruits were getting up, looking for their clothes to get ready for the day. The hymn continued to fill the air and I could not move a muscle.

Israel García came quickly to the side of my bed, and told Ferrer and me, "It's fantastic; they woke us up with a church service!"

Then, we heard a voice that all of us recognized. "Dear radio listeners. The Word of God teaches us that...."

"That's Domingo Fernández!"[2] screamed Israel.

It was the voice of the well-known Baptist preacher on a radio transmission broadcasted from the United States. When they realized that it was a religious program they quickly changed the station. But, it was just amazing to us to realize that the message of God and the beautiful tune of an old hymn of faith could get all the way to the fields of Camagüey.

Israel García began to repeat the stanza of the hymn: *Rock of ages, Cleft for me, Let me hide myself in Thee.* He looked me in the eye, approached my bunk bed and hugged me. He knew intuitively, as did the others, that I was not doing well.

"It won't be long, brother." He told me, "We have to hold on to the Rock. Someday this will be over."

"Do you think so? Don't you think that it's been too long?"

"Yes, it's been too long but God is going to help us. You'll see."

I looked into his eyes and I discovered that they were damp. Then I said, "Look, Israel, I am very happy for all those who have been able to leave. But why hasn't God gotten us all

---

[2] **Domingo Fernández Suárez** was an eminent Baptist pastor, writer and radio preacher. He directed "The Baptist Hour" for many years, a weekly radio program of the Western Baptist Convention. He immigrated to the U.S. in the decade of the 60's, and was a pastor of many churches in the City of Miami. He preached on the radio for many years and also published various books. He passed away in the City of Miami.

out? He can do it! How is it possible for us to be here in this hell and for the other brothers to be back in the seminary? Why has God punished us so?"

Israel gave me a serious look and another strong hug. Ferrer climbed up, sat in my bunk bed and patted me on my knee. Given the love and acts of affection from these two brothers, I felt the need to open up my heart to them. Recently, I had been avoiding contact with them.

"I have so many doubts and I feel terrible. I won't be able to return to the seminary when I leave here." It was the first time that I had admitted in front of my brothers that things were not going well.

"Don't say that! We all go through our crises, but you'll see that in a little while you'll feel better. Do you want me to give you some advice? Don't pay much attention to yourself, and soon you'll see that all of this will be over," said Israel.

Ferrer put his hands on my chest and advised me, "You have to draw closer to the Lord. We are all desperate, but you are backsliding and we're very worried about you!"

We could not continue talking, because they called us to fall in for breakfast and the whirlwind of the day had begun. We had breakfast quickly; they only gave us a glass of powdered milk and then we went immediately to the fields to continue cutting cane. We had to walk that day because the unit's tractor had broken down. The field was a long walk and it was full of tangled canes, which made the work much harder. The harvest had been very long and the rains, which would put an end to it, still had not begun.

During that day, both Israel and Ferrer tried to approach me, but I once again closed myself off in silence and did not want to share my feelings, which were not good, with anyone. Since the day when I felt like killing the sergeant, I had not been the same person. I felt a hatred that had never been a part of me before. Although it is painful to confess, I resented the brothers' company. After the moment of truth that morning, perhaps brought on by the dream and the hymn, *Rock of Ages*, I did not want to talk to anyone about my situation again.

Too Tired and Empty to Pray

What had happened inside of me that I was capable of desiring to kill someone? While I was cutting cane, I thought about everything that had happened over and over again. I told myself that the sergeant was a poor ignorant man who could barely speak, a soul for whom Christ also had died. But to me, he had become a living and hurtful symbol of all the injustice and barbarity in which he was involved. The day was long because we worked until dark. They took our lunch to the country on a cart pulled by oxen, and it only consisted of mashed bananas and sardines. The food was not always like that because usually there was a good supply, but we also had hard times and this was one of them.

We left the country and took a path along a dirt road looking for a shorter way to get back to the unit. The field was on the other side of the bamboo-lined river, a kilometer and a half from the dirt road, and about three from the unit. As we walked on the dirt road returning to the unit, I saw one of the most beautiful sunsets I had ever seen.

Absorbed in my thoughts and troubled by my feelings, I barely heard when Ferrer started singing: "*If the light of the sun hides away, and my faith hesitates, I lift up my prayer and claim: Christ, is my pilot*". But the chorus of the hymn took me away from my seclusion: "*My pilot shall go with me, and I shall fear nothing, the furious sea does not frighten me; in Him alone shall I trust.*" It annoyed me that Ferrer would sing that hymn and I began to talk with other recruits in order to block it out. A wall of impenetrable coldness had risen up in my soul, which made me insensitive and resistant to emotion. I wanted Ferrer to know that I was not listening to him.

I had been unable to pray for days. Why should I talk to a void? God had closed His ears to me. My communion with him had been broken. Ferrer continued singing all along the way, but I ignored him. They were hymns that I knew from memory, but now they could not reach my heart.

That very night, after dinner, when the mail was delivered, I received a letter from Miriam.

Ciego de Avila, April 28, 1967

My love:

> *Yesterday, I started to write you a letter, but in the end I tore it up, because I was writing nonsense. I received yours and I felt bad about everything that you said. I don't want you to get angry, or think that it is easy for me to say these things because I am not in your shoes.*
>
> *I know that everything that you are experiencing is hard for you. But I think that in the same way that I rest in your arms when we are together, you should rest in the arms of the Lord, being sure that He shall sustain you throughout. Now I remember the stanza of the hymn that says:*
>
> *If faith shall abandon me, He shall sustain me,*
> *And if all threaten me, He shall sustain me.*
> *He shall sustain me; He shall sustain me.*
> *My Jesus who loves me so much, He shall sustain me.*
>
> *I know that faith has abandoned you, because I feel it and because I see you, but I also know that He has not abandoned you. My love, look more to the Lord and you shall obtain more victory. Please, honey, don't worry right now for how and on what are we going to live when you manage to leave. Everything will be arranged. You know what? I married you knowing where you were and that I wouldn't even have you by my side. When at last I have you I am going to be so happy that nothing else worries me at all.*
>
> *I only ask you to remember that faith can abandon*

you, and you can be full of doubts as you are now, but that doesn't mean that the Lord is going to abandon you. Hold on to that, someday you and I will tell of these experiences to our children...

I had started to tell Miriam everything about how bad I felt. I tried to hide it for a while, but she knew. Then I began writing letters that were full of accusations against God and making her even a part of the struggles of my heart. Sometimes they were very unpleasant letters. When I read them now I am embarrassed. If she tried to comfort me, I took offense. It must have been very difficult dealing with me then.

I became adept at silencing her arguments by telling her that because she was not in my shoes it was easy for her to accept the situation; that one had to be immersed in this hell in order to understand all the despair and discontent that one begins to feel. I also wrote letters to my mother and others. In my rebellion I wanted everyone to know how much I was suffering. Among other things, I felt that my family, especially my father and my brothers, were indifferent to all that I was suffering. They did not believe all the atrocities that were taking place in UMAP, which had made me feel so miserable.

Kicking Against the Goads

I had even begun to tell Miriam that I would not go back to seminary when I left there. I knew that I was not worthy of the ministry, especially in the spiritual state that I was in. But then, what would I do? Although the possibility of getting out of there was remote, I began to torture myself with this. What would become of my life? How would I start a family? If society had labeled me as social scum and sent me to UMAP, would there be any employment opportunities at all for me after I left there? Now everything is easier to explain, but at that time there were many unknowns. My letters were full of complaining and blaming of others. Miriam always answered them by trying to encourage me, and with arguments that might help me dig out of the pit of depression and spiritual apathy into which I had fallen.

Why do I share this part of the story?

It would be dishonest to leave the impression that all the time that I spent in UMAP I was victorious and strong in the faith. In that case, some might think that I am pretending to be a martyr, or a triumphant Christian hero in the midst of difficult circumstances, through which I was passing by the will of God. This is far from my purpose in writing about this experience, and the truth is that it did not happen that way.

Eleuterio Figueredo, another young Christian, recruited in June, 1966, faced the ordeal of UMAP with a far more Christ-like attitude, even though his situation was far more difficult. His father, the pastor of the Baptist Church in Vueltas, was in prison. His brother David was also sent to UMAP and his other brother, Samuel, was also arrested. The tremendous difficulties that his family faced prevented him from receiving any visits during the first six months that he was in UMAP before being able to go on leave. But he constantly prayed and he was filled with peace. Each time that he approached the Lord in prayer he experienced the new strength that God promised for those who wait on Him as described in Isaiah 40:31. *"But they who wait for the Lord shall renew their strength; they shall mount up with wings like eagles; they shall run and not be weary; they shall walk and not faint."*

Nevertheless, sometimes the desperate idea of escaping from that place consumed him. On one of those dark days, he was hoeing in a cane field that was hellishly full of weeds, and he just could not do it any longer. His hands refused to continue pulling on the hoe. The railroad tracks were closeby, and the temptation to escape became overwhelming and urgent. He became very distressed and could not see another way out. The fact that we are Christians does not mean that we do not share human feelings! He began walking through the cane rows where he had been working in order to escape without being seen. On the brink of fleeing, following the path that would lead him to the railroad, he saw lying in the middle of a pool of mud, in the rotting vegetation, a beautiful lilac-colored flower. Desperate and troubled as he was, he stopped and took it in his hands. Then a miracle occurred.

It was as if the flower had told him, "If I can live in this muddy swamp, you can survive in UMAP." By means of that wild flower, God spoke to him. For a long time afterward, he kept that flower in his New Testament as a reminder.

To the Christians who read these lines, my story should serve as a warning. I was in the church from the time I was born and surrendered to the Lord when I was ten or eleven years old by personal decision. I still remember the place, the pew where I was sitting in the Presbyterian Church in Cárdenas, the preacher and the hymn that they used in the calling. I was baptized while a young man, also by my personal choice, and very aware of what I was doing and what was expected of me. I felt the call to the ministry when I was very young, decided to serve the Lord by giving up my dream of studying architecture and entered the seminary without much difficulty. All had been favorable. Now, for the first time, and in a terrible way, my faith and commitment to the Lord were being tested.

When Faith is Put to the Test

I am now convinced that God had a purpose for everything that was happening to me. I had to learn what a spiritual crisis was in order to understand and help others. My faith had to be tested; such things as despair, anguish, doubts, rebellion, insecurity, unbelief, and blindness always test true faith. If, after suffering through these things, faith can emerge victorious, then it is based on truth. But, it is an unavoidable path. Every Christian must pass this way eventually. The difference between biblical faith and superstition, between spiritual reality and intellectual knowledge, and between our own will-power and the power of the Spirit of God working in us, is revealed on this difficult path of trial and suffering.

How did Elijah feel when he sat under the juniper tree in Beersheba wishing to die, and said to God, *"It is enough; Lord, take my life"*? He had experienced great spiritual victories, but the announcement that Jezebel was seeking to kill him caused this man of faith to flee, and plunged him into depression. That depression and the testing of his faith made him know God in a way that he had not known Him before.

After having broken the tablets of the Law written on by the finger of God, how did Moses feel when he saw the infidelity of the people? He prayed, *"Now therefore, if I have found favor in your sight, please show me now your ways."* [3] This man of faith was confused, disoriented and afraid. *"If your presence will not go with me, do not bring us up from here."*

How did Joseph feel when he, as an adolescent, was sold into slavery, far away from his father's home and of the privileges that he had once enjoyed? What a tremendous spiritual pilgrimage and how many battles must have been waged against his soul, until he reached the moral stature that allowed him to say, in a key moment of his life, *"I am your brother, Joseph, whom you sold into Egypt. And now do not be distressed or angry with yourselves because you sold me here, for God sent me before you to preserve life."* [4] And again, *"As for you, you meant evil against me, but God meant it for good… Do not fear, for am I in the place of God?"* [5] Many years had passed, but along with the years, many storms must have crushed the heart of this magnificent, very intuitive and sensitive man according to what we know of him from the biblical account. We are not given details of his agony in the midst of injustice and the difficulties of life, but the man who wept out loud before making himself known to his brothers must have asked himself countless unanswered questions after crying alone in the desert. His character was tempered by the tests, but we should not think that achieving it was easy, nor that his ascension to an eminent position was painless.

---

[3] Exodus 33:13-15.

[4] Genesis 45:5.

[5] Genesis 50:19-20.

How did Job who was an example of affliction and patience, according to James,[6] feel in the midst of his great suffering and cries of despair? He had moments of despair, unbelief and self-absorption, and only at the end was his faith in God finally renewed, recovered, and deepened. He came to a knowledge of the Lord and of himself that was much more real and spiritual than he had known before.

The Psalmist wrote, *"Deep calls to deep at the roar of your waterfalls; all your breakers and your waves have gone over me...I say to God, my rock, 'Why have you forgotten me? Why do I go mourning because of the oppression of the enemy?' As with a deadly wound in my bones, my adversaries taunt me, while they say to me continually, 'Where is your God?'"* [7] Was he experiencing any peace when he said these words? No, certainly not! He was in the process of discovering it in the midst of the agonies of life, the only place that the indescribable peace of God can be understood and found.

What did Jesus experience when He called His three most beloved disciples to pray separately, and said with obvious despair, *"My soul is very sorrowful, even to death"*? How did He feel when He saw that they were not even able to stand watch, but were insensitive to His suffering, even sleeping while He was writhing in prayer, asking His Father, *"Father, if you are willing, remove this cup from me"?* [8] Luke says that He was in agony, praying so intensely that His sweat became droplets of blood that fell to the ground. What tremendous spiritual anguish is behind these words! We read them as if Jesus were saying, "All right, Father, I can handle all of this without any problem." We are so accustomed to reading the stories of the great men of the Bible without internalizing their feelings and struggles that were often terribly agonizing.

Sometimes we demand that those who go through the

---

[6] James 5:10-11.

[7] Psalm 42:7-10.

[8] Luke 22:42.

great conflicts of life continue smiling as if nothing were happening and tell us, "Don't worry; I have everything under control." But the Christian life is not like that, and Christians are not like that either. Unless we are Pharisees hiding our struggles, inward questions, and doubts behind an arrogant and hypocritical mask, we will have to recognize that true faith emerges triumphantly only after a long journey. Everybody, or almost everybody, will pass through questions and suffering.

Only the Christian who is able to hold on to God at all costs when he does not understand anything else, nor see any light on the horizon, comes to experience what true faith really is. Just like a drowning man that clings to a stray board after the sinking of a boat, is he who holds on to the small fragments of his faith (that faith that appeared so firm and powerful as long as he did not have to face a real storm) and finds peace and glory. The cry on the cross, *"It is finished!"*[9] seemed tragic, but ultimately it was the radiant victory over the power of sin. It came after another cry, so human and repeated throughout the history of humanity: *"My God, my God, why have you forsaken me?"* [10]

The Long Road Ahead

That is why I do not mind telling about my crisis experience nor share the weakness of my faith. Although my faith faltered when it was strongly shaken by UMAP, by the grace of God He gathered up all the pieces of my life and with them I serve the Lord today. I am no longer a young Pharisee, proud and arrogant, but one who learned how low he could descend, then being horrified, clung to God with more humility and dependence.

Months later I would understand it, but at the end of the 1967 harvest I was at the height of my crisis, my despair, and my doubts. Miriam was right about what she said in her letter; *faith could abandon me, but the Lord would not.* He would be

---

[9] John 19:30.

[10] Matthew 27:46.

patient and merciful, and he would show me his love a thousand times, while I, as the psalmist said, *"With my voice I cry out to the Lord; with my voice I plead for mercy to the Lord. I pour out my complaint before him; I tell my trouble before him. When my spirit faints within me, you know my way!"*[11]

So I was when the harvest ended. We left again on a ten-day leave on June 16, 1967. I had spent a year, six months, and twenty days in Las Marías. The night before leaving, the group of Christians sat down to talk with each other and to share our plans that we had for the leave. It was a beautiful moonlit night, and in the small park of rustic benches that was beside the barracks, overshadowed by the avocado trees, we were eagerly waiting for the hour to go to bed. The last official leave had been six months earlier in December. I had benefited from a few extra leaves, but the rest of the recruits had spent half a year without going to their homes.

"Can you imagine what it will be like the day we finally get out of here?" said Israel Cordivés. "I am not coming back to Camagüey, not even as a visitor. If I ever have to travel to Oriente, I'll go by plane. I never want to step foot in this province again."

"I hate all of this," I said, "and it seems incredible to me to have lived here for a year and a half. I've never felt that I belong here. It has nothing to do with my life. At least I'm going to put it behind me for ten days again."

We went to bed late. The nights before the leaves we could never sleep, because of the anxiety and excitement. Waiting for the sun to rise seemed endless.

It was raining when we awoke that morning. All of us got up quickly when the morning shout to fall in rang out; none of the usual protesting was heard. We fell in fast for the daily count and for breakfast. Because it was drizzling, they wanted us to count quickly. Israel García, always with a witty

---

[11] Psalm 142:1-3.

remark at hand, said as we fell in, "Come on kiddos! Count fast! This is the last time we have to yell out our numbers here."

He was an unwitting prophet; we would never again fall in at Las Marías to be counted. We yelled out our numbers for the last time. That day, although I could not imagine it, I quit being 41.

I Am No Longer 41

An hour later, under a tremendous downpour, we climbed into the truck that would take us to the battalion. When we left Las Marías that morning, we had no idea that our stay in that place had ended. While our time in UMAP was not over, we would all be transferred when we returned. Since I had changed my mailing address to Ciego de Ávila, in the province of Camagüey, I would be separated from all my companions and sent to a different camp. We were ignorant of all that under that downpour that day, but we were full of joy as we boarded the truck. From there we went to Senado Sugar Mill where the buses were to take us to our destinations. An hour and a half later, we came to Ciego de Ávila. Since Miriam lived on the Central Highway, the bus stopped and dropped me at the front door of her house.

When I got off the bus and stood on the sidewalk, I shouted to the brothers who were waving their hands at me through the windows, "Have fun and take care! We'll see each other in Las Marías on the 26th!"

But that would not happen.

I did not see those brothers who had accompanied me during that eighteen month-long trial again, until the day we were released from UMAP, some thirteen months later.

The worst part of the experience was yet to come. From then on, I would have to handle it alone. I would struggle with my faith in crisis, without the company of the brothers who could help me and who understood me. I also did not know that more than a year was still to come before I would leave that place. During the coming year, very few Christians would be by my side.

What remained of my pride had to be torn down and my self-sufficiency abandoned.

God had His own plan for accomplishing it and the test ahead would be harder still.

9

Peace Returns

In the days leading up to our leave, there were persistent rumors of changes and transfers that would take effect upon our return. I had read in the monthly work plan that the most disciplined recruits would be selected to work on military construction.

I had a break just after the harvest was over in May before the leave when several recruits were chosen to attend a workshop for teachers. The purpose was to prepare us to give remedial instruction to those recruits who had not completed a 6th grade education. José Ferrer, Israel García, and I were among the attendees, and together we were taken to a camp at Nuevitas for the workshop.

The course was really like a working vacation, because the conditions were completely different from those in Las Marías. The barracks were well painted, clean, and refreshing. They were made of masonry and located beside the sea, where we could swim every day. Our only responsibility was to attend training sessions in the mornings. It was being said that from that point forward in UMAP, we would work in the morning as usual, but that in the afternoon our time would be dedicated to improvement classes. The workshop lasted for one week and we returned to the unit. As they had directed us, we worked in the fields in the mornings, and began teaching classes in the afternoons. But only three days later, there came the new order for us to work all day and teach the classes at night. This regimen was maintained for the second week, and then we went on leave.

The leave arrived, and Miriam and I spent our wedding anniversary together. As always, I managed to forget everything, and I was happy and rested until the return day approached. Normally when I went on a ten-day leave, I did not go back at the required time, but stayed one extra day, because I could not find the strength to head back to the unit. This time, we did not ever leave Ciego de Ávila due to financial problems. My mother had come to see me in May, so we decided to relax at home without traveling.

I particularly enjoyed that leave. I longed for the solitude of a family environment. Miriam, as usual, took her vacation to coincide with my time away from UMAP. We avoided the topic of my spiritual state because I had no desire to listen to a sermon, and because she was hopeful that after spending some time at home, my spiritual outlook would improve. I did not wish to provoke any arguments or ruin the few days that we had together. The last few times I told her that I would not be returning to the seminary when I got out of UMAP, she answered, "Let's not talk about that now. One should not make decisions in the middle of a crisis." I listened; I knew that she was right. I attended church as usual and pretended that all was well. As before, I declined the pastor's invitation to preach.

Without the Strength to Return

My ten-day leave flew by fast. Miriam, who had requested the same number of days off, went back to work. She did not want to miss another day because she wanted to be sure to accrue enough time off for the next time that I was able to go on leave. She said goodbye to me that morning, assuming that when she returned I would be on my way, but she found me still at home when she came back.

"Don't worry, I'm leaving early tomorrow," I told her.

The next day, when she got up to go to work, I insisted on staying in bed to sleep a little longer. "Go and please don't worry. I'll get up later, and then I'll leave. If I'm going back a day late, it makes no difference whether I arrive there in the morning or at night."

She hugged and kissed me saying, "Please! I just don't want you to get into trouble." She left for work after making me promise that I would leave by mid-morning. She returned that afternoon not expecting to find me at home, but she was wrong. At that point she began to insist that I leave, worried about the consequences that I could suffer if I did not report back to the unit as soon as possible. "Don't you realize that this can have consequences and that we might suffer even more?" She was upset, sad, and worried. Although she wished I could stay, she tried to prevail upon me to leave as soon as possible. "Don't you realize that all I want is to be by your side?"

I could not stand to hear anymore of that! "I can't take it anymore! Don't you understand? Don't you know what it means when I tell you that I can't take it anymore? I'm going, you can be sure of that. But don't force me, please. It makes me feel that you want me to leave, and that is harder than being in the unit!"

She looked at me with her eyes full of tears. She did not know what else to tell me to persuade me, and yet at the same time she was terrified that I would have even more problems.

"I know what I'm doing, trust me. I have gained some experience at least, inside of that inferno. I know how everything works." Then I told her in an attempt to ease her fears, "Now there are going to be some transfers and changes made. Many recruits said that they were going to do the same, to stay home for a few more days. You know that sometimes I've returned late and I have never had any problems."

She gave up. She did not want me to leave either, and

thought that it was grossly unfair that the leave was so short considering the whole situation. "But you know that we *have* been together and you have had other opportunities. Would the Lord be pleased if you took such a risk?"

"I'm sure that it's fine with Him; otherwise He would convince me to go, wouldn't He?"

I stayed not only for one more day, but for five! I left on the sixth day after she left for work. I did it very reluctantly but I understood that it had been too long. My staying at home had made everyone tense for fear of the consequences that could cause our difficult situation to deteriorate further. Miriam's parents were very respectful and they did not say anything to me, but their faces and demeanor reflected a lot of fear and sorrow.

Each time I returned from leave was more upsetting than the time before.

Farewell to Las Marías

I made the trip back through Morón. I took the morning train that stopped at every station rather than the nighttime express train, and I was able to get off at Truffín, the stop that was only two kilometers from the unit. I got off at two in the afternoon and took the road to Las Marías. I was, of course, a little afraid. After all, I was coming back after sixteen days. I realized that I could not invent some excuse, and as I made my way back, I asked God not to have Lieutenant Marrero waiting at the door. When I arrived at the grove where we received visitors, I took a shortcut that led directly to the unit, and immediately noticed something strange. It was too quiet in the camp.

When I entered, it startled me to see that the unit had been deserted. The recruits were gone. The dining hall and kitchen were closed. So was the office. I noticed that that the door to the officers' bedroom was open, so I went in. There I found a military man whom I did not know sleeping in Lieutenant Marrero's bed. I was so desperate to know what was going on that I did not hesitate to wake him. "Everyone has been transferred from here," he told me. You'll have to go to the battalion to see where you've been assigned."

At that point, I began to panic. I remembered Miriam and her warnings and the increasingly worried looks from my in-laws. "Now I have really messed things up!" I thought.

My bewilderment was so evident that the soldier hastened to calm me down. "Don't worry, recruit. Very few have returned from their leave. I'm certain that from the battalion they will take you to the unit where they're segregating everybody according to their province, because you're going to be transferred. Go to Jagüeycito so that you can find out where you will be going. Everything is a total mess right now, and nobody knows when the transfers will happen. They left me with the order to stay here and look after the unit and to direct those who are still trickling in."

I left quickly, already convinced that there would be no problems. In fact, I was so convinced, that instead of heading to the dirt road toward the battalion, I went to the grove. I sat down to seriously consider the possibility of going back to Truffin, and then taking any train that would go through Morón, in order to go back home for a few more days. After all, the soldier did say that everything was in chaos, and that he did not know when the transfers would take place.

Lying under the shade of the tree where Miriam and I used to sit down during the visits, I studied every facet of the situation. After much thought, I decided to go to the battalion for two reasons. First, I did not know what time the train would come by, so I would have to walk more than five kilometers to Sola to board it. Besides, I knew that if I returned home, the same anxiety would start over again when it was time to leave, and that my return would cause everybody there a great deal of stress.

I stopped. I looked closely at those trees and that place, realizing I was leaving forever. I had experienced so many emotions there! What an indescribable joy every time that Miriam came and what pain and agony when she left! Heaps of laughter, countless tears, more numerous than the dry leaves that covered the ground, had made for intense and unforgettable moments spent in that grove. It is funny how we learn to love places much like we love people. I had been in Las Marías for a year and a half, and under the shade of those trees I had also spent many hours writing letters and my horrible and gloomy poems.

I leaned against that tree as I watched its huge, beautiful, green branches, under which I had spent so much time. I was tempted, in spite of the fact that I had always found the practice distasteful, to write Miriam's name and mine on its bark. I did not do it because it would have been like hurting an old friend. "I'll come back here someday," I talked to the tree as if it could listen, "and will bring my children to tell the story."

It was hard to walk away. I walked down to the dirt road and then on toward the battalion. When I rounded the corner at a place from which you could see the camp, I turned my head back to take one last look at Las Marías. It was startling to remember what I had said seventeen days before. The night before the leave, sitting in the small square of the unit, I had expressed with all the bitterness that I could muster, "I hate all of this. This place has nothing to do with my life." Incredibly, leaving Las Marías made me feel sad now. We humans are sometimes contradictory. Really, is the place at fault for what men do there? Somehow, for some mysterious and inexplicable reason, the land that has been watered with our tears becomes a little part of us. I viewed the camp from a distance. Because all the cane fields had been cut, it was all clearly visible, including the grove, the grocery store, and the white house across from the unit.

I turned my back to Las Marías with profound sadness. Crossing the river and then losing sight of the unit, I felt that I would be tied to that place forever.

Changes, but More of the Same

Where would they send me now? I wondered as I walked to the battalion. The old saying is exactly right: "Better the evil that you know than the good that you know not." All the recruits whom I knew who had been transferred before said that transfers were disastrous. All the previous relationships were broken and it was very difficult to adapt to new chiefs, to new recruits, and to the conditions of a different place. What I did not know then was that I was to be transferred at least ten times during my remaining time in UMAP.

When I arrived at Jagüeycito it was after six in the evening. The camp of the second company of the battalion, like in Las Marías, was deserted. I found only the Chief of Staff, who also reassured me by insisting that few recruits had returned from their leaves, and that all of us would be transferred.

"Three others arrived a little while ago. Look for them in the barracks. Tomorrow we will take all of you to the temporary transfer center with everyone else," he explained to me.

I thanked God that evidently there would be no problems. I regretted again not having stayed at home for a few days longer. The chaos was widespread, and incredibly nobody was enforcing the return of the recruits. Several times that night I woke up and thought about going home for a few more days. The next day they took us to a unit bordering the town of Mola. I discovered that not one of the brothers was there who had been with me in Las Marías. Everything was disorganized, because recruits had come from several different camps.

We were told that we would wait there for our permanent transfer orders. The man in charge of the camp happened to be the same sergeant who had accompanied me to the Senado Sugar Mill the day I wounded my leg, and who had taken me to the battalion before I went on leave. On those occasions he had proved to be a very good friend. As soon as he saw me coming, he joyfully greeted me, "Well, well! We haven't seen each other since you got married. How is your wife?"

"Fine. How lucky you're here!" I answered.

"I'm the lucky one, because now I have somebody who can work in the office and get things organized here. This is a total mess, 13," he remembered my first number in UMAP, "and we don't know which, or even how many recruits will be coming here. I have been ordered to make a list of everyone in order to better organize the transfers when the time comes."

His presence in the unit was detrimental to my plans to return home. If I had been a stranger to the only officer who was in charge, I would certainly have left. The recruits continued to return from their leaves, and I started working by making lists by each recruit's province of origin.

More than a few of the recruits escaped and went home for a few more days. Everyone knew that enforcement was almost nonexistent at the moment. One day, brother Federico Fernández[1] who was a member of the church in Catalina de Güines, arrived. We talked together, and I knew that he wanted to return home again. Seeing what the others did, he spoke constantly about it. He would not dare do it because his father-in-law, a prominent member of the church in Catalina de Güines, had made him promise several times that never, under any circumstances, would he escape. Federico had a lot of respect for his father-in-law.

One day, when the sergeant assured me that the transfer was going to be delayed two weeks, I went to look for Federico.

---

[1] **Federico Fernández.** He was originally from Vueltas. He was a member of the Baptist Church in Catalina de Güines when he was taken to UMAP. Later he was the administrator of the Baptist Camp. He is currently living in New Jersey, United States, where he works as a Baptist pastor.

"The transfer will not be coming for another fifteen days. Do you want to go on leave?"

"I'm already gone. How do we do it?" He asked.

"No problem. Since I'm working in the office I can make a pass, stamped and all; you'll be on your way!"

The permit signed by me was totally worthless should an officer have stopped him. However, with all the chaos that was going on at that time, it was very unlikely to happen. Outside of Camagüey, the permit would be valid under all circumstances because it was stamped and was official. With it he could also reassure his father in-law that he could stay at home. It was the same system that Lieutenant Marrero had used with me, and I was very pleased to be able to offer Federico the opportunity, especially since I was tied up due to my relationship with the sergeant.

"I'll mark you down as present every time that they call the roll," I continued, "but just make sure that you come back at the end of the ten days, because if the transfer comes I won't be able to do anything for you. Only God knows what will happen then, because you could be reported as an escapee."

I spoke with the sergeant before giving Federico a pass and he agreed, but he did not sign the pass so that he would not be compromised.

"That's your business. You sign it, it's just the same." He said. "I'll just warn you that I won't be able to do anything for him if he isn't here when the time for the transfer comes."

The move was risky but Federico was all set. When he arrived at Catalina de Güines, his father-in-law would not at first let him in the house. He did it to protect himself, because he did not want to have any problems.

"But I do have a permit!" Federico protested.

"Why are you on leave, if you just left a few days ago? Where did you get that permit from?"

"Alberto González gave it to me," he answered.

"Alberto González...the seminarian? And who is he to grant passes?" Manolo Martínez, his father-in-law, knew intuitively that there was something strange about the situation, and he was wary. Federico took out the pass and showed it to him. It was the official form, stamped and all, but signed by me with a scribble. Manolo, still suspicious, told Federico, "Don't you go cheating on me!"

Federico enjoyed staying at home during the ten days of leave and returned in a timely fashion. When he returned he went straight to the office. He handed me the pass and then very humorously, with a smile that went from ear to ear, he stood at attention before me, stating, "UMAP soldier Federico Fernández reporting my return from leave on time, my captain!" And he added, "and for the record of Baptist history, Captain Nobody gave me ten extra days of honeymoon." And looking both ways, just in case someone might hear, "Can I go again? I did what you told me, but if I can, I will get out of here as fast as lighting. What do you think?"

We laughed like two children at the stunt that we had pulled off. But both of us knew that he could not do it again. I had checked him present in the daily report. Three days after Federico's return, his transfer order came. One night (why would they always do the transfers at night?) we were taken in a caravan of trucks to Vertientes, south of the province of Camagüey. Unfortunately, Federico and I were placed in different units. I was transferred to a place called Sabanilla, located fifteen kilometers south of the Vertientes Sugar Mill. During the entire trip, I held onto the hope of finding some of the seminarians in the unit where I was going, but it would not be so. From that time on, I was never accompanied by another Christian recruit in any of the units to which I was sent.

Better Alone than in Good Company?

I must confess that one time I wished to be the only Christian in the unit, and I even asked God for that. Since I had good relationships with the chiefs, many times I had to stand up for the brothers when they had some difficulty. At first, I was proud of doing it, but as my spiritual crisis grew, it began to bother me. In my absurd selfishness, I began thinking that if there were no other Christians in the unit I would be more comfortable and everything would be better. How horrible it all seems when I remember it now! The devil was expanding his trap in a subtle way.

God had mercy on me, and later when I found myself all alone, I began to seek Him more. The process was long. God used, among other things, Miriam's letters which often came full of encouraging words. The same was true of her visits. God gave her patience and wisdom in order to bear with me during those difficult times. God used her because I clung to her as my lifesaver.

She and I had a beautiful experience a short time after I was assigned to the region of Vertientes. We had communicated by letter, but due to the time that lapsed waiting for the transfer to Mola, we went a month without seeing each other. One Sunday when there was no scheduled visit while sitting in the barracks talking with a few of the recruits, I began to feel sure that she was nearby. I tried to remove the idea from my mind so as not to get my hopes up, because there was not much chance for that to be true. While trying to think of anything else, the idea kept coming back repeatedly and I really felt that she was nearby. I mentioned it to one of my companions. He replied, "Now you *are* going crazy! How could a woman get in here?"

I could not stay quiet, because I sensed that Miriam would arrive at the unit at any moment. How can I explain it? Undoubtedly love has means of communicating that are beyond the purely physical. As the certainty of her closeness grew stronger by the minute, I left the group and quickly rushed out of the barracks. Another of the recruits followed me; we stopped outside and looked down the dirt road. Far away, we could see two people walking toward the camp. Due to the distance it was difficult to recognize them. A tall, thin, black man was being accompanied by a young, short, and red-haired white woman.

"Your wife is a blonde, so, calm down," said the recruit.

Miriam had told me in her most recent letter that she had dyed her hair red. It was she! As she got closer I could definitely recognize her. My heart could no longer fit inside my chest for the emotion I felt. How was it possible for me to sense her presence nearby? As much as I had tried to block the idea from my mind, it had returned again and again. The resources of human love are infinite.

My wife came accompanied by Luis Figueredo, the pastor of the Baptist Church in Vertientes. When she arrived the day before at his home, planning to visit me, this brother had set aside his duties as a pastor and decided to accompany her, in spite of the fact that it would be on a Sunday. He knew where I was, and that the trip was dangerous for a young woman. To get there, one had to take the train from Vertientes to Santa Cruz del Sur, get off at a bus stop, and walk down a winding road for many kilometers. The chief of the unit authorized me to receive her, even though it was not a visitors' day.

Letters of Love and Hope

When the visit ended, Miriam was miserable because of the spiritual and emotional condition in which she found me. A few days later a letter came and among other things she said this:

Ciego de Ávila, August 25, 1967

My love,

> *Don't worry, I'm not going to either scold you or advise you. I just want to tell you that I love you very much and that I am more and more convinced that God is not going to abandon us. I do have faith and I am*

> *not "in your shoes" as you say. I know that most of it is because you are "inside". That is why I have hopes that everything is going to end, and I do not stop asking God to help us and give us strength to endure this terrible experience.*
>
> *I think that everyone has his doubts, his highs and lows. So, even though I am worried, I am sure that you will find peace. Eventually, we need to seek God, and not until we do will we find peace. We fight against Him, we rebel, and do not accept as good the things that He allows. But in the end we see His purposes fulfilled. In these cases the best thing to do is to be reconciled with Him and we will have peace, although we may be in the middle of difficulties. I know, my love, that this episode that you are living is more terrible than one can imagine, but you shall have the reward sooner or later, honey. Now it seems that it will never come, but everything in life passes!*

A few days later another letter arrived, in answer to the one that I wrote after that visit.

> *Today I received your letter, and I know how you must have continued. I am just like you. But, what's the use of worrying so much about the future and what we will do? Don't we have enough worries now in the present? Remember, "Sufficient for the day is its own trouble." In this respect I am different from you, and I look for the easier solution. It seems to me…please don't get angry!… that you want to drown in a glass of water. Why, honey? Just as all good things come to an end, so also the bad things, although of course, it's after a lot more work, but it's done with, anyway. Don't despair, my love, we have almost won the victory. A little courage and strength and we will get there; how can we not get there?*
>
> *Don't be too worried over your state of mind; it happens. What, you no longer have faith? What,*

doubts? It doesn't matter; God is not going to abandon you for that, nor do I think that it is a sin. On the contrary, this experience will allow you some day to help others, you will see. Whenever there are tough tests, doubts and questions come.

I don't want to criticize you, nor scold you, nor do I want you to change your character, because I like you just as you are. On the other hand, I also want you to tell me all the thoughts that go through your mind, whether sad or happy, pessimistic or not. I want to know everything. And I will not condemn you. Do you know why? <u>Because I believe in you, and because I know that all of this is going to pass.</u>

Another letter arrived later, on September 3rd.

Are you still discouraged? My darling, not even my letters cheer you up? Give me the comfort of knowing that even if they aren't good, at least they are helping you a little to go on.

Have faith that a bright day is coming for us. God is going to help us. He never abandons his children, and he will help us to emerge victoriously some day. Remember what Paul said in Philippians 4:13. "I can do all things through Christ who strengthens me." Was he, by chance, going through an easy time when he wrote that? You know that he wasn't.

Paul wrote it when he was having a very difficult time. I am going to turn the tables on you; I am going to send you one of your sermons, which you wrote and preached when you were doing well. Maybe remembering what you intended to teach others will help you. But remember that whatever comes, I will be by your side and I will be praying a lot for you. I am sure that you are going to move forward, <u>because I believe and I trust in you</u>, and above all, because I believe and trust in God.

Her letters, written with so much love and wisdom, were penetrating my heart. When she visited with me in Sabanilla, sitting by the side of the cane plantation, I spoke to her about my doubts and my rebelliousness in a bitter and very ruthless way. She cried with such a deep sadness and left so depressed that after she was gone I felt guilty. She did not argue with me nor did she criticize me. She only caressed me, listened, and cried. Seeing her leave so shattered, for the first time I realized that my bitterness, besides destroying me spiritually, was also hurting her and our relationship. I understood that my attitude made everything more difficult. What remained, the sensation of happiness and total communion that we experienced when we were together, was being demolished, because I was acting more and more wickedly, being far from God. If we could not even enjoy the time when we were together, then what did we have left?

"Maybe my life is destroyed," I thought as I watched her climb with immense sadness into that truck with some other people that had also come to visit other recruits, ***"but I have no right to make her unhappy."***

I went back to the unit convinced that I couldn't go on behaving like that, although I was unable to find a way to get rid of the anxiety that gnawed at my soul. I was not interested in reading the Bible, much less praying. Was God, by chance, having mercy on me? The idea of going back to the seminary was repulsive. I thought that I had wandered so far away from God that it would be impossible to even begin to come back. I was unaware that God was already taking care of the situation, and in the following days, a chance encounter would help me get out of the crisis.

The Impact of an Unexpected Encounter

Shortly after receiving the last letter cited, I was sent with another recruit to the office of the battalion; I do not remember the reason. At midmorning we happened to run into Pastor Manuel Morales Mustelier. As always, he came over and gave me a happy and lively greeting.

Manuel Morales and I were good friends during the time when we were students in the seminary. A trivial incident led me one day to treat him in a cruel, harsh, and derogatory way. In my locker, I kept a coat that my mother had knit; I had not yet worn it for the first time because I was waiting for cooler temperatures to arrive. I liked that coat a lot. I had shown it proudly to all my friends at the seminary.

One night, the temperatures dropped suddenly, and upon returning from our usual walk following the evening service and before beginning to study, I went straight over to look for the coat to wear it for the first time. To my surprise it was not in my locker. When I spoke of the matter with some of the seminarians, they mentioned having seen Manuel go out wearing my coat. **"How could Manuel take it without even asking me?"** I fumed.

Manuel was going out with Ernesto Ruano, my roommate. As they went out, they realized that it was cooler, so rather than climbing the stairs to his room on the third floor again, Manuel grabbed my new coat and put it on. Since I was not there, I took his action as a personal affront, an inexcusable intrusion into my things.

Shortly after, he came back smiling, not expecting me to be so offended. He took off the coat and told me very gently, "Look "*Yiguiri,*"(an affectionate nickname, I do not know where it came from; we often used it with each other), "I borrowed it because it was very cold, and it was the first jacket that I could find; is it okay?"

"No, it's not okay!" I answered angrily. "My mother knit that coat and I haven't even worn it yet. Who told you that you could take something from my stuff to wear? I have never offered you this trust because I have always thought that you were careless. Now I am outraged that you put on my coat!" I used worse arguments to justify my displeasure, but I am too ashamed to write them here.

When Manuel heard me he drew back. "Don't get so

worked up," he said trying to calm me down and then he gave me an affectionate pat on my arm.

"Don't touch me! Get out of my room; I never invited you in here."

Manuel lowered his head and left without answering me back. A few days after the incident, he finished his studies at the seminary and graduated. He was in the class of students who were three years ahead of us. Because I was too proud, I had never apologized to him, in spite of the fact that I had felt bad later and regretted the whole affair. Ernesto insisted that I had been cruel, and that I had had no right to offend him. Although he should not have taken my coat without asking, the issue was not that bad. But I was unwilling to humble myself after all that I had said.

That day before meeting in the battalion, I had not seen him for about two years. Our relationship after that incident was purely formal. Manuel arrived at the battalion when I was talking near the front door with a group of recruits. My attitude and vocabulary were not exactly becoming of a good Christian. I noticed that after greeting me and then sitting down a short distance from us, he continued to watch me closely.

"It's time for pay back," I thought, *"he will surely write letters to Havana telling them that I am on a spiritual decline and in a few days all the Baptists will know about my crisis. Fine! I will not have to explain anything to anybody."*

I could not have been more wrong. Manuel would teach me an unforgettable lesson, for which I will always thank him. He taught me, in a loving way, who he truly was, and made me face once and for all the condition that I was in.

When I was about to leave the battalion, Manuel approached me and insisted on talking with me in private.

As we walked away, separating ourselves from the group, I thought, *"Here comes a sermon, and he is going to take advantage of this and pay me back for what I told him a couple of years ago."* I got ready to cut off the conversation and to strike back at him with all my bitterness and with my new foul language, so that he would leave me alone. But Manuel did not give me that opportunity. Contrary to all that I expected, he put his arm around my shoulders very slowly and with a great tenderness that I did not deserve, told me, "Look, Alberto, the man that I saw here today is not the gifted, consecrated, and well-mannered young man that I knew in the seminary, and although you may not believe it, whom I always admired.

I looked him in the eyes, ready to answer him back with an expletive and was stunned to discover that he was crying. He hugged me more strongly and continued to tell me, "We're living in an inferno. I know perfectly well that you're going through a crisis. Look, <u>I believe in you,</u> and I am sure that you're going to get past it. You are going to be the man you were before coming here, a young man whom God wants to use for his work in order to bless many. Don't forget that."

I stood completely still. His words were the same as those that Miriam had written to me. His attitude toward me was what I had least expected; his love and wisdom disarmed me. I started to explain but he did not let me continue. "You don't have to explain anything to me. I am simply going to forget the man that I saw today because I know that he is going through a bad time. I won't tell anybody that I saw you, or of your present condition. This is a matter that only you can sort out with God. But please, brother, do it soon for your own good. You're suffering with this attitude and destroying yourself. I promise that I will pray for you."

Manuel hugged me again to say goodbye and then told me: "I know that you're going to get over it, you'll see!" He tried to smile, but tears were running down his cheeks.

Manuel moved me more than he could have imagined. God spoke to me through him. His kindness toward me, in spite of the fact that I had treated him so badly, broke down the wall of hardness and coldness that had imprisoned me for the past few months. I made the trip back to the unit by repeating his words, shaken by the loving and Christ-like way with which he had treated me. I, who had thought in the seminary that I was superior to him, was really a pitiful wretch.

Doctor, Heal Yourself

When I arrived at the unit "by chance?", I received another letter from Miriam. Actually it was not a letter; inside the envelope was the sermon that she had promised. It was one that I had preached on Psalm 39:7. *"And now Lord, for what do I wait? My hope is in you."*

After dinner I went away to read it. I marveled at the things I had said in the sermon and how well they could apply to my life now. My thesis, based on the discourse of the psalmist, was that life is often so frustrating and contradictory that our only hope is for our lives to be in God's hands. Why is He the only hope for man? I asked myself, and then answered myself:

First: because there is no hope if we look inside ourselves, where we can only find sin, complaints, and fragility.

Second: because there is no hope if we look at the world around us, where we can only find injustice and vanity, and,

Third: because there is no hope if we abandon the faith, because then we are completely alone and destroyed.

I ended the sermon by quoting Psalm 73:21-26, which I transcribe below:

"When my heart was embittered,
And I was pierced within,
Then I was senseless and ignorant;
I was like a beast before You.
Nevertheless I am continually with You;
You have taken hold of my right hand.
With Your counsel You will guide me,
And afterward receive me to glory.

Whom have I in heaven but You?
And besides You, I desire nothing on earth.

MY FLESH AND MY HEART MAY FAIL,
BUT GOD IS THE STRENGTH OF MY LIFE
AND MY PORTION FOREVER."

I remembered the sermon, but I had forgotten its structure and teachings. I shuddered as I read it because I could now apply every word to my own life in a literal way.

I would not have imagined when I preached that sermon in San Antonio del Río Blanco, on Sunday, January 10, 1965, that it was going to be directly applicable to my life a couple of years later. How could Miriam have kept that sermon? Evidently, I had given it to her on some occasion. In precisely the right moment, in that wonderful way that God works, she found it and sent it to me with the thoughtful comment, *"Maybe remembering what you intended to teach others can help you."*

And it helped me tremendously! Reading it again made me face reality. And what hope is left for me if I walk away from God? At the same time, Manuel's words hammered me, *"The man that I saw here today is not the gifted, consecrated, and well-mannered young man that I knew in the seminary, and although you don't believe it, whom I always admired. What we're living in is an inferno. I know perfectly well that you're going through a crisis. Look, I believe in you and I am sure that you're going to get over it. You're going to be the man you were before coming here. A young man whom God wants to use…"*

That night, when I lay down, I could not sleep. I tossed and turned constantly looking for a comfortable position that I could not find. I knew there was something that I had to do and it could not be put off any longer. I could not sleep until I did it. I do not know how long I lay there. Suddenly, without thinking, I jumped out of bed and went outside the barracks.

I walked towards the benches that were in a secluded

place behind the dining hall. Above me a starlit sky, as can only be seen in outside of the city where there is no electric power, was glimmering brightly. I did not know where to begin, because I had not prayed for a long time. I did not close my eyes but kept them open to watch the wonder of the sky. Looking at the sky I began to settle my account with God.

"I know that You haven't listened to me for a long time," I said, "but I'm going to tell You everything that I feel...." How could I tell of my experience? I confessed all my rebellion and I expressed all the complaints that I kept in my heart due to my UMAP experience. I also told God that when I was seventeen years old, I had felt the call to become a pastor. I had surrendered my life to Him and I did not want to do anything else. I asked Him to forgive me and to take away all the struggles of my soul that were obstructing and harming me. I told Him about all the bewilderment, all the horror that I felt when I walked away from Him and ceased to be what I had been before this nightmare started. I confessed to Him that I was being cruel to Miriam and I knew that I was hurting her with my bitter expressions of rebellion and with my behavior.

Then the miracle occurred.

I began to cry. But it was a different kind of tears from those on November 27, almost two years ago in Las Marías, when I covered my head in order not to see the sky and cried desperately for all I had lost in just one day. It was completely different from the bitter and helpless tears that I shed while working in the country on Thursday June 16, 1966, when Lieutenant Marrero suspended my leave when I was just about to get married. It was also different from so many other times when Miriam and I had cried, hugging each other, and lamenting the constant separation and loss of our dreams.

This time I did not cry for the things that I had lost, but for those I did not want to lose. It was a cry that cleansed me little by little, by slowly wiping away all my rebellion and bitterness. It was the thawing of my frigid soul that I had been waiting for and had needed. My heart, at last, broke through the prison of coldness and bitterness that had kept me distraught and hopeless. I felt for the first time in a long time that God loved me. He had not abandoned His purposes for my life. He did not turn his back on me even with my complaints and spiritual anguish. I knew that God forgave me and accepted me definitely. I felt His presence like I had never experienced it before. I felt the embrace of the grace of God, a strong, tight, consoling, and invigorating hug.

It was an intimate, sweet, and very special experience. I was not conscious of how long I cried, nor when I knelt down on the grass. When I stopped crying I lay on my back and stayed completely silent, looking at the stars, without wanting to move even a muscle. I was afraid to break the sensation of tranquility and indescribable comfort that I was enjoying. I felt that my soul was healed completely of all the wounds that I had suffered since November 26, 1965.

When I got up from that place, I was the same young man full of dreams and ideals that had gone into UMAP almost two years earlier! The bitterness and doubts that had taken over my heart were gone. Peace had returned to my soul, although I was still in the Military Units to Aid Production, and there would be other lessons and experiences still to learn.

From that moment on, everything began to change. God had prepared some of the most extraordinary experiences of my life for the coming months. I went back to the barracks and went to bed. I lay on my back a long time asking myself how it was possible to feel such an indescribable happiness. Still, I was in UMAP and there was no end in sight. Then I understood that I had won the battle. The Military Units to Aid Production would no longer be a tragedy for me.

After a long, sad, and desperate road, God had given me victory.

10

"I Was Also a Baptist"

My crisis was only spiritual and did not have any ethical implications. Despite the corrupt environment where I was surrounded by many sinful situations, God protected me. After that experience, I understood very clearly what it means in 1 Peter 1:4, 5; *"You, who by God's power are being guarded."* My spiritual condition had made me vulnerable to temptations, which, had I given into them, probably would have changed the entire course of my life. Due to my spiritual crisis, I had no inner strength, but God was faithfully watching over me.

During the time I worked as a counter and as an accountant in Las Marías, I frequently had to go to the farm office in La Gabriela where a young woman employee began acting very friendly toward me. After discussing various work matters with her, there was always something that she wanted to talk with me about. She did everything possible to arrange it so that I would stay with her for a longer time. Then, she started to send me small notes through the chief of the allotment. Her hints were obvious. She pleaded with me to visit her house because her family wanted to meet me. Rarely did I go to the office without her asking me, "When are you going to drop by my house? If you ask the lieutenant for permission on any Sunday, he will let you go."

She knew that due to my work, I could move around the area with relative ease. She was attractive and had a nice personality. What she did not know, or did not want to know, or understood but did not care to know, was that I was truly in love with my wife. She was probably unaware that I was married when she began to be friendly toward me, but when the day came that I told her, she almost screamed, "But you're not wearing a ring! Are you trying to hide it? You have kept it very quiet."

And then she burst out laughing and said, "All you men are alike!"

"No, you're wrong," I said to her, showing my irritation. "I want you to know that I am very much in love with my wife. Neither she nor I wear a ring, because we have not had the money to buy them."

"Hey, don't get so upset, man," she said, while exhibiting her best smile. "I'm not worried about it."

"Well, I do love my wife—very much!" I quickly responded.

Even so, her advances continued every time we met. I had an unavoidable working relationship with her, so I pretended not to notice her interest in me. I am not sharing this experience to pretend I was a saint. She was a real temptation. I believe that God was merciful and took care to prevent me from becoming entangled in a relationship that could have put an end to His plans for my life. What would have happened if I had decided to go to her house some afternoon to meet her family, just to have a little entertainment or to deepen our friendship? Would I not have started to spin a web into which I likely would have fallen and completely changed the course of my life?

What I did immediately was to tell Miriam. There was quite a reaction!

People, Christians included, do not make every life decision ahead of time as if in advance we decide, "I am going to get tangled up in this," or "I am going to change the course of my life with that." The process of our behavioral change is gradual and seemingly harmless. In my case, perhaps I could have thought that by meeting a family in La Gabriela, or by visiting them on a Sunday afternoon, or by dropping by for a while when I was going to the farm office, I could have helped my situation become more tolerable. What harm could come from sitting down to talk with a pretty girl? Since I was honest and told her that I was married and that I was deeply in love with my wife, where was the danger? It may seem prudish not to have taken advantage of that opportunity. It could have resulted in a simple visit and nothing else, but it is difficult to imagine that it would have happened just once. That first visit could have been the beginning of a relationship that, little by little, would have put me in a vulnerable and dangerous position. Because in my situation I was abused, frustrated, and confused, far from home and able to see my wife only sporadically, anyone who might offer me a little understanding and affection would have caught me when I was emotionally vulnerable. Nobody knows how all this could have ended, although I am sure that at some point I would have regretted it and realized my mistake.

The more I think of that situation the more I am convinced that the conditions were ripe for me to become involved in an adulterous relationship. I went to the farm office almost daily. At night, I took the report to the battalion and nobody knew at what time I left or when I returned to the unit. At that time, I didn't have to fall in to be counted in the mornings either, so I would have had plenty of opportunities to spend some time with the young woman. Even the chief of the allotment, who had helped me on many occasions to go on leave on weekends to be with my wife, acted in collusion with her by bringing me papers and then would tell me frequently, and at the same time smiling mischievously, "Why don't you go take a walk to La Gabriela, eh? There are people there who love you. If you came to my house, we would have a good time, but you could have a much better time in another place that you know."

Temptations are Never Lacking

Although the chief of allotment insisted, I never went to see him, in spite of the good friendship that we had. Neither did I visit her. It was always clear in my mind that such an action would be a very dangerous step that I should never take. The Sundays that I did not go on leave, I preferred to stay in the unit writing letters. I never went to the farm office unless specific work issues forced me to. As I tell this story, I ask myself, how was it possible for me not to succumb to such agreeable and tempting circumstances? I was twenty-two years old, and therefore I cannot deny that I had plenty of energy...and desires.

Even though I did not fall into that trap, it was not due to my spiritual strength. At that time, my Christian integrity was in tatters. The whole stage was set for the play. I thank God that he took care of me. What could my life have become, "tangled up" in La Gabriela, or leaving a child behind? Would I have the family stability and happiness that I enjoy today? While speculating about the past may seem silly, there is no question that a few slips could have led me to lasting and regrettable mistakes. The entire course of my life would have changed. A little bit of self-pity in the midst of a difficult situation, allowing me some small consoling pleasures (*ah, and I was suffering a lot, so why not have a good time?*) would have been at the least a very bad move, one that could have easily led the way to checkmate. Today I understand better the wonderful ways in which God protected me.

The same thing happened on other occasions when more coarse and degrading situations were present. One of the camps, where I stayed in the area of Vertientes was next to a village, and during the harvest a prostitute came from Havana. The woman was young, elegant, and very attractive. It was said that she led a normal life in the capital, but during harvesting times, she came to the house of some relatives to make money by working as a prostitute. The house in which she practiced her occupation was across from the unit. Every night, a line of men, UMAP recruits and volunteer cane cutters, would wait in front of the house in lively conversation in order to utilize her services.

The arrival of the woman turned into a party in the unit. Many visited her and told with great detail of their incredible experiences with her. All repeatedly insisted that I go, too. To be honest, I did not lack the desire, but I did not go; God took care of me once again. Even if my faith was in a crisis, my principles, some of which were deeply rooted, were not compromised. Thus, God prevented the crisis in my faith from having moral complications. When I resolved my spiritual problem, I did not have to deal with the consequences of having committed immoral sins.

Although I must confess that I faced many temptations during this tumultuous time, I definitely stayed true to my principles. The Lord did not abandon me despite my rebelliousness, and He kept me from actions that I would have regretted later, or would have led to further degradation, as often happens in the lives of Christians.

Everything Began to Change

Once I settled things with God, everything began to be different. A few days later we were transferred to a place called Los Sitios, much further to the south of Sabanilla and twenty-four kilometers from Vertientes. The harvest had not yet begun, and the unit was working to clean up the cane plantations. The chief of the unit, Lieutenant Rojas, was a soldier of a peasant origin. He must have been about forty years old. He was very serious, spoke softly and always with very few words. He was direct, very disciplined, and yet very personable. I do not know how he found out that I had worked as a counter, but after I had been there a week, he called me to his office.

"Is it true, 27," that was my number now, "that you worked as a counter in the Senado group? If so, you can do the same work here starting tomorrow. Now, let me warn you of something."

"Yes?" I replied, not knowing what he might possibly say.

"I want to be clear with you that you must be exact in your measurements. I don't like the company doing little, but I don't want to cheat the farm either. Do you hear me? Your report must be truthful at all costs. Tell me about any problems immediately. You can go."

"Excuse me lieutenant," I held back, wanting clarification. "I don't understand what you are trying to say. I have experience in this work and measurements are measurements. One measures the work done and it's always exact."

He smiled. He rose from the table, turned around and stood by my side. Taking me by the arm, he led me to the door and spoke to me while looking directly into my eyes. "I know what I said, 27. I want a true and an exact report. Ok? Any problem, come see me immediately."

"Don't worry, lieutenant." I answered but still not understanding.

I soon found out what he was referring to. The first platoon had been working by cleaning up a few cane fields, which, because they had not received enough attention, were completely covered with grass. Then I noticed that the platoon had cleaned up three consecutive fields in one morning's work. When the lieutenant told me that I could go measure the work, I thought it strange.

"Are they done already? Those fields were in very bad condition. Are you sure?" I asked him.

"My platoon takes its business seriously, guard. It is finished already! Undoubtedly we'll win 'The Emulation[1].'"

The three fields certainly appeared to be clean, especially on the sides by the outer edge and the outside

---

[1] "The Emulation" was an expression coined after the Revolution to recognize those who were the most productive workers and hold them up for others to emulate.

furrows. The work was so perfect and the time used was so little that I was suspicious. I went through one of the outer furrows and went deeper into the field. I then discovered that they had only cleaned the sides and only the furrows that were five or six meters from the outer perimeter, only what could be seen standing from the outside. From that point on, the grass was not touched. I went to the next field and walked all along the furrow to the end and I confirmed that five or six meters from the outer perimeter it had all been cleaned up neatly like the first field. Then, I crossed the field and went deeper into the back part of the field. I discovered that each of the three fields had been cleaned in exactly the same way.

Without measuring the fields I went directly to find the lieutenant of the platoon. The first platoon was (what surprises life gives us!) the "outstanding" brigade of the company. I found him watching the work in another field and I told him about the result of my checking.

"But your mission was not to check on the fields, guard. Your mission is to measure them."

"Pardon me, lieutenant," I responded, "my mission is to measure the work that has been done."

Then he got defensive. "Are you implying that I knew that the fields were like that? Be careful guard, don't make that mistake!"

"I'm not implying anything, lieutenant," I quickly responded. "Can you imagine what will happen if the chief of allotment goes into the field to check them before signing the report? It's me they'll come looking for."

"The chief of allotment never checks anything, guard," he said as his annoyance grew.

"And the chief of the unit, Lieutenant Rojas?" I asked.

He turned pale. He took off his cap and ran his hand slowly through his hair lowering it to his neck and ended up clutching his chin. He looked down to the ground a couple of times, then looked up, breathed deeply as if he was offended, and at last he decided to say, "What a completely sh**** thing the platoon has done to me, man. I trusted them! And he took off into the field where his platoon was working.

"We'll work this out tomorrow," he shouted, as he got lost in the furrows of cane. "I'll take the platoon back again so that the fields will be redone."

I remained confused. Was it possible that the lieutenant was cheating on the chief of allotment and on his own chief of the unit in order to make his brigade look good? Was it because of him that Lieutenant Rojas gave me the warning? If not, how was it possible for the chief of the platoon not to check the fields before sending someone to measure them? Did he not constantly supervise what the recruits were doing while they were working? Could the recruits cheat on him so easily and thus win "The Emulation"? It was hard to believe (although he had tried to help me along) that he was unaware of what had happened. It was also difficult for me to accept that he was consciously lying to the farm and to the army.

Was this chief of platoon re-educating the social scum that he had under his command?

With God or With the Devil?

That night, when I was already lying in bed, a good friend from the first platoon approached my bed. "Hey, 27, be careful. The lieutenant says that he is going to tear you to pieces."

"What?" I answered sitting up in bed, "who is he going to tear into pieces?"

"Yes, because he said that you messed up yesterday's work and that you're playing with fire."

"Then he did know what the platoon had done!" I answered.

"Don't be stupid, man. What planet are you from? We do it like that because those are the orders that he gives us." Miguelo explained to me that the lieutenant had taught them how to clean up the outside borders of the fields, called "desorillos," as if they were serving food on them. Afterwards they should make sure to perfectly clean the furrows as far as they could be seen from the road and nothing more. The only furrows that were cleaned completely were those parallel to the road; a few of them had to be cleaned so that from the outside all the fields would appear to be clean.

I could not believe it! Their own platoon leader taught the recruits how to swindle the farm!

"Why do you care, man? It's all the same," Miguelo insisted.

"What I care about is doing my job well." I answered.

"And I'm going to tell you something, brother. Don't get mad, eh? If you tell on him, you'll bring misery on all of us. All in all, working this way is easier than getting tangled up in those devilish fields full of grass. And you can't do any more for seven pesos. Which side are you on? Remember that these people have us here by force."

"I'm not on anybody's side, Miguelo." I answered him uncomfortably. I felt that I was being trapped or blackmailed, and I added, "Hey, are you my friend or not? Did the lieutenant send you to tell me this?"

"Hey, what's up, buddy? Let's be clear. I am my own man! Look, my brother...and he came closer and whispered, "That guy is worthless. How could I defend him? I'm defending your fellow recruits, you and me! They want us to work like animals and we have to defend ourselves somehow! Right? If that guy lets us do that because he wants his platoon to win 'The Emulation,' it's better for us! If he is cheating on the farm, the army, and his revolution of which he speaks so much, that's his problem!"

I was facing a tremendous dilemma. On the one hand, Lieutenant Rojas was trying to do his job with honor. I liked him from the minute I met him. He never abused anyone; he only required that we do our job well. On the other hand were my fellow recruits, who benefitted from this scheme. At least, they thought that they were benefitting, but they were being taught to work in an undignified and fraudulent manner, which in the long run would not be beneficial to anyone. The cane fields would definitely be damaged if left like that. In how many other fields, and for how long, had the brigade been working this way?

I had read and saved a series of articles that the provincial newspaper "Adelante" (Onward) had published about the five UMAP associations. In one of them, journalist Armando Boude had written,

> *The function of UMAP, besides contributing to the production of material goods for the nation, is to give back to our society men who have been trained with a new attitude toward life, with the idea that what matters is being useful to society.*

Is this the way they were training the recruits of the first platoon? If the idea of working fraudulently had come from the recruits, the situation would be more understandable. But the fact that the lieutenant, the chief of the brigade, was training them like this, I could neither understand nor accept. I said nothing to Lieutenant Rojas the following day when the first platoon returned to the same fields and spent two full days "redoing" the fields that they had cleaned in a single morning.

That afternoon when I went to the shower room, Miguelo was already there, showering. There were about ten showers but there were no partitions between them. I took off my clothes and went to the shower that was available, next to him, turned it on and I started to lather my body.

Miguelo immediately stretched out his arm and turned

it off. Half jokingly, he said, "Look, buddy, how about if you look the other way and stop pretending to be the patriot. Because of you, we had to work like crazy today."

"Turn on the tap, please." I told him, pretending to ignore what he told me.

"Yes, I'm going to turn on the tap, but I guarantee you that if you keep tattling on us, out of that same shower will come fire, or gas, like in the concentration camps. This place is pretty similar to those!" Miguelo was a nice guy and witty. Over time, he had proved to be a good friend.

"Ah, stop messing with me, Miguelo. Don't tell me anything else because my mind is in a mess," I told him, while I finished lathering my body. And then I added, "I'm thinking of quitting as a counter and of going to the country with you."

"Don't be a fool, Alberto. That's exactly what the lieutenant wants."

"But, what can I do? If I tell the lieutenant, it's against you. If I accept the job like this, I think that I'm doing something immoral. I'd be better off to go hoeing, and the problem would be over with."

Miguelo burst out laughing and told me, "Immoral! What's so important about morality? It is immoral that we are here. If you quit the job and go to the country, it will be you who leaves the fields full of grass, because we have to obey orders. You're "fried" either way buddy. We are in UMAP, papa! Have you forgotten?"

I finished taking my shower, got dressed and went straight to the office to see Lieutenant Rojas. I had almost decided to ask him to send me to the fields without any explanation. At least I wanted to talk to him, although I did not know if I dared to tell him about the problem. When I was almost at this office, I suddenly stopped and turned around because the chief of the platoon was also there.

I was so confused that I truly did not know what to do.

Social Scum...but Who?

A week later I had another conflict with the first platoon lieutenant. The platoon carried out the first cleaning in a few other newly planted cane fields. In a field like this one it is impossible to falsify the work because the canes are very small and one can see the entire field. I measured the area that they had cleaned up that day and it was only 480 meters. The lieutenant was watching me closely all the time while I measured. When I finished, I sat down by the edge of the field in order to make the report of the work done, which had to be completed in triplicate. I had to have it ready so that the chief of allotment could sign it. This was the field of an elderly farmer, a serious man, hardworking and respectful. He was an innocent-minded person who trusted others because it never occurred to him that he might be cheated. I had already figured out why the platoon chief wanted to do his fields! The farmer, a man of honor and of his word, trusted blindly in what a military man would say to him.

The lieutenant approached me; he sat by my side and told me, "Look, I'm going to teach you how to do things once and for all," he said as he grabbed the book including the forms out of my hands. He continued, "As you know the reports are filled out in triplicate. The first one goes to the farm, the second goes to the chief of allotment, and the third goes to the army."

"Yes," I told him while concealing my irritation, because I had mastered all of this far better than he had. His detailed "explanation" seemed pointless to me.

"Well, on the first copy you write 480 meters, which is what the brigade did. But, *before* you do that, you take out the carbon paper between the second and third forms, so that when you write, 480, it only appears on the first and second forms. Is that clear?"

I still could not figure out what he was up to. "And what do I do with the third form?" I asked him.

He quickly replied, "Well, there's the trick that you have just learned, man. There it is!"

"What trick, lieutenant?" I wanted to know where he was going with this.

"Don't worry, guard, I'm going to teach you all about everything. Take the carbon paper and place it on top of the third form. Figure out where you're going to write the meters that have been cleaned up and then write on top of the carbon paper '960 meters.'"

"What do you mean 960 meters?" I asked him leaping to my feet. "The platoon only cleaned up 480, lieutenant!"

"Of course, man! We both know that. But there is no problem because when you place the three forms together once again for the chief of allotment to sign them, he sees the report that tells about the 480 meters and signs it. He doesn't check the forms below because as they have a carbon paper, he thinks that all of them contain the same information. Do you get it, guard? Then you detach his and give it to him. It also has 480 meters! The one that goes to the farm has 480 meters, right? Well, everything has been solved. You see? The form that goes to the army has 960 meters and that gives a *little help* for us to win 'The Emulation.' Understand, guard, how you have to do it? Do you understand?"

I was outraged. Due to the anxiety that the situation aroused in me, I answered him almost at a shout, "I can't cheat on this farmer like this. He is an honest man, apparently more than…!" I restrained myself. Although I was absolutely right, I did not finish saying *"apparently more than you."* I had already determined that the lieutenant was an unscrupulous man and it would not be very smart to offend him directly. "Don't count on me for that." I just told him. I left the lieutenant in the field with the book in his hands and left for the unit. When I was about twenty meters away, I heard him call out to me.

"It's an order! Come back here immediately! That's an order!"

I kept on walking without ever looking back. I arrived at the unit and told Lieutenant Rojas about the incident as calmly as possible. "I'm very sorry, but I can't write a false report. You tell me what I must do."

Rojas listened to my entire story very seriously and without saying a word. When I finished he just said, "Ok. You can go rest. I'll let you know what we'll do afterwards."

When the company returned from work, both of the lieutenants locked themselves in the office and argued for a long time.

An Exception or the Entire System?

That night, Miguelo who knew it all, came to tell me, "Hey, buddy, I would hate to be in your skin."

"Why?"

"They say that the chief of the first platoon is being transferred. And everybody is asking what you're going to do."

"What? I have nothing to do, Miguelo."

"Look, brother, wake up and open your eyes. You live on the beach but you don't see the sand. You look like a smart guy but you're acting like an idiot. Be careful, because religion is making you a fool." I continued looking at Miguelo, expecting him to finish what he wanted to say. "Come down out of the tree, buddy…the other chiefs are doing it just like him."

"No, that's not true," I told him, but asked, "are you joking, Miguelo? Are you sure?"

"By my mother, I swear it to you, Alberto. Everyone is cheating on Rojas, who is a conscientious guy. Poor guy! So, carry on doing your patriotic crusade and unmask all the enemies of honesty that prowl around this prestigious place. You have plenty of work ahead, buddy. But don't count on me, baby. I don't care about anything. What I do care about is doing the least amount of work possible, and getting the hell out of here as soon as I can. It's your problem if you want to become a savior. Get ready to be crucified!"

It was difficult for me to absorb the shock because I could not believe what Miguelo was telling me. How was it possible for all the other officers to be altering the data deliberately? If that was so, what was true about the work reports of the units that were published in the provincial newspaper and in the bulletin *Sin Tregua (Without Any Truce)*? How many companies were operating under the same system? I know for a fact that in Las Marías it didn't happen that way, at least during the time when I was working as a counter or an accountant. Could that have been the reason why there never was an outstanding platoon there, and no matter how hard we worked, the unit was always behind in the "The Emulation" compared to the other battalions?

I remembered the insult from the captain, the chief of the battalion, when he found out that I was doing the job of a counter and not one of the chief officers of the brigades, like in the other companies. He so insisted and fought that he succeeded in convincing Lieutenant Marrero to remove me from that job. Could it be that the system had already been used there and I was the one who didn't fit in? I cannot be certain of that, but from that time on, I questioned the achievement results that I had read in the newspapers. The reporter may work or inform out of good faith, but it can also be that some place in the chain, before the data got to him, some carbon paper was removed as it was done in Los Sitios and then replaced, thus altering a number.

The next day, I sat down with Lieutenant Rojas in his office, and without telling him what I knew, I begged him to free me from my job as a counter. He could not understand and I dared not tell him the details because, after all, I did not have any proof and my position as a UMAP recruit was very vulnerable. But Rojas was an honest man who believed in what he did. He insisted that I should go on working as I had done so far, but finally, he let me choose. And I chose to go to the fields the next day.

"You've failed me, 27," he told me as I left the office.

"No, lieutenant. I haven't failed you. I refused to hand in falsified data just as you ordered me to, but there are some things that are beyond... and I prefer not to have to deal with them."

Once Again in Administrative Work

A couple of days later Rojas offered me the supply position for the company. The recruit that had been working in the position was being released due to an illness. The day for a visit from "Control and Help"[2] from the UMAP association headquarters in Vertientes was drawing close. The lieutenant wanted me to organize the storeroom and to have everything ready in one week for the inspection. I took pleasure in this, and I did the best that I could. I knew the job of handling supplies because I had also done it for some time in Las Marías. It mainly consisted of managing the control of the storeroom for food and clothes for the unit, besides making up the menu for daily meals according to what was in stock while, at the same time, following the rules. I had to keep the storeroom tidy, deliver the food to the cooks daily so that they could prepare it, and stock the goods every time that the battalion truck brought something. The unit in Los Sitios had a good storeroom. It was large, spacious, and it was well stocked. I ordered everything, updated and made new cards for the incoming and outgoing stock, and painted the entire storeroom. I worked every day until very late at night. At the appointed time the storeroom was ready for the inspection. The night before the "Control and Help" visit, Lieutenant Rojas could not believe his eyes! He congratulated me and left very enthused.

"With the work that you have done," he told me, "we will certainly win 'The Emulation'."

---

[2] A group that performed inspections.

And so we did. The following morning, at the appointed time, the officers of the association arrived. I knew from the first instant that my work had impressed them. Lieutenant Rojas was proud. "There is no storeroom like this one in any of the units," said the visitors.

I knew that it was true. For the first time since I was in UMAP I had done a job that I truly loved and that had employed all my capabilities. My motto was the Bible verse: "*Whatever you do, work heartily, as for the Lord and not for men,*"[3] and the results from that attitude were evident.

Captain José Durán Bravet,[4] (called Captain Zapata) chief of the UMAP association in Vertientes, extended his hand to shake mine, and told me, "I congratulate you, soldier. How long have you been working in supplies here in the unit?"

"A week, captain." I responded.

"You have certainly done a great job. Join us in the dining hall because I want to talk to you."

There he asked me what my level of education was and he wanted to know if I had worked as a supplier before. He wrote down my first and last name on a piece of paper and put it away in the pocket of his uniform.

When they left, Lieutenant Rojas called me into his office. "I'm not sure, 27, but I think that we're going to lose you."

"What?" I asked. I wasn't sure of the meaning of his expression, "we're going to lose you."

"If I'm not mistaken, they're going to take you to Vertientes to work as an assistant to the Chief of Services of the association. I won't know anything definite until

---

[3] Colossians 3:22.

[4] **Captain José Durán Bravet** (Captain Zapata) Officer of the FAR. He fought in the Rebel Army in the Second Eastern Front "Frank País". He was chief of the UMAP association in Vertientes. He is presently retired, and lives in San Miguel del Padrón, in Havana City.

tomorrow."

It was going to be my third transfer in the two months since coming to Vertientes: another new place, new mates, new chiefs. I was beginning to miss the stability of Las Marías!

A Turning Point in Vertientes

I did not know whether to be glad or not, because I had felt happy during the week's work in the storeroom. I had prepared a corner where I could sit down to work without being disturbed, to write or to read whenever I had time. I had done my work in absolute tranquility. Besides, I knew that with Lieutenant Rojas, I would never have any problems. The only benefit that I saw from the outset was that the association headquarters was in the sugar mill of central Vertientes, only twenty-six kilometers from Camagüey. From there it would be easier for Miriam and me to see each other more frequently. What could be better than that? God was blessing me and I was happy. My attitude had totally changed and God was improving my situation. The next day, very early, a jeep from the association came to pick me up.

The UMAP association headquarters in Vertientes was in the central part of town adjacent to the sugar mill of the same name, today called "Panamá". It was a single story, brick building with a concrete roof, a porch, a lobby area, and then a long central hallway with different rooms on each side. To the left of the office were a couple of wooden huts, supported on very old posts. One of these was the storeroom. On the other side of the complex were the bedrooms, the dining room, and the kitchen. The office was located beside a railroad, and beyond and parallel to it was a wide and beautiful central avenue. A majestic line of palm trees bordered an asphalt walkway that passed right in front of the office, between it and the railroad tracks. It seemed like paradise to me when I saw it all for the first time.

I encountered a UMAP soldier from my hometown of Cárdenas, working there. I had known him since I was a child, because he lived a couple of blocks from my parents' house. When he saw me arrive with my belongings, he said: "Look who is going to be the new assistant to the Chief of Services!" He showed me around the entire facility, took me to the dormitory, and explained to me how things were there. "Here we only work eight hours a day from Monday through Friday. When you finish working, you can do as you please in town, because we are not prohibited from leaving here. On weekends we have leaves and can go to Camagüey or anywhere we want, as long as we are back here on Monday morning."

I could not believe what I was hearing. Being a simple office employee, free to do what I wanted to when my working hours ended, and with the possibility of going to Camagüey, which for me meant Ciego de Ávila where Miriam lived, was more than I could imagine. I was at the height of joy when my compatriot warned me, "Now, don't tell the captain when he interviews you that you're religious. If you tell him that, you won't be here long."

"Well, look, friend," I told him starting to lose all my enthusiasm, "then it is better for me not to unpack."

"Don't be a fool, man. Don't you realize the advantages that you're going to lose? I'm not telling you to quit your religion. What I'm telling you is that you can't tell the captain."

I began to discuss with him whether faith is a private matter that is only one's personal business, or if it is something that we are obliged to share with others. He was of the opinion, as were many in Cuba for many years, that a person could be a believer without having to outwardly confess his faith. There were unfortunate consequences associated with such a confession, due to the Marxist-Leninist ideology prevailing in the country. I insisted that I could not hide my faith. I was not going to do so in order to work there, even with the benefits that place could offer me.

Great Excitement in a Blackout

It was true that I had to go to a preliminary interview with the captain, where he would examine my records and ultimately decide if I could work in the association. I waited for the pending interview all day long, but the captain was visiting various units and did not arrive until evening. He summoned for me at eight in the evening. I spent the entire day uncertain whether or not I would be able to remain there. The delay allowed me to confirm the freedom that I would have in that place, to see the office where, *if I were not religious*, I could work. I walked around town, and then fed on a feeling of heroism because I had decided to spurn all of that and go back to Los Sitios. Now that I was enjoying a renewed spiritual relationship with God, I was not willing to hide it away or deny it ever again.

At eight in the evening, nervous but determined, I knocked on the door of the captain's office, which was the last room on the left in the long hallway of the building. Zapata was sitting behind a large desk. I saluted him militarily, but then he stood up, leaned forward and offered me his hand. After shaking it, he pointed to a chair next to his desk.

"Please sit down, soldier," he told me. At that exact moment a blackout occurred. It went completely dark in the office. He waited a bit, thinking that it was a momentary interruption, but seeing that the lights did not come back on, he started to interview me. "Well, it looks like we have to talk like this. Let's get to the point!"

"What is it, captain?" I told him.

"The point is, soldier, as you have probably seen, this place is different from the units and here you will have much more freedom."

"I realize that, captain." I said, even while thinking that I would not be experiencing any of that freedom, and that in just a few minutes I would be out of there like a bullet shot out of a gun.

"We're very careful with the UMAP personnel who come to work here. I am impressed with your work in Los Sitios and I believe that you will be very helpful in the association. But we have a problem."

"What problem, captain?" I asked, prepared to sacrifice myself completely and finish, once and for all, that strange interview in the dark. I was sure that he was referring to my status of being religious and I wanted the moment to arrive when I would tell him that I was a Christian and that I would gladly go back to the unit, for nothing in the world could make me renounce or hide my faith. I had rehearsed my speech a million times during the afternoon, sitting in the square of the boulevard of the town under the palm trees across from the association.

The captain went on, "The problem is that your records were requested from Havana, but they aren't yet here in the office of the chief of staff. We don't know the reason."

"Look, captain, my father, who lives in Cárdenas, is a member of the Communist Party. He requested an investigation as to why I was sent to UMAP and is trying to make arrangements so that I can be transferred to a regular unit of the SMO. Surely that is the reason why my records are not here."

I should explain that I had written to my father telling him not to do anything, but that I would rather stay in UMAP. I was thankful for his interest and concern (at last!) to get me out of there, but there were two things that I did not like. One of them was that he read aloud to his companions of his cell of the party the letters that I sent. They were very intimate and private letters. Why did he have to read them to his party leaders? I was annoyed at the comments and the conclusions that some of them came to, and that he told me in good faith.

According to my father, some of his friends from State Security, with whom he had discussed my situation in an effort to help me, had asked if I planned to emigrate after I left the service. A letter that I received from my sister, Olga, who worked at the University of Havana, had arrived with the same question. According to her, the chief of my sister, Enna, who worked in the 1089 Unit, asked my father if I was going to "pack up and fly away" when I left the service. Although my family was obviously concerned about my stay in UMAP and was taking steps for me to be transferred to a regular unit of the SMO, I was no longer interested in such a transfer. UMAP was no longer a tragedy for me.

The interview with Captain Zapata continued on in the dark, but I knew that at any minute it could end, and with it, my hopes of working there. So, I was nervous and expectant.

Sincerity Can Bring Surprises

"OK, I see why your records are not here. But we need to know what you did on the street. You well know that all sorts of people have come to UMAP. This is the headquarters and not just anybody can work here. I must warn you that I need you to tell me the truth. Even though your records are not here today, they could arrive at any time now. I need to know what you did on the street before you were recruited, in order to know if I can let you work here.

I breathed deeply, sat more comfortably in the seat and in the dark, because the blackout was still on, and said, "Captain, I don't need to hide what I did before I was recruited. I was a student in the Baptist Seminary in Havana and worked as a pastor in a Baptist church in San Antonio de Río Blanco."

I said it all at once without taking a breath, like somebody who is being sacrificed on the altar. Due to my nervousness and the dark that prevented us from seeing each other's face, I think that I spoke with a loudness and speed that was out of place. So I kept waiting for the captain's answer. For seemingly an endless amount of time, there was just silence. The captain did not respond. I expected that soon he would hit the table with his fist and say something like: *"And* did you think that you could work here?" or, "Pick up your belongings and go back to your unit."

But the captain remained silent in the middle of that completely dark room. Every second that passed made it more unbearable.

"Captain?"

His slowness to respond bothered me. His silence seemed to last for an eternity. Very slowly, with a much warmer voice and with a tone obviously nostalgic, he said, "I was also... a Baptist!"

There in Vertientes, in the middle of a blackout, with the captain and me alone in his office, I felt that my heart was about to explode. Did I hear that right? Could it have been possible for him to have ever professed to be a Christian? The tone of his voice was sincere and he gave me the impression that he wanted to go on talking about the topic. When I got over the surprise, I lowered my voice and was careful to speak slowly in a very respectful tone, but amicable, I told him, "The difference, Captain, with all due respect, is that you were a Baptist... but I am one!"

Zapata seemed not to be listening to me. Probably he was sifting through his memories. When he spoke again, he didn't respond to me, but said to himself, "That was a very good time in my life, and I haven't forgotten the principles of honesty that I learned in the Baptist Church." Then, suddenly, the captain slammed his fist on the desk, just as I had been expecting, but in order to say, "You are just the man that I need here!"

In all the years that I have lived, as I write these lines, I think that was the closest I ever came to having a heart attack.

My New Responsibilities

After I had changed my attitude of self-pity and rebelliousness, everything began to change. Now, just when I had thought that the fact of my being a Christian was going to close the doors to an opportunity of improvement and comfort, it instead opened them. When Captain Zapata said, *"You are just the man that I need here,"* he shattered my plans for martyrdom. I expected to find myself going back to Los Sitios satisfied and in control because I was willing to pay the price for being a Christian again. The reality was that I was not being persecuted! The interview with Zapata, from that moment on, continued in a more friendly tone. The captain began to address me in a familiar way.

"OK, you will be the assistant to the Chief of Services and be in charge of the storeroom. I hope you organize it like you did in Los Sitios!"

"I'll try, captain." I answered.

"You have to work on the controls because many things have been lost from that storeroom."

The captain told me that he had been a member of the "William Carey" Baptist Church, in El Vedado. He asked me about Pastor Juan F. Naranjo,[5] and was also interested in other pastors that he knew. He told me that he also had a very good relationship with Pastor Domingo Fernández, who had also been his pastor and was now living in the United States. We spoke for a long time about the situation of the pastors who were in jail from 1965, and he became interested in all the details of those events. Zapata had fond memories of his time in the church. He stated that he knew very well what was taught in the church and insisted that since I was a Baptist and a student of the seminary, he knew that he could trust me. We chatted in his office until the lights came back on. He instructed me about my responsibilities and emphasized that if any difficulty arose that I should not hesitate in asking for his help.

When I was at the door to say goodbye to him,

---

[5] **Juan Francisco Naranjo**. Baptist Pastor. He was a pastor in Aguacate, Colón and William Carey in Havana City. He held various leadership offices in the Western Baptist Convention. He passed away in January, 2000.

thinking that the interview was over, he said to me, "Wait, there is something else that we need to talk about, you and I." I went back inside his office and sat down. "I'm going to ask you a favor. Tell me if you are willing to grant it to me."

It surprised me that the captain would ask me for a favor. It was going beyond the normal protocol of a superior-subordinate relationship. The relationship with the chief of the association in Vertientes was taking an unexpected turn.

"You'll be a free man after six each evening and able to go anywhere you want to. Now, you must sleep in the association and above all, be very punctual and in the office at eight every morning."

"Don't worry, captain. What's the favor you were talking about?"

"You don't have to hide that you're a Christian here in the association, but you need to be prudent. It is possible that some officer could harass you for your firm stance on religion. Surely, you'll visit the pastor here in Vertientes and will spend time with his family. However, I would like to ask you not to attend the church here in Vertientes. The weekends when you go to Camagüey you can attend there and there is no problem if you even want to preach there. But if you go to the church here in Vertientes, you'll complicate things for me and it will be difficult to keep you working here. And your presence here is very important to me. Do you understand?"

For a moment I hesitated to accept his petition. My initial impulse was to head back to Los Sitios. It seemed to me that the arrangement would mean making too great of a concession. But the captain talked to me as a friend. He had shared with me his experiences that probably had been well kept in his heart. Knowing the dynamics of the Christian life, he had taken for granted that I probably had a relationship with the pastor in Vertientes and his family. He told me that I did not have to hide my faith but that I should behave prudently. He only asked me to refrain from visiting the church in Vertientes, which meant not going to services that were held during the weekdays, because on Sundays I would be either in Camagüey or in Ciego de Ávila. Although I wanted to go to the church in Vertientes, I probably would not be able to do that every week anyway, because I would be checking in the monthly distribution of food, and we had to work even at night. That took at least two weeks each month.

The captain had asked me this as a favor to avoid a difficult situation for him. I decided that if I did not agree I would be taking a fanatical attitude, which would be disrespectful and unnecessary in light of all the concessions that he was making for me.

"All right, captain." I responded.

"Explain it to the pastor. I'm sure that he will understand."

Did I do the right thing by granting his request? Maybe some think not. I confess that I had my doubts too. I prayed a lot and thought about it that night. I came to the conclusion then, and I still believe, that I did the right thing. Everyone in the association knew that I was a Christian. I had my Bible there and I did not try to hide the fact that I read it. What church could I have attended on weekdays if I was in one of the units in the country? Since I had returned from my leave in June and had been transferred to Vertientes, I had not been able to attend any services at all. Now I would have the ability to go to Sunday school and the service held by First Baptist Church in Camagüey, as well as participating in the meetings with the youth on Saturday. The only opportunity to attend church in Vertientes was, at the most, two services in a whole month, and maybe only one, depending on my work. In the end, I had to obey orders, and if I had work to do or if I were on duty, I would not be able to go anywhere.

Zapata had not prohibited me from interacting with the pastor and his family. Had he done that, perhaps I my decision would have been different. In that case I would have had to avoid contact with these fellow Christians, which would have made it awkward for them to relate to Miriam when she came to Vertientes and stayed in their home, while they were unable to even communicate with me. But it was not so. I could visit and stay in contact with them. Besides, the captain had not given an order, but had asked as a favor.

I believe that granting his request was a good decision.

11

God Doesn't Come In My Office

Zapata treated me like a son while I was working in the association headquarters office. Just as he expected, an officer, specifically the chief of personnel, was a thorn in my side from the moment he found out that I was a Christian. He made my life miserable and constantly tried to antagonize me.

"Don't pay any attention to him," Zapata advised me. "He wants to create a problem with you so then he can make me send you back to your unit. As long as you work well and respect him, he can't do anything to you. Everything he says to you is just an attempt that you might answer back to him in a rude manner so that he can say that you have been disrespectful. Ignore him! As time goes by, he'll get used to your presence here and he'll let you be."

The man was persistent and was determined to get me out of the association. Rarely a day would go by when he would not look for an opportunity to say something derogatory about Christians or blaspheme God in my presence. The same thing happened when we met in the dining room. He enjoyed the twisted and evil pleasure of provoking me every time that I was nearby. Making matters worse was the fact that very few people worked in the association and the chances of avoiding him were minimal. Unfortunately, in order to do my job well, I had to be in close contact with the personnel office. We had to update the transfers, and the ever-changing number of recruits in the units, because the food was supplied according to the regulations and the number of recruits in each unit.

Other from that, working in Vertientes was a blessing. It was undoubtedly the best time that I spent in UMAP despite the fact that we worked hard in the association. INRA[1] informed us about the available food and we, according to the established regulations and the number of recruits, had to invoice the quantities that corresponded to each company. It was a tedious and slow job, because INRA worked with pounds as a unit of measurement while the army worked with kilograms. At that time there were no calculators to do the conversions automatically. We had to calculate invoice-by-invoice and unit-by-unit. After having prepared the monthly bills, it was also our responsibility to pick up the food and produce in Camagüey with army trucks to deliver them to the units. Some of the food had to be purchased weekly, like meat, eggs, and chickens when they were available. In addition, I had to look after the storeroom and the control of incoming and outgoing merchandise. At times, I had to work late processing the bills for the monthly distribution of food, but most days I was a free man at six in the evening. There was a movie theater in town, or I could go to the square to talk with the other recruits who worked there, or simply take a walk. There are small pleasures in life that can provide a lot of satisfaction that we don't value often enough.

How many times while confined in a unit had I longed to walk freely without the awful feeling of being restricted within the perimeter of a fence! There was a sidewalk in front of the office that was lined with royal palm trees, and continued all the way to the sugar mill. It was a lovely place to take a stroll, just to enjoy the breeze and the calm of the evening. I was so happy to see the trains go by, or just to sit quietly in the park below the trees, watching the people move

---

[1] National Institute for the Agrarian Reform.

around from here to there to get to their busy jobs or interests.

Privilege in the Midst of a Trial

How different and full of color is life and the great variety it offers when you can see it without being locked behind a fence and forced to work under an oppressive routine! The pastor of the church in Vertientes, Luis Figueredo, and his wife Leonor, were a channel of blessing during that time. And so was Zapata. He was always attentive to my needs and he set aside time to talk with me, asking me about the Baptist work with much interest.

Miriam and I could see each other every weekend. Sometimes she arrived on Friday afternoons, and we went to the movies or we talked while we walked around town. She slept in the pastor's house and on Saturday we went to Camagüey. There we would take part in the activities of the First Baptist Church. We often stayed at a hotel.

Other times, Noel Fernández[2] and Ormara Nolla[3] let us stay in their apartment, sharing the little that they had with us with much love and happiness. Noel was raised in Camagüey, and Ormara, Miriam's lifelong friend at church, was from Ciego de Ávila. Noel was also recruited to UMAP but he was released early due to an illness. We went to church with them. We enjoyed times of fellowship that strengthened a friendship that has managed to survive the passing of many years during the ups and the downs of life. Generally, I got up

---

[2] **Noel Fernández Collot.** A member of First Baptist Church in Camagüey when he was taken to UMAP. Afterward he was a member of the Baptist Churches in Ciego de Ávila and Güaimaro. He was Secretary General of COEBAC (Spanish acronym for Baptist Student-Worker Coordination of Cuba). Ordained a pastor in 1995, he was the pastor of the Emanuel Baptist Church in Ciego de Ávila, affiliated to the Fraternity of Baptist Churches of Cuba. He is now retired and lives in Ciego de Ávila. He is the Regional Coordinator for Latin America of the Ecumenical Disability Advocates Network of the World Council of Churches.

[3] **Ormara Nolla Cao.** Noel Fernandez Collot's wife. She was a member of First Baptist Church in Ciego de Ávila, First Baptist in Camagüey and Guáimaro. She lives with her husband in Ciego de Ávila. She is a coordinator in the Council of Churches in Cuba in the province of Ciego de Ávila and a coordinator of the World Prayer Day in Central America and the Caribbean, of the World Council of Churches.

at midnight and made the trip back to Vertientes very early, to assure that I would arrive on time to start work in the office.

One Friday night, after talking with Miriam until late in the pastor's house, I went back to sleep in the barracks. After I fell asleep, Zapata woke me up. "What are you doing, sleeping here?"

I awoke frightened and did not understand why he was asking me. "What happened, Captain?" I asked.

"Why are you sleeping here? I saw that your wife arrived late this afternoon. Why didn't you stay in the pastor's house with her?" He asked.

I sat up in bed and said, "But, Captain, the leave is tomorrow. You warned me that I could leave at night but that I had to sleep in the association."

"And do I need to know that you're not sleeping here? I don't have to know it, man! I am not used to walking around the dormitory or checking the beds." He winked an eye and left.

That night I went out again and then returned to the barracks at six-thirty in the morning. The roll call in Vertientes was at seven. The captain, who already knew Miriam well, saw her when she got off the bus that afternoon. I do not know if he went to the barracks for another reason or just to see if I was there. It was a nice gesture that demonstrated to me that he was a good man and that he was looking out for me. Zapata did all that he could so that I would have the best time possible while I was at the association.

It is important to note that only a very few of the other recruits enjoyed the kind of freedom that I had in Vertientes. The vast majority of them were forced to remain in the units in the country. I belonged to a tiny minority who were able to work in the association. These small pleasures that made my life more comfortable were not available to the typical recruit. Thousands and thousands of young men had spent more than two years having been subjected to a get up-work-eat-sleep regimen. The only thing they could look forward to was to have a leave once every six months at the end of harvest, and family visits once a month. This was the reality of life in the Military Units to Aid Production. It is true then they were beginning to grant leaves for a few hours on Sundays. But not many of them could enjoy this due to the location of the units, since the majority of them were working so far out in the country that it was impossible for them to leave, get to a worthwhile place for a few hours, and return on the same day.

The other seminarians who were still in UMAP, and had been my mates in Las Marías, José Ferrer, Israel García and Israel Cordovés, still remained in their units working under the same regimen without the privileges I enjoyed. They, like the vast majority of the recruits, spent their entire time in UMAP working under the worst of conditions.

However, little by little, improvements were being made for some of the recruits.

God Helped Others Also

There were other Christians who also saw their situations improve. About that time, some personnel were selected to be transferred to regular military units in Havana to work on the construction of military facilities. The criteria for their selection were discipline, work ethic and good behavior. Among the forty-five recruits that were chosen from our association in Vertientes, were three brothers from the Batabanó Baptist Church: Rodolfo Luis Delgado,[4] Roberto Luis Delgado,[5] and Moisés Hechevarría Luis.[6] Eduardo M.

---

[4] **Rodolfo Luis Delgado.** A Member of the Baptist Church in Batabanó when he was taken to UMAP. He later matriculated in the Baptist Seminary and was a pastor of the churches in Artemisa and Guanabacoa. He is currently living in New Jersey, in the United States.

[5] **Roberto Luis Delgado.** A member of the Baptist Church in Batabanó when he was taken to UMAP. He is currently a deacon of the same church.

[6] **Moisés Hechevarría Luis.** A member of the Baptist church in Batabanó when he was taken to UMAP. He is currently a deacon of the same church.

Díaz,[7] who was a member of the Baptist Church in San Antonio de los Baños, had been working in the association in Vertientes.

The forty-five young men were subjected to a rigorous interview. Senior UMAP officials reviewed their records with them and determined who was suitable to leave UMAP and transfer to regular military units to work on construction projects in Havana.

When Eduardo Diaz was being interviewed, an official told him, "It's a shame that a young man like you with such a great record, not only as a civilian, but also here in UMAP, still believes that God exists."

Eduardo had come to UMAP at nineteen years of age. He had been employed at the time, and therefore was not within the limits of the official UMAP recruit profile. He had simply been a Baptist. At the end of the interview, in spite of his Christian beliefs, the official told him, "We understand that there is no one more deserving than you to be transferred to his own province."

From the group of forty-five young men who were interviewed, only sixteen were selected. Among them were the young Christians mentioned above. They were transferred to a camp close to the Ignacio Agramonte Airport in the city of Camagüey where they joined other chosen personnel from different associations. Felipe Cabrera Rentería[8] of the "Bethel" Baptist Church in San Antonio de los Baños was also among them. The final group was made up of 102 recruits, selected as the best in UMAP. In that small elite group were five Baptists.

---

[7] **Eduardo M. Díaz.** A member of the Baptist church in San Antonio de los Baños when he was taken to UMAP. Later, he was a member in the Second Baptist Church in Bautista de Güira de Melena. He was away from the church for several years, but he returned and was a member of Second Baptist Church in San Antonio de los Baños. He is currently living in Fort Worth, TX.

[8] **Felipe Cabrera Rentería.** A member of the "Bethel" Baptist Church in San Antonio de los Baños when he was taken to UMAP. He is currently a member of the same church.

When the day came for their transfer to Havana after they had stayed in the aforementioned camp for about a month, there was a farewell event in which Captain Felipe Guerra Matos spoke. He told them, "This is an opportunity that you've been given because of your good behavior and hard-working attitude. But know once and for all, that, if anyone engages in misconduct, he will return to UMAP again." None of them did. The word UMAP continued to be a threat; it never became pleasant or prestigious. Nevertheless, it was good to see young Christians, who had not abandoned their faith, distinguished for their conduct. There is no better preaching than that of good behavior. The Christians in UMAP gained recognition and had a good reputation due to their hard work, much like the prophet Daniel, who was one of the few true believers serving in the highest offices of a heathen empire, was found to be faithful, reliable, and respectable.

The Woman and the Transferred Son

My job at the association in Vertientes ended abruptly because the chief of personnel finally succeeded in getting me to demonstrate my contempt for him. One night when it was my turn to work as an assistant duty officer, I saw a woman arrive about ten. She was elderly, well dressed, and was carrying a heavy bag that bent her body over when she was walking. I went out to the porch to see what she wanted. She explained to me that some recruits, friends of her son, were told that her son had some type of problem and had been transferred. Upon hearing the news, she was very worried because she did not know what problem her son was experiencing. So she had traveled all the way from Havana to Vertientes, beginning at sundown the day before. She arrived after twenty-six hours of travel, extremely fatigued and worried.

I told the chief of personnel, who miraculously met with her at that hour, although he did it in a crass and callous way. The son and his mother were Seventh Day Adventists. The recruits who had told her of the problem were also

Adventists. From my post on guard duty, I heard the chief of personnel get into an argument with the woman. She wanted to know if the problem with her son had to do with religion. The official refused to give her any information. When the interview was over, standing at the door, the woman begged with tears, "Please, surely you too have children. I only want to know where he is and what happened."

"When your son writes you, he'll tell you. I can't say anything else."

"But I have come all the way from Havana to find out."

"Well then go back the way you came, lady. Nobody told you to come and look for him. Go back and expect a letter from your son; he's a grown man, now."

"Please, don't you realize the effort and the trip that I have made to get here? How hard could it be for you to tell me where he is and what the problem is?"

He was furious because the woman would not tell him the names of the recruits who had informed her of the son's problem. He said that they had revealed a military secret and had violated military discipline. The woman defended them, saying, "How is it a military secret, lieutenant? If they had weapons, or if this were a combat unit, I'd understand that. My son is only a farm worker. Why is it so important where he is working? I just want to know where he is now."

"If you don't tell me who notified you, you'll leave without knowing anything!" He roared.

"Well, I'm not a military woman," answered the woman, "and I don't have to tell you."

"OK. Then beat it back to Havana without finding out anything."

"God will let me know about my son, lieutenant, I can assure you."

"I don't know how!" He answered. "God doesn't come in my office, citizen!"

"What did you say?" The woman inquired, confused at what she had heard. She did not understand what he had said because the officer had spoken quickly.

Then he straightened up even more, and raised his voice, much more emphatically, "That God can't come into my office, citizen! I don't know how you're going to find out where your son is."

The woman was angry and hurt. Already on the porch, as she was leaving, crying, enraged and helpless, she turned and told the chief of personnel, "Anyway, I know that God takes care of my son, and I also know that you can't harm him."

"Well, if he doesn't behave, you'll see whether we can harm him or not." He responded and burst out laughing, very loudly, for the woman to hear it. She walked away from the office without looking back.

The lieutenant kept on watching her and laughing as she crossed the rail line that was adjacent to the building. When he saw that the woman had definitely left the association, he came into the room. When he realized that I was sitting at the table of the assistant to the guard, he stopped quickly. It seemed that he had forgotten about me and then he realized that I had heard the entire conversation.

He went to the door that divided the living room and the place where I was, leaned on it, and very slowly began to talk, taking care to pronounce each word to me so that I would understand clearly what he was saying, "All religious people are SOBs[9]!" He remained at the door, leaning on the wall, watching me closely, to see what I would do. I raised my head and saw that he laughed cynically.

I confess that I did not think about it; it was an instant explosive reaction. I stood up, looking at him directly in the

---

[9] The word was actually far more vulgar than this.

face. I got out from behind the table and moved over to where he was. Then I said with all the strength of my soul, "Don't you know lieutenant...that I know many SOBs...?" and I mimicked him by talking as slowly and emphatically as he had himself had done, looking into his eyes, "I know, lieutenant, many SOBs who *are not religious people at all!*"

The chief of personnel got the message loud and clear. With an obvious look of triumph, as one who had just won a long-awaited victory, he told me, "With those stupid words, you have signed your death sentence, soldier. Enjoy your guard duty tonight because I assure you that it's the last one you'll do here." And he locked himself in his office after slamming the door behind him, which must have been heard all over town.

After he left, I walked to the living room and sat there. I knew that I had messed up, but I had to confess that I was not sorry for having stood up to him. I enjoyed every word that I had said. The lieutenant had worn me down with his constant attacks. One of his helpers, another UMAP recruit working in the office was in the living room. He knew the lieutenant very well.

"You just won the lottery, Alberto. *El viejo*[10] will not forgive you for that."

"Fine! But you don't have to endure his attacks; he has no right," I answered.

The poor woman had left the association thinking that she had made the entire trip in vain, which turned out to be untrue. When the deputy chief of personnel saw that the lieutenant had gone, he told me, "Look, if *el viejo* comes back and asks for me, tell him that I went to get cigarettes at the barracks. I'm going out the back door to tell the woman that her son does not have a serious problem. I had just discussed it with the politician of his unit and he was transferred to another company. I know where he is and I'm going to tell her."

---

[10] In the association they called the chief of personnel "the old man," because he was the oldest among the officers.

He left the association to find the woman. He found her crying in the bus station. He explained to her the problem of her son in detail and took the heavy bag with food that she was carrying for her son, promising that he would deliver it to the recruit.

And the chief of personnel believed that God does not come into his office!

On the Verge of Another Heart Attack

The following morning, when Lieutenant Zapata heard from the lips of the outraged chief of personnel how I had treated a superior officer in a profoundly disrespectful way, he told me, "It's unbelievable that you allowed yourself to be provoked by that idiot. Look at all the times that I had warned you, man!" The lieutenant insisted that I had to go back to the unit. Zapata decided to give me a five-day leave.

"Give me some time to see what I can do," he told me.

When I returned, something else happened that forced me to leave that place. The associations in Vertientes and Esmeralda were merging, and the latter came with its chief of services and UMAP assistant. The chief of personnel arranged for the UMAP assistant of the chief of services in the Esmeralda association to take over my position so that I would be sent back to the country. Another young recruit, named Joel Ajo,[11] took over my place, my bed, and my office in the association in Vertientes. The chief of personnel got rid of me, but he had to deal with another Christian. Joel Ajo was recruited while a pastor in the Methodist Church in Alcides Pinos, in Holguín.

Together with Joel Ajo, another recruit named Rigoberto Cervantes came to work as a cook. He was a Baptist pastor. The chief of personnel, so proud of himself because he

---

[11] **Rev. Joel Ajo.** Methodist pastor. He was a pastor of the K and 25 Methodist Church in the Havana City. He was also Vice President of the Council of Churches in Cuba, and served in administrative offices in international ecumenical organizations. He now lives in the United States.

kicked out a Christian from the association, did not know that the end result of his scheme was that two more Christians would be working there.

So, God didn't come in his office?

The next day I returned to Los Sitios. That was the fourth time I had been transferred since I had left four months earlier to Vertientes. The chief of personnel took pleasure in taking me back on his own truck to the same unit from which I had been chosen to work in the association.

We left at about ten in the morning. In the vehicle, his assistant accompanied the chief of personnel. Among the boxes of food and produce, and covered by a canvas, was the bag of food and the letter for the Adventist recruit. It just so happened that we needed to stop by his unit to leave those boxes filled with various things that had to be delivered to that camp. God, though He had not been granted permission, not only went to the office of the chief of personnel but also used his vehicle and took a trip with him.

Even after losing all my benefits, I praised the Lord all the way, and also, why not say it?—laughed inside at the chief of personnel. He was proud and happy because he had brought me down at last. He was completely oblivious to the great way in which God was mocking him. He threw a Christian out of the association, a seminarian, but now he had two pastors. Even though I lost all the benefits of my position in Vertientes, I was quiet, confident, and even happy for having stood up to him like that. So, I accepted the return to Los Sitios as something natural. If two other Christians would be working in the association, I could step away quietly.

I was tempted a few times, when I got off the truck, to tell him, "So, God doesn't enter your office, lieutenant? If I were you, I wouldn't be so sure. Besides, there are SOBs that aren't Christians." I did not dare because I knew that he would answer back with one of his favorite blasphemies.

I also kept quiet for another reason. When Lieutenant

Zapata said goodbye to me in his office, he hugged me and whispered in my ear, "Don't worry! You are in the final stretch. When the harvest is over there will be a general demobilization. UMAP is going to be dissolved. Don't say anything about it; it's still a secret."

Without a doubt, Captain Zapata's office in Vertientes was a very dangerous place…very dangerous for my heart!

12

In the Final Stretch

Back in Los Sitios I had to return to working in the country. During my time in Vertientes, another recruit had taken over my job in supplies. The harvest had not started yet, and the unit was at work cleaning up the cane fields. The chief of the first platoon, the person with whom I had previous problems, had been transferred. When Lieutenant Rojas welcomed me, he told me that the first chance that he could, he would give me back my old job.

I was working in the country again, and with genuine enthusiasm. Since I had begun to apply the principle that Paul expresses in Colossians 3:23, "*Whatever you do, work heartily, as for the Lord and not for men,*" everything had changed for me. Why did it matter that I had been taken to UMAP unjustly? When I was working, I could do it as if I was working for the Lord. And why did it matter if I was only receiving a salary of seven pesos?

When Paul wrote that exhortation he was referring to work that was done by slaves. Some might interpret his words as biblical support for a system of oppression and exploitation. But there is nothing further from the truth. The secret is that when a person puts his heart into his work, whatever it may be and regardless of the compensation, he obtains a personal satisfaction that allows him to victoriously overcome any difficult and oppressive situation.

We all know very well how much we enjoy it when we do something that we really like and that has genuine value, whether for ourselves or others. Time passes quickly and without our even realizing it, any sacrifice ceases to be one. The delight of seeing how our work progresses and the anticipated joy of seeing it finished, gives us the strength and enthusiasm to go on. Sometimes we are not even aware of how much time has passed, or how tired and fatigued we have become, until the moment we finish.

Whether we like it or not, we were made to work. In the biblical account of the creation, God placed man in the Garden of Eden *"to work and to keep it."*[1] Long before sin entered the scene and disrupted man's relationship with God, the fact that man was to be busy in his work was the divine plan. It is one of the many things that God created and declared, *"was very good."*[2]

Now, all of this can be very easy to accept and understand when we can choose our job. But sometimes, work is forced upon us, and the job has not been our choice, but somebody else's. What if we must work at something we dislike? I think that work itself has an intrinsic value. As incredible as it seems, a well-done job produces in a person a strong sense of well-being.

I once read (I do not remember where, or I would gladly credit the author), *"success in life consists not in doing what we like, but managing to like what we are doing."* I think that putting our heart and soul into our job is like the magic wand of fairy tales. It has the power to turn the unpleasant into something beautiful.

The Bible absolutely condemns laziness because it degenerates and destroys a person. So, (as in so many other things in life!) the secret is found in the mental and spiritual

---

[1] Genesis 1:28 and 2:15.

[2] Genesis 1:31.

attitude that one brings to his work situation. It is tragic when a man rejects or shows that he does not care about his work, because even though it might be humble or poorly compensated, it still has genuine value. Working raises our self-esteem and gives us the ability to live a full life. When a man is unwilling to work, performs his work grudgingly or carelessly, is satisfied with mediocrity, or cheats his employer, the greater damage done is to himself because of the apathy and frustration with which he burdens his own life.

Displaying this different attitude now, and having resolved my spiritual problems, I was not affected by the loss of the privileges in Vertientes, and the return to the unit was not a tragedy, nor was the fact that I had to return to the hard work in the country. I did my job with genuine enthusiasm. I met my quota of work very early and then continued to work even longer.

My friend Miguelo, who tried every day to work as little as possible, told me, "Take it easy, Buddy; we have to make this last! What kind of brainwashing did they do to you in Vertientes? Patriotism has gone to your head now!"

I enjoyed working now because of my new attitude adjustment, and the time went faster this way. I had lost all the advantages of working in the association, and I could no longer see Miriam every week, but I knew that, as Captain Zapata had said, I was in the final stretch. Besides, there would be leaves again in December and it was said that they would give us additional days if we exceeded our assigned quota. So, in the first month after returning to the unit, I was chosen as "Vanguard" in the competition for "The Emulation." They held a ceremony and gave me a red flag as an award.

Comrade Vanguard

I do not know who came up with the brilliant idea that comrade Vanguard would delight in the great privilege of constantly carrying around a red flag. They looked for a long wooden rod so that I could carry that flag everywhere I went. I had to tie it next to my bed. In the morning, I had to take it to the country with me and place it next to the furrow where I was working, so that comrade Vanguard's location was visible at all times. I also had to take the flag to every roll call.

That blessed flag, rather than a prize, became a punishment. Sometimes I would forget about it in the country. My fellow recruits would hide it, and then, not seeing it when I finished working, I would forget about it and leave it there. Then when we were en route back to the unit, someone would say, "Excuse me, comrade lieutenant. comrade Vanguard forgot his flag in the country!"

And the lieutenant would immediately issue the order, "comrade Vanguard! Go back to the country immediately and pick up your flag."

So, I had to retrace the path to the place where I had worked, pick up the flag and walk back to the unit with it, while those responsible for the joke had a great laugh. Rarely there was a day when the red flag of comrade Vanguard did not provide hilarious moments. I decided I had to get rid of that flag and so the next month I worked much less! I did enough to feel good, but I consciously avoided being outstanding. The incentive that they offered me to work hard was actually a deterrent. Walking around with a red flag in tow, rather than making me proud, was humiliating and absurd, at least for me! What a great way of rewarding somebody for his hard work: force him to carry around and display a red flag twenty-four hours a day! Whose spectacular idea had this been?

We left on leave by the end of December. We were given the ten regular days, but the earlier promise of receiving extra days for exceeding the norm was broken. Miriam and I rang in the New Year together for the first time since we had been married. On December 31, 1967, at twelve midnight, while in church, we held hands and asked the Lord that the words that Zapata had said to me would come true. That New Year came with the hope that the end of the great trial was approaching.

According to the law, I should be demobilized by the end of November. If it occurred when the harvest was over, I could go out five or six months earlier, which would enable me to attend classes at the seminary in the upcoming academic year. If I were not demobilized until the end of November I would not be able to go back to the seminary until the following year. But the harvest was ahead, and that was always a difficult time. Officially, we would have no leaves at that time. The situation was complicated for us by the fact we were located in Los Sitios, a considerable distance from Vertientes with poor access to any form of outside communication. Traveling to Los Sitios was a major feat, and I did not want Miriam to travel any more. Transportation to Las Marías had been reliable as far as La Gabriela, and from there, only seven kilometers remained. But it was thirty kilometers from Vertientes to Los Sitios, and it was in a far more isolated and deserted area. We agreed that she should not even try to travel there.

We said goodbye to each other on January 3, prepared for the likelihood of another four or five months without seeing one another, until perhaps some favorable circumstance provided it. I was hoping that the nightmare would end sooner than that, and I did not want Miriam to continue making the trips that were always so stressful. Usually, the harvest was over by the end of April or early in May when the rainy season began. One factor that made this separation more palatable to us was that my spiritual state and attitude were now different.

I have come to see in my years of ministry that when a person is having trouble spiritually, he becomes selfish. He demands attention and support, which leaves the people around him exhausted. The constant need for human crutches is always a sign that the relationship with God is not very close. One can rely on others, but should not constantly demand sacrifices from those who are helping him; such sacrifices are sometimes beyond their strength to give.

The harvest began in early January. Getting used to the pace of work during the harvest was a tough experience. This time, the biggest incentive was the hope that it would be the last one, so much so that we had actually been looking forward to its beginning. Even Miguelo, who was never enthusiastic about working, got up on the first day of the harvest, shouting all over the barracks, "Let's go, recruits! For something to finish, it must first begin!" When he passed by my bunk bed he added, "You look and find a way to ask God for springtime to break so that it starts raining early and the harvest can be over quickly. He can give us a little help sometimes, don't you think?" Then, when he had walked a few steps past me, he turned back and approached me, and told me in a lower voice, "I already have it all figured out partner. I'll cut cane for a month and a half. Then I'll cut a tendon and I won't work anymore until I get out of here."

"Don't be a fool, Miguelo," I answered him. "Hurting yourself just to avoid working isn't right."

"What isn't right is cutting cane for seven pesos a month, patriot. I have already made up my mind, my brother. I'm only working one more month for these people! What do you think? Afterwards, the wound won't heal until after I am released. You'll see."

After about two weeks of cutting cane, a rumor began to circulate that we were about to be transferred. For me, it would be the sixth transfer since I had left Las Marías. I had been in Mola, Sabanilla, Los Sitios, Vertientes, Los Sitios again, and now God only knew where we would be taken. We were never informed of the transfer in advance. My hope was that it might be some place near the city of Camagüey where Miriam could come see me more easily, if we were granted leaves on Sundays.

An Unexpected Gift

We left Los Sitios, having climbed on the trucks with our belongings once again at night. When the caravan left

Vertientes and took the road to Camagüey, I was filled with hope. When we got to town, I thought that we would take the road of Nuevitas, which is the way to Senado, but when we reached the Central Highway, we turned left, toward Ciego de Ávila. When we went through the city of Florida and continued our trip along the Central Highway, my hopes had grown higher. Could it be possible that God would send me to a place near Miriam? There were several sugar mills in the area around Ciego de Ávila. If we were going to cut cane for one of them, she and I would be able to see each other more often.

When we arrived at the junction of the Baraguá Sugar Mill and we turned left, my heart almost burst with joy. Baraguá was about forty kilometers from Ciego de Ávila and there was reliable transportation between the mill and the city. The caravan passed by the mill and went into the fields. I could hardly wait to arrive at the camp because I wanted to be within walking distance to the mill, which would make things easier. The truck continued going for eighteen kilometers more and finally stopped in a bleak and dilapidated camp, in front of some old barracks that appeared uninhabitable. We had traveled for more than 150 kilometers since leaving Los Sitios.

The camp was a disaster. There was no electric power. The bunk beds were made of rustic wood and of burlap sacks. The wooden walls were rotten and full of holes. The cold was overwhelming inside the barracks. Neither the showers nor the latrines had a roof. The water had to be carried a bucket at a time from an artesian well. Arriving at a place like that in the middle of the night and then having to stay there was very unpleasant. Exhausted from traveling, I fell asleep as soon as I could make a bed. I was happy because I would not have to wait four months to see Miriam. I began to dream about it and anticipate the joy of surprising her at her house on Sunday. I had never been in a camp that was this close to her house. One way or another, we had a much better chance of seeing each other soon.

The following day, during the roll call before breakfast,

Lieutenant Rojas recognized all the discomforts of the place. He exhorted us to work very hard in spite of the conditions, and finished by saying, "Anyway, I have good news for you. There will be leaves on Sundays for those who behave well and stand out at work."

"Is what I'm hearing true?" I asked Miguelo who was standing next to me at the roll call.

"It's all true buddy, but don't get too excited. You know what things are like here. Tomorrow another order will come and turn everybody upside down. Where are all the extra days they were going to give us for our leaves in December?"

On Sunday, when Miriam least expected me, I showed up as a surprise at noon. When she saw me, she could not believe my story that I would be cutting cane for the Baraguá Sugar Mill.

"God is good," she said. "We are suffering, and look what He's done for us!"

I had walked eighteen kilometers from the camp to the mill with a group of recruits. I spent the entire afternoon at home. At night, Miriam and I went to the service together, and at ten, I met up with my mates again for the long trip back. We took the last bus to Baraguá, which left at eleven from Ciego de Ávila. Since we had walked the entire distance that morning, the eighteen kilometers back at night was much more difficult. But, we were young and we made the trip anyway. We passed the journey by talking, sitting down to rest at times, and at other times, jogging part of the way. We arrived at the camp just as they were giving the shout for roll call.

I felt immensely happy. Although the official announcement had not yet been made, there were persistent rumors that they were preparing to demobilize. The following Sunday, I made the same trip all over again, although nobody else wanted to join me this time. What did walking thirty-six kilometers matter if I could be with my wife at home for a few hours and then attend the service with her at night? I was

In the Final Stretch

strong and very healthy.

Every week that I stayed in Baraguá, I did the same thing Sunday after Sunday. I worked hard during the week in order to ensure that I was given the leave. On Sundays, I would leave early and energetically make the long hike to the mill with the group of recruits who, due to their work, were also given the leave. I was the happiest one of them all. They had as an incentive going to town and walking around some, but I was going to see my wife and spend a few hours at home. Sometimes I walked back alone at night. Other times, a recruit who had stayed late would keep me company. The majority preferred to return early because in the early evening they could always find transportation back to the camp in time to go to bed. I was able to see Miriam every Sunday for the six weeks that we cut cane in Baraguá.

Being able to see my wife meant walking thirty-six kilometers and staying up all night, but I did it with great pleasure. After all, she had sacrificed a lot to visit me for more than two years, regardless of the distance or difficulty she had encountered, just to be able to spend a couple of hours at my side. Now, on my Sunday journeys along with the other recruits, we were occasionally able to catch a ride on a truck that happened to be heading to the mill, but at night it never happened. The return trip was completely on foot. I do not know where I got the strength to cut cane the following day. I worked enthusiastically all week long in order to win that Sunday leave. It would have been great to have spent the entire harvest cutting cane there. I was a happy man during that month and a half.

After a month, they began telling us that we were nearly finished cutting the cane there, and that we probably would be transferred again. A couple of weeks later, on a Friday, the order came and suddenly we found ourselves back on a truck with our belongings, headed for a new camp.

Stumbling Over the Same Rock

It was my seventh time to be transferred. Every time we prepared for a transfer, I remembered how much we had complained in Las Marías for always having to stay in the same place. Now, I realized that being transferred was much worse. We were never given any information as to where we were going, what the conditions would be like when we got there, nor how long we would stay. It was all treated as classified information.

For me, this transfer was the worst of all. When the truck we were on got to the Central Highway and turned towards Camagüey, moving further and further away from Ciego de Ávila, it was a struggle not to feel depressed. Time and again, I kept telling myself that I did not have the right to feel that way, but should be grateful for the unexpected transfer to Baraguá, which had truly been a gift. Standing on back of the truck with the wind in my face, I began to look up and notice the beauty of the starry sky and I praised God for the blessings that we enjoyed while in Baraguá. In this way, I was able to free myself of the sadness and the pain that I felt. I thought of the following Sunday when Miriam would still be expecting me.

Whenever a transfer took place, I always had one wish: to meet up again with one of the other seminarians in UMAP, or perhaps just to meet another Christian. But such a circumstance never came to pass, though I longed for it with all my heart.

This time we were transferred back to cutting cane for the Senado Sugar Mill. First, we were taken to a camp on the outskirts of La Gabriela, on the road that comes from Senado. We stayed there fifteen days. Afterwards, my eighth transfer took us to another camp about five kilometers further ahead, in the direction away from Jagüeycito. This transfer was more than just changing locations; they split up our company and joined a part of it to the one that was already staying in this camp.

When I arrived there a great surprise was awaiting me. The chief of that unit was the same lieutenant with whom I had problems in Los Sitios for refusing to falsify the data. I could not believe it! And then, while trying to get over the shock of that news, I was confronted with an even greater surprise. There was nobody to organize the supplies, and when the lieutenant recognized me among the recruits, he ordered me to do the job.

The camp was somewhat similar to Baraguá, but they had a nice and spacious dining hall, a good kitchen and storeroom. There was also a windmill attached to a well, which provided us with an abundant water supply. It was a beautiful place, surrounded by trees on a small hill. Across from the camp there was a house made of masonry and concrete, where an elderly married couple lived. I became acquainted with them immediately, due to my ability to move about freely while working as a supplier, and of constantly staying in the unit. The worst thing of all was the barracks where we slept. The conditions were at least as bad as those in Baragúa. But because there was space in the stockroom, the lieutenant authorized me to sleep there. Once again, God provided for me a quiet place where I could do my job, and also read and write without being disturbed.

The lieutenant and I continued to have an uneasy relationship. He had not forgotten about our confrontation in Vertientes, and I kept expecting him to order me to do something unethical. He began to frequently come to the storeroom and help himself to a can of condensed milk or of meat. He would take it while saying, "Discharge it, supplier; I'm hungry!" He was the chief of the unit and I could not stop him from coming into the storeroom, but he came almost every day and usually at different times. Each unit that received supplies had to keep a careful accounting of it. One can of condensed milk was the normal amount used for breakfast for four recruits. If the lieutenant took a couple of cans daily, he was consuming the milk that had been planned for eight recruits. Since the milk that was provided had to last for an entire month, I had to water down the milk for breakfast. Obviously, he thought that he had the right to anything in the storeroom at anytime he desired. That really bothered and upset me, and my bad feelings toward him because of our altercations in Vertientes increased.

When I worked with supplies in Las Marías I never once saw Lieutenant Marrero do anything like that. In Los Sitios, Lieutenant Rojas never went to the storeroom to ask for anything for himself. While working at the association, neither Captain Zapata nor any other officer, including even the chief of services, did such a thing. But this lieutenant acted as if everything in the storeroom belonged to him.

A Letter for the Lieutenant's Girlfriend

Although the lieutenant was married, one day he came into the storeroom and told me with a lot of pride that he had a girlfriend in La Gabriela. After that, he started to take cans of milk, meat, and other foods to her every time that he went to visit her. "Discharge them, Supply," he repeated every time he came to take something, "and see to it that nothing turns up missing when you do the accounting."

I always wanted to tell him that nothing would be missing when I did the accounting, but it would certainly be missing when the troops had to be fed. Although I did not want to have any more problems with him, he was about to push me over the edge, and I knew that eventually, at some unexpected moment, we would end up squaring off again.

That occasion came when the lieutenant insisted that he wanted me to write a letter to his girlfriend. I inferred that he did not know how to write well, and that he simply wanted to dictate a letter, because he had seen and liked my handwriting. So I responded, "Any time, lieutenant. Drop by and I'll do it."

He looked at me with a strange expression as if he didn't understand, but left anyway. At lunchtime he asked me in the dining hall, "Have you finished writing the letter to my girlfriend?"

His question seemed very odd to me, so I said, "Come to the storeroom with me if you can; we will do it."

I went to my work desk, looked for paper and a pen, and sat down to wait for him. I did not like the idea of being a scribe for the lieutenant. What would he tell his "girlfriend"? But I wanted to get rid of him as soon as possible. I thought that the lieutenant was coming immediately, but I kept waiting with a piece of paper and a pen in my hand. Eventually, when he did not come, I started to prepare the food that I had to deliver to the cooks so they could prepare the evening meal.

An hour later the lieutenant came into the storeroom. When I saw him arrive, I put the paper on the table, took the pen and sat down. When he saw the paper was blank, he complained, "But you haven't finished the letter to my girlfriend yet!" And he added as if he was mocking me, "Look, it appears to me that you don't know how to write letters to a girlfriend. Ha! Ha!"

Then I answered him, annoyed and slightly insulted, "You're the one who doesn't know how to write to his girlfriend. When I write to my girlfriend, lieutenant, nobody has to help me, because I know how to write very well. So, just sit down there," I said fingering authoritatively to the chair that was next to the table where I worked, "tell me what you want to say to your girlfriend. She's your girlfriend, not mine!"

"You're giving *me* orders!" He protested furiously.

"I'm not giving you orders, lieutenant. I'm explaining to you how to write a letter to your girlfriend."

"Yeah, don't tell me you're not. You're giving me orders. You're still as mistaken as when you were in Vertientes. I'm your superior! Do you hear me? Your superior!"

Raising his voice even louder, he put his two hands on the table, and leaned towards me, and repeated even angrier, "I'm your superior, don't you ever forget that!"

I decided to keep quiet. The letter to his girlfriend was the trigger to display my frustration for the other things that I could not tell him, like his daily taking of food from the storeroom. I breathed deeply and asked God in silence to give me patience. The lieutenant looked at me with a very clear expression of hatred, and told me, "You've disrespected me several times and that will end up costing you dearly."

He immediately turned around to leave the storeroom, but not before going over to the place where the condensed milk was and grabbing two cans. He turned again to me and showed them. "Since you can't write a letter to my girlfriend, I'll take these. Discharge them!"

From that point forward my relationship with the lieutenant was very tense. I knew that he was waiting for the chance to get back at me. He had said in Vertientes that he would do it. Now, he came daily into the storeroom, taking food with a harassing and threatening attitude.

One day I told him, "The recruits are protesting because the milk is watery."

"They're not at home; they have to drink whatever they're given here." He answered.

The lieutenant did not have another supplier to replace me and what he was doing was resulting in more work for me. One day, the recruit that was a health care worker got sick and had to be put in the hospital in Camagüey. The lieutenant came into the storeroom and told me, "You're going to have to take care of the job of being the health care worker too. I can't afford to keep another man away from the country for that."

The health care worker took care of minor wounds and referred any case that he could not resolve, or recruits who needed an appointment, to the battalion doctor. In addition, every morning, if anyone claimed to be sick, he had to determine if it was true or not, because the health care worker was the only person who could authorize a recruit to stay back in the unit rather than go to work. It was a thorny job. The recruits were constantly making up illnesses. Sometimes the chiefs wanted the recruits to go to the country even when they were actually sick. The health care job was quite difficult to manage without having problems from one side or the other.

A Man with Menstruation

One of the most perplexing experiences that I had in UMAP occurred during the week when I was doing both jobs. The lieutenant ordered me to go to the barracks to check on a recruit that refused to go to the country because he was sick. I went into the cabin and found him in his underwear, lying face down in bed. I recognized that it was the recruit that everyone said was a homosexual. "What do you have?" I asked.

Without turning over, he answered me: "Uh, supplier...the truth is that this happens to me every month. But I could not tell the lieutenant."

"What?"

"Yes, every month. Don't you know what happens to women every month? I'm having my period."

I burst out laughing thinking that it was a joke and told him, "Listen, buddy, don't make my life difficult, okay? My wife has her period every month and she doesn't stop working for that. Surely you understand that I can't certify that you're having your monthly period, okay? Make up a better story if you don't want to work today, because this one won't work."

The recruit became outraged. He was totally convinced that he was having his period.

Although this one turned out to be an unusual case, the recruits tried to escape from work every day by making up all sorts of illnesses and ailments. Discerning between which ones were true and which were false was sometimes impossible. Between the extremely exhausting work and, at times, the inhumane demands of the chiefs, made many recruits seek a way to defend themselves by escaping from work. There were no doctors among the officers. Recruits were chosen as health care workers if they claimed to have only a small amount of medical knowledge, which was not true in my case. Frequently, the health care workers helped the recruits, but it was a very frustrating position because the chiefs often ordered the health care worker to send recruits to the country even when he knew that they were actually sick.

Thank God, the health care worker returned the following week.

Miguelo Keeps his Promise

One day, they brought Miguelo back from the country after he had suffered an "accidental" wound to his left hand while cutting cane. He was immediately sent to the battalion, and from there to the hospital in Camagüey for surgery. The machete had cut two tendons. Due to the injury he was given a release from work for forty-five days. Miguelo had kept his promise.

The method he used was very common and many recruits practiced it. While they were cutting cane in the country, they hid from the chiefs' view and looked for a big rock on which they could lay the left hand. Then they placed the blade of the machete over the hand and with the file that was used to sharpen the machete, or with another rock, another recruit would strike the machete. They pretended that it had been a machete accident while working. If the recruit were right-handed, the blow would be to the left hand, or vice-versa if he were left-handed. After the operation, the wound would immobilize the hand, and the recovery process was slow. Some were even able to get released from UMAP if the hand failed to heal properly.

"You see, Patriot?" He told me showing me his bandaged hand, "Now I will just sleep and eat until they release me. Nobody is going to exploit this Cuban any more."

Not long after, his wound became infected. Then he said that he could not close the fingers of his hand and that the operation had not been done well. He spent the rest of his time going from one appointment to the next and did not work another day until he was demobilized. There were three other recruits in the camp with a similar situation.

I had great affection for Miguelo because he had a high regard for friendship. I shared the gospel with him many times. He enjoyed listening to me and asked a lot of questions, but he never made a decision to receive the Lord. I know that he admired me. He would tell me about his problems and aspirations. He was always joking and laughed at everything because he was a typical Cuban practical joker, always enjoying pulling pranks, but deep inside, he suffered intensely. His decision to injure his hand was a desperate act to flee from something that was very difficult to face and to overcome.

Another recruit in the unit had been fighting for months to get his release after he had done the same thing. He insisted that the index and ring fingers of his right hand had no feeling after the operation. He would show his stiff fingers to everyone and he went months without working in the country. He was taken to the medical board where they conducted many investigations and different treatments. But his fingers remained stiff. The day before Miguelo's return to the battalion they sent the order for the recruit's demobilization. He rushed to the storeroom to tell me the news and to say goodbye.

"Do you see? I did it, supplier! It took me several months, but I finally did it!" He was beaming with happiness. He gave me a hug and headed for the door. Then he stopped, looked outside to make sure that nobody was looking, and then he lifted up his hand to show me that all his fingers were working perfectly. Incredibly, he had managed to fool the medical board, and all the other recruits, by keeping his fingers stiff for several months. "They won't be exploiting me anymore!" he said as he burst out laughing.

My Wife Stayed in the Unit

My mother came to the unit to visit me. That was her last visit while I was in UMAP. The demobilization was approaching and I asked her not to come anymore. She had to make a long and exhausting trip just to see me. Mothers are always willing to make any sacrifice. She had suffered in silence, enduring my bitter letters when I was doing badly, and had written constantly to encourage me. I accompanied her back to La Gabriela and said goodbye happily because I thought that she would not have to come back to see me. "Next time we'll see each other at home, OK?" I told her as we said goodbye.

"Yes, but if it takes you too long to be demobilized, I'll be coming back to see you." She was very happy because my attitude had changed and she left smiling on that little bus that traveled between La Gabriela to the Senado Sugar Mill. She would have to travel from town to town all night long, not arriving at home until very late the following morning.

Miriam also came to the camp. Her visit coincided with Miguelo's return from the hospital. He met her in La Gabriela and accompanied her back to the camp.

Miriam's visit proved to be unique. The elderly married couple that lived in the house across from the unit invited her to come on Saturday and then stay over in their home until Sunday afternoon. I wrote to her immediately. The next Saturday, after receiving the letter, she appeared. Miriam tried to surprise me, but actually she was the one who was surprised. That weekend the elderly couple had left to visit some relatives. When Saturday afternoon came and she arrived at the unit accompanied by Miguelo, the house was absolutely closed and vacant.

In spite of my poor relationship with the lieutenant, and at the insistence of the recruits who were my friends, of the cooks, and especially of Miguelo, I asked him to allow her to stay in the unit that night. He agreed to allow it. By the time that Miriam arrived that afternoon, it was impossible for her to have returned. There was no available transportation out of there.

So, we prepared the infirmary, a hut that was in terrible condition, but was separated from the main barracks and the dining hall. We carried a couple of beds and bed sheets there and arranged the place so that the two of us could spend the night together.

In the end, it was an uncomfortable experience. She was the only woman among 120 recruits in the camp where there were all kinds of men. That night a movie was shown in the dining hall, and we stayed up until very late talking with the recruits who were my friends. However, it was comforting to me that the vocabulary used in the camp that night was completely different, and the men were careful in their behavior because the supplier's wife was there. When it was time to go to bed, everybody left and Miriam and I went to the infirmary.

So she, against all regulations, became perhaps the only wife of a UMAP recruit ever to have slept in a UMAP unit. The respect with which she was treated by everyone, the affection that my friends showed her, and all the effort that everybody expended for her to feel as welcome as possible, turned the uncomfortable experience into another evidence that human solidarity has no borders or impossibilities.

Not a single incident occurred that would have made the experience difficult for her or for me. That night I felt very happy, valued, and even appreciated by my fellow recruits. They responded appropriately to the unusual circumstance of having a female visitor in the unit all afternoon and night. My UMAP friends, comrades and all the officers, including the lieutenant with whom I did not have a good relationship, behaved splendidly. The next day Miriam stayed in the unit all morning, and after lunch I took her back to La Gabriela.

The Lieutenant Fulfilled his Promise to Harm Me!

A couple of weeks later there came an order for a transfer, which would be my ninth. Working as a supplier, I was responsible to pack everything and to make sure that nothing got lost in the transfer. There were confusing rumors about the transfer. Some said that we were going back to Vertientes. I asked God that it would be to Baraguá, but they just took us to the camp in La Gabriela. It all went very quickly. We heard the rumor in the morning, and by that night we were on the truck. The transfer offered the lieutenant the opportunity to "harm me" that he had been waiting for.

When we arrived at the camp in La Gabriela, we discovered that another unit was also coming. We were approximately a month away from finishing the harvest; the cane cutting was coming to an end, and they were focusing on areas where there was still more cane to be cut. When I arrived with the supplies for the storeroom of the new camp, the other unit with which we would be working had already arrived. The person in charge of supplies for that unit was also there; only one of us could continue working at that job.

In the storeroom, the other supplier and I organized all the supplies that we had brought from our camps, while the chief of personnel from the battalion and our lieutenant, who was going to be the new chief of the unit, watched us. I knew from the outset that the chief of personnel wanted me to keep the job. When the new chief of the unit went into the storeroom, the chief of personnel took the opportunity to ask him if it should become my job. The lieutenant looked at me and smiled as if to say, "Here's my opportunity!" and asked the chief to leave the storeroom with him to discuss it.

After a while, the chief of personnel came back and told me, "Go back to the country. The other comrade will be the supplier for the company."

When I left the storeroom, the chief of my unit stood there with an expression of victory. Then I remembered what Miguelo said six months earlier, *"the lieutenant is going to harm you."*

In a very cynical way, he asked, "Oh, weren't you asked to continue working as the supplier?"

"No, lieutenant." I answered him calmly and trying not to reflect either in my voice or with a gesture, that I was the least bit uncomfortable, "the other recruit is going to take over."

"That's just to take you down a peg or two so that you won't be mistaken so easily as to who is in charge," he answered back.

I smiled. I knew very well the lieutenant's moral condition and I was not at all surprised by what he did. Besides, I knew that there was less and less time remaining, and going back to cut cane was no problem for me. Working directly with him *was* a problem for me, so I felt I had been liberated. After that, he was assigned to another nearby company, and I would not be under his command anymore. This event was, in itself, a blessing.

He Who Laughs Last Laughs Best

The lieutenant's victory was short-lived. One of the most amazing verses of the Bible is in Acts 7:9, where it says: *"And the patriarchs, jealous of Joseph, sold him into Egypt; but God was with him."* If God wants to bless a person, any man's efforts to harm him are useless. Paul said the same thing in Romans 8:31: *"What then shall we say to these things? If God is for us who can be against us?"* The last thing that either the chief of the unit or I expected was about to take place.

After the chief of personnel left our camp, he picked up two military men in his jeep, who were walking to La Gabriela towards the battalion. One of them happened to be Lieutenant Rojas. After saluting him, the chief of personnel said to him, "I just came from La Gabriela camp. There we combined one of the units that you led in Los Sitios with one from another battalion."

Lieutenant Rojas, who knew me very well, advised him, "Then you have a good supplier. That boy worked in the association in Vertientes with Captain Zapata and was the assistant to the chief of services."

The chief of personnel stopped the jeep and turned around to Lieutenant Rojas, surprised by what he was hearing. "What did you say? Who is this you're talking about?"

"The recruit that was with me in Los Sitios and who was working as a supplier near La Gabriela. He did such a great job of arranging the storeroom that when Control and Help came we won 'The Emulation.' Then Zapata took him to work in the association. He is the best supplier that I have ever met."

The chief of personnel could not believe it. Somewhere there was a mistake. The chief of my unit had told him that I did not know how to work, that I was very disruptive, that I could not manage the records, and that he had wanted to remove me as the supplier for a long time. Then Lieutenant Rojas told him about the problems I had earlier with this man in Vertientes. He also told him about my confrontation with the chief of personnel at the association, because he had given Rojas all the details. Rojas was a man who inspired confidence and had very good intentions.

That night, shortly after dinner, while I was talking with some of the other recruits outside of the barracks, I saw the chief of personnel return in his jeep, accompanied by Lieutenant Rojas. Shortly after, I was summoned to the office. As I reported in and greeted them, I heard the chief of personnel ask Rojas, "Is this the recruit?"

"Yes." answered Lieutenant Rojas, as he extended his hand to greet me.

I looked at both, as if to ask what was going on. The chief of personnel added, "Pick up your belongings and get back to the office as soon as possible. You're going to be transferred from here."

I left quickly and was very worried. Had I done something wrong? Had the chief of the unit said something worse about me? But, the smile of satisfaction from Lieutenant Rojas calmed me down. I said goodbye to my mates without being able to tell them what was happening, and reported back to the office. I climbed in the jeep with the chief of personnel and Lieutenant Rojas. (I regret that I am now unable to remember the name of the former. It would give me tremendous pleasure to note it.)

When I left the camp the chief of personnel told me, "I can't stand it when they want to do a *número ocho*[3] to a good man. Rojas explained to me why the lieutenant has it out for you. Now I'm going to make you feel good, and I'll do it right in front of his face so that he can see you every day."

Lieutenant Rojas smiled with satisfaction.

A Month Working as a Civilian

The chief of personnel took me to work as the supplier for the civilian dining hall at the gathering center[4] in Jagüey, only a couple of kilometers from La Gabriela. I was there alone with only three other recruits who worked as cooks. In the dining hall, they prepared meals for the civilian truckers who transported the cane from the plantations to the gathering center, and then to the sugar mill. My job was to be in charge of the storeroom, develop the daily menu, and keep the place clean. The main benefit of working in the dining hall was that there were no strict rules for the food like there were in the army. Here they cooked plenty of food and the meals were excellent. When I needed something, I just had to ask the driver to take me to the town of Minas to pick up the supplies.

The cooks and I were the only ones who slept in the room next to the dining hall and storeroom. There were no officers who constantly watched us and gave us orders. There was a timetable for the food to be served. The drivers could eat all they wanted. The place was frequently visited by officers who would stop and eat there, because of its pleasant conditions and because it was, to some extent, supervised by

---

[3] Popular expression that means "to harm."

[4] Installation where the cane cut by machines is taken before it is carried to the sugar mill.

the army, since the four of us worked there.

The first time that the lieutenant, the new chief of the unit at La Gabriela, came to have lunch, he asked me immediately, "What are you doing here? Why aren't you working in the country in the La Gabriela unit?"

"No," I responded, "the very same day that our unit went there, after you were transferred, the chief of personnel and Lieutenant Rojas brought me here." He turned pale and it took a great deal of effort to conceal his displeasure. For me, I confess that I took great pleasure in what I told him. "And I so enjoy being here, lieutenant! God has been very good to me and has given me a magnificent job, where I am comfortable and very happy!"

Yes, God had been very good to me. But so had been the chief of personnel and Lieutenant Rojas as they reacted against the injustice of which I had been a victim. Both showed a sense of justice and integrity, which the chief of my unit had lacked completely. When they left me in the gathering center that night, the chief of personnel had told me, "You'll be here until the harvest is over."

A few days after I was transferred to the gathering center, Miriam came to visit me. She came because we had not seen each other for a month, and because it was relatively easy for her to get to my new location. It was a trip with which she was very familiar since she had done it many times before. The gathering center was near La Gabriela. One Sunday, she arrived early with a smile that she always had on her radiant face, as if she had not been traveling all through the night. I introduced my wife, proudly, to the recruits who worked as cooks and to the drivers that ate there that day.

We stayed until after three in the afternoon talking under a tree outside the dining hall. We did not cry anymore, as we had in the grove in Las Marías. Now we talked about plans for the future. The coming demobilization seemed like a dream to us. Our times together had long ago ceased to be distressing and now were full of hope. At about four in the afternoon, I walked her back to the dirt road to see if we could catch some vehicle to give her a ride to Senado. After a short time, we saw a truck with two men inside, and I signaled for it to stop. As I saw her leave alone with two strangers, I asked God to protect her and to provide some means of transportation for her to return home from Senado.

The two men treated her with a great deal of respect. When they found out that she was going to Ciego de Ávila, they told her, "Well, we're going to take you to the door of your house; it just so happens that we, coincidentally, are going to Jatibonico, and we need to pass by Ciego de Ávila."

Coincidence? Christians believe in the providence of God rather than in coincidence or chance. Miriam made the entire journey, from La Gabriela, to Senado, then to Minas, Camagüey, and finally to Ciego de Ávila,[5] without ever having to get off the truck. They made a few negotiations in Camagüey and then at about ten o'clock that night, the driver stopped right in front of her house. Her mother was on the porch, concerned because she had not returned. When she saw that she was alone, at night, on a truck with two strange men, she was horrified. Miriam noticed the fearful expression on her face, so when she greeted her, she comforted her by saying, "Don't worry; nothing happened. They were very proper with me."

"Thank the Lord, my daughter!" she answered, as she shut the door, greatly relieved. That would be Miriam's last visit.

Miriam's parents suffered the entire experience with us, and always encouraged and helped us. They acted with remarkable wisdom. They were humble people who did not have many resources to help them grow intellectually. They used every opportunity that the church gave them, and acquired a great deal of spiritual maturity. As Christian

---

[5] Approximately 170 kilometers (105 miles).

education elevates and dignifies a person, his culture and knowledge are also elevated. My mother-in-law was a great Sunday school teacher. Today, as I write these lines, I am the same age that they were when their youngest daughter married a UMAP recruit, who had no money and no future. I admire them and recognize the greatness of spirit that they exhibited. They always understood and recognized our love for each other. They were sympathetic with our suffering and supported our plans in an unconditional way, even when the family was suffering from very difficult economic times. They never objected to any of our decisions, and when I left on leave they made all the necessary arrangements for us to enjoy privacy even at the expense of their own peace and comfort.

The Long Awaited Demobilization

I worked at the gathering center for another month until the harvest was over. Afterward, I went back to the camp in La Gabriela to await demobilization. We worked some days cutting pastures, but there was not the same rigor in the work, and life was much easier.

Just as Captain Zapata had told me, UMAP was about to be completely dismantled, and the normal tension inside the units was gone. The harvest was over and the records of the recruits were being prepared for the general demobilization. Since everyone knew that we were in the final days of an inevitably dying organization, there were no demands. All of us were waiting eagerly for the order that would put an end to a shameful history of more than two-and-one-half years, which would be remembered with sadness.

For two consecutive weeks it rained and we could not work. Then the unit worked cutting cane for seed in nearby fields, one kilometer from the settlement. On June 29, 1968, at five in the afternoon, the order was given to stop the work and to leave the country. The order of the general demobilization had been given. Everything was ready for the recruits to go home and to return to lives as civilians. Total joy immediately broke out in the fields where the UMAP recruits were working.

The men tossed their hats into the air and started to clink their machetes one against the other. Friends hugged each other strongly. Many others joined in the embrace, which became a giant group hug. Others were running from one side of the cane field to the other, shouting, singing, laughing, and crying like children.

Even the chiefs enjoyed the general happiness.

That day, thank God, the ill-fated Military Units to Aid Production died.

Never has a funeral provoked so much joy.

13

The Happy End

*When the Lord restored the fortunes of Zion,
we were like those who dream.
Then our mouth was filled with laughter,
and our tongue with shouts of joy;
 then they said among the nations,
"The Lord has done great things for them."
The Lord has done great things for us; we are glad.*

*Restore our fortunes, O Lord,
like streams in the Negeb!
Those who sow in tears
shall reap with shouts of joy!
He who goes out weeping,
bearing the seed for sowing,
shall come home with shouts of joy,
bringing his sheaves with him.*[1]

"I am the Lord, the God of Abraham your father and the God of Isaac. The land on which you lie I will give to you and to your

---

[1] Psalm 126:1-6

> *offspring. Your offspring shall be like the dust of the earth, and you shall spread abroad to the west and to the east and to the north and to the south, and in you and your offspring shall all the families of the earth be blessed. Behold, I am with you and will keep you wherever you go, and will bring you back to this land. For I will not leave you until I have done what I have promised you."* [2]

When the jubilant atmosphere quieted down, we went back to the camp. We did not have to fall in as we normally would. We walked and talked with whomever we wished. We did not fall in at dinnertime either, nor were we counted. UMAP no longer existed! Who was going to escape then? We hardly slept that night. Some spent the entire night beating drums, celebrating the demobilization, but the majority talked until sleep finally overcame them. The next day we were taken to the Senado Sugar Mill to board the busses that would return us to our homes.

Everyone in the company awoke by themselves before dawn. Finally, around nine in the morning, the trucks that were to take us out of there arrived. When we got to the mill everything was in chaos. All the recruits from the entire area were there, and there was not nearly enough transportation. The busses arrived one by one, and everyone was desperate to leave. Some even tried to leave on their own, but it was not allowed.

"This is a total disgrace right up to the last minute!" I heard a recruit who passed by me say, trying to board a bus. But I was enjoying a profound sense of peace and was willing to wait as long as was necessary.

Israel García, José Ferrer and I hugged each other with excitement when we met. We had not seen each other since we

---

[2] Genesis 28:13-15

had left Las Marías a year before. As we waited, we exchanged the stories of our experiences and we laughed a lot about the situations that previously had greatly troubled us. There, we also saw other brothers from various churches. What a joy every time we found somebody we knew! After so much suffering and hard work, so many questions, and so much confusion, the time for joyful laughter had clearly arrived.

The busses began to arrive, little by little, and all of us were leaving. On Sunday, June 30, 1968, at one in the afternoon, I got off the bus full of recruits, which would travel on to Havana, right in front of my wife's house. I had the demobilization letter in my pocket. I had yearned for that moment for so long that I was surprised that everything seemed so natural. I simply arrived and greeted everyone.

I have learned that when the greatest and most anticipated moments in life arrive, they usually come in a normal and natural way. How many times had I dreamed of coming home after being demobilized! I had always thought that when it finally happened, I would be lost in indescribable emotion.

It did not happen like that. I went into my house naturally and greeted everyone the same way as the many times when I had come home on leave. Maybe deep down, I still doubted that it was true. It was the same kind of disbelief that I faced in the beginning of my experience with UMAP. Great sorrow produces disbelief and denial, and in much the same way, great joy can leave us numb and in shock. When a person has longed for a deeply joyful event, and it finally comes about, he can only assimilate it slowly.

Life is different in the movies. The cinematography, the lights, and the music play an important part in the greatest moments in film. But, there is no music in the background in real life: no special effects or a message indicating that "The End" of the film has come, as the camera moves away and the theme song is played. In real life, after the outcome of a meaningful event, another experience begins, or the experiences that have begun to develop alongside the completed event simply continue on. Everything seems so normal and natural that sometimes we miss the greatness of these events.

The dismantling of UMAP came into my life quietly and serenely. It had to be that way, because what was aberrant was the experience of just being in UMAP. Now everything resumed its normal course and the nightmare was simply over. It was like a long night of experiencing a terrible nightmare, when the morning never seems to come. But, thank God, in spite of our worst predictions and fears, the dawn always puts an end to the darkest night. Each sunrise is the glorification of new hope, even though it comes every day in the same usual way.

In September, when the fall semester began, I went back to the seminary along with the other brothers who were demobilized. We were all welcomed with open arms. In the interview that I had with part of the faculty in order to apply for my re-entry, I felt that it was my responsibility to share with the professors about my spiritual crisis that I experienced during my time in UMAP. I did not think it was honest for me to let them think that I had been faithful the entire time. Even though my crisis did not have any ethical consequences, I thought that it was appropriate to explain how far I had fallen and to share my regret.

Dr. Rafael A. Ocaña, who was the rector then, interrupted me, "We didn't know anything about what you are telling us, Alberto. The news never reached us. Everyone, every now and then, is overcome by doubt and discouragement. What is important is that the Lord helped you through it, and now you are here again." This confirmed that Pastor Manuel Morales, as he had promised me, had indeed forgotten about our encounter in the battalion. Undoubtedly, this brother gave me excellent counsel and then kept the secret when he returned from UMAP.

I also wanted to make it clear that if I had the

opportunity, I would definitely leave the country, when Pastor Juan Francisco Naranjo interrupted me, "Who hasn't thought of leaving, son? What is important for you is to serve the Lord and to let Him guide you. Maybe you will never be able to leave. Your thoughts of doing this and even your following through on that desire if one day you are presented with the opportunity should not be an obstacle to the completion of your studies. The work needs pastors, and you are here now."

Naranjo did not know that his prophecy would come true. Every brother who had been interviewed that day ended up emigrating later; I am the only one who has remained in Cuba for my entire ministry.

I completed my final year, which I had left unfinished when I was recruited, and graduated from the Baptist Theological Seminary in Havana on June 19, 1969. That same day Miriam and I celebrated our third wedding anniversary. Ernesto Alfonso, Israel García and José Ferrer graduated with me, as did Segundo Mir[3], who had not been recruited to UMAP. All of my dreams that the UMAP experience had seemingly curtailed were now fulfilled. Miriam and I went to serve in San Antonio de Río Blanco, in the province of Havana, just as we had longed to do years before. We returned to the house where we had always wanted to live. We pastored the church there that we loved so much and that had helped us with our needs many times during the difficult trial. We started our ministry there, and I was ordained as a pastor on May 26, 1970.

A couple of weeks later our first son, David,[4] was born. Three years after that, Liliam[5] was born. They were very happy times that we enjoyed immensely in spite of the fact that it was a very small church with difficult circumstances, and our

---

[3] **Segundo Mir Almaguer.** This brother had matriculated in the seminary in our absence. He was a pastor of the Baptist Churches in Candelaria and Guanajay. He later left for the United States, where he works as a pastor in Washington D.C.

[4] **David González Daniel.** Firstborn of the author. He and his wife are members of the McCall Baptist Church in the City of Havana. He works in Baptist Publishing.

[5] **Liliam González Daniel.** Oldest daughter of the author. She and her husband currently are the administrators for the Baptist Camp in Yumurí.

financial situation was always very precarious. We, who know the pain of being separated, have always realized the tremendous blessing of being able to be together our entire lives. We learned through the separation that we had suffered during the UMAP experience that what is most important is not the place where we are located, nor the things that we have or do not have, but the people whom we are with. Even though we have often gone without, but our needs have never prevented us from being content and happy. We learned once and for all how to discern between what is truly valuable and what is not. When we are together with the people that we love, we can do without many things.

In 1974 we moved to Pinar del Río. Three years later, our youngest daughter, Leydis,[6] was born. We served the Lord for twenty-three years in that church, where God blessed us abundantly and where we enjoyed an exceptionally rewarding period of our lives. In spite of the difficulties, struggles, and normal concerns of life and ministry, God has been very good to us and has given us many satisfying years. It would be impossible to list them all! We have certainly been extremely happy and blessed.

If it had been possible in UMAP to look into the future and to see what would become of my life later, I would not have had even the tiniest reason to be as distressed as I was. In the most difficult times in life, we should never give up our faith and hope. I am ashamed for having fallen into such despair and anguish in an experience that was unavoidable, but transitory. I have asked God for forgiveness for that. It is shameful for a Christian who is undergoing affliction not to trust and wait on God as patiently as he should. In our weakness, we sometimes dare to question everything, as I did. It is something very common and very human. Nevertheless, it is true that we should never forget those times, because in

---

[6] **Leydis González Daniel.** She is the youngest daughter of the author. Her husband is the director of the children's ministry for the Western Baptist Convention. They live in Havana where he is an associate pastor of the Baptist church in Almendares.

them is the secret of victory.

Elie Wiesel, in his book, *Night*, tells a sad but wonderful story. When he was in the concentration camp in Auschwitz, one day while returning from work, he was forced to witness an execution. Three victims were chained and waiting to be hanged. One of them was a boy, a sad-eyed little angel. The three condemned people were placed together on big chairs, as they tied the rope around their necks. At the signal, the three chairs were removed and the three bodies were hanged. A deep and long silence resonated across the entire camp.

The adults that were hanged died instantly. But the boy, due to his lack of weight, was hanging for half an hour, struggling between life and death in a slow and horrible agony. Then Elie heard someone behind him, ask, "For God's sake, where is God?"

Then, a voice inside his heart answered him, "Where is He? This is where – hanging here from this gallows."

There is no doubt that God suffers with us when great sorrows come into our lives. He does not get offended if we despair nor does He leave our side. He has his ways to help us face them, by preparing us, through them, to enjoy the future without any bitterness or resentment. He enables us to go on in spite of everything. He also prepares us to receive the blessings, which in his loving purpose He has prepared for us…later. When affliction arrives, we must wait patiently until the bad times pass. The Psalmist, David, described this process in a wonderful way:

> *I waited patiently for the Lord;*
> *he inclined to me and heard my cry.*
> *He drew me up from the pit of destruction,*
> *out of the miry bog,*
> *and set my feet upon a rock,*
> *making my steps secure.*
> *He put a new song in my mouth,*

> *a song of praise to our God.*
> *Many will see and fear,*
> *and put their trust in the Lord.* [7]

It is beyond question that if we can trust and hope in God, we will suffer much less during our difficult trials. If instead of waiting patiently by holding on to faith and the hope of a better future, we choose the path of resentment and bitterness, the pain of our suffering only increases. Truly, God never abandons us, even though we may constantly protest and worry. He will always be on our side during every painful moment, and he will not leave us until he finishes his loving work in us. The Father displayed His love for us by sending His Son to die in our stead. He further reveals that same love for us by sending His Spirit to be with us always, but especially during times of affliction. He does not do this as a passive spectator, but as a participant. We are so united, our Lord and His people, that what happens to us is felt by Him, and done to Him. It is His presence, patience, company and support that allow us to find peace and victory in and through the trials of life.

When my dreams were shattered by one of those tough situations that life can often give, God—for the simple reason that He was there with me—picked up the pieces of my life and put them back together. In the heat of suffering, where no one like Him can create such masterpieces, He fused them back together and the result was that I was cleaner, brighter, and more able to do His will and live according to His purposes. In UMAP, I learned that it isn't simply fulfilling our dreams and aspirations that brings happiness in life, but searching for and accepting His purpose for us. God's plan will always be more wonderful than the greatest aspirations that we may have, or the best plans that we could conceive.

In many ways, my life has been different from what I imagined. Shortly before I was taken to UMAP I had decided

---

[7] Psalm 40:1-3

to leave the country. I did not want my children to be born and to grow up in Cuba. Convinced that I no longer fit into the society that was so quickly changing, I, like so many other people, decided to emigrate. My first attempt was thwarted miserably. When I was in UMAP, what was said and believed about us—*so they believe that I am social scum?*—reinforced my decision. After I was demobilized, existing laws prevented my departure. Later, I started my ministry, always feeding on the hope that someday an opportunity would present itself to leave Cuba for good. In the meantime, I gave myself to do the work where the Lord had put me.

Slowly and indiscernibly, I began to understand that not all the pastors could leave, and that I had been called to stay. Somebody must preach the gospel and serve the Lord in Cuba. Who was going to talk about the Lord to the Cubans? Who was going to teach and disciple the new believers? Who was going to stick with and pastor the people, the brothers and sisters that stayed over, through their difficult moments and everyday lives filled with a multitude of inconveniences? In the meantime, the children started to come. Miriam and I devoted ourselves to teaching them the values of the Christian faith, despite the fact that the surrounding society denied them. It was no easy task. We always understood that the time devoted to the children was an important part of our ministry. They never knew parents who were so busy in the work of the Lord that they hardly had time for family life, games, walking together, communion, counsel or discipline. We never thought that the time invested in our family was time taken from the work of the Lord—quite the opposite.

Now today, when I see how God has blessed our ministry and all the opportunities that He has given us, I feel humbled and thankful. By the grace and mercy of the Lord, I have been able to be an instrument of God for the blessing and salvation of many people. I have also committed mistakes. As a pastor, I have failed in the way I treated certain people and issues. It is painful to realize the things that I should have done but did not do, or did wrongly. In spite of these things, the Lord has used me, and I am the one most amazed by it. Every time somebody approaches me and tells me that in some way God has used me to bless them, inwardly I lift up a prayer of gratitude. I am amazed that He uses so unworthy an instrument.

When I see our children who serve the Lord with dedication, I worship Him even more. God has given them gifts and they use them to serve Him. They grew up and were educated in an adverse environment, but when they had to make a decision, they made it for Christ. They are all married. If we had chosen their spouses, we would have selected the same people that they chose, for they are marvelous people with strong Christian values. We are proud of them. What greater happiness could we have experienced? Our seven grandchildren have been our last and most wonderful gift.

Our greatest satisfaction has come through the blessings we have received in the service of the Lord. Although God has always supplied our needs, we have suffered through many difficulties and lack. However, the blessings from Christian ministry and our family life have given us abundant treasures in the kingdom of heaven, where they cannot be taken away and where the happiness or misery of human beings will be decided.

The young man that was taken to UMAP did not interpret life that way.

The one who returned most definitely found a new set of values.

14

Thirty Years Later

On Tuesday, August 16, 1995, I returned to Las Marías. It was a trip that I had long desired, and now knew that I needed to take. I wanted to know how I would feel visiting the place where I had suffered so much and where it once seemed that all my hopes had been dashed.

Many times during those first few years after being demobilized, I had a recurring nightmare that I had been recruited once again, and that I had returned to Las Marías. The dream was always the same: I was on a truck in the middle of the night, shivering from cold, and I would start screaming, "I have already been here! Why are you bringing me back?" And I then I would struggle, desperately trying to jump off the truck.

Every time that it happened, I would scream in my sleep, and Miriam would wake up very startled, since my howling was unnerving. When I managed to wake up, a great deal of effort was required on my part to overcome the nervous agitation that the nightmare produced. The UMAP experience was traumatic, and it took some time for me to recover my emotional stability. The nightmares began to be more infrequent until they finally disappeared with the passing of the years.

Although Las Marías was not the only place where I had been, it was the camp where I spent the most time, endured the greatest suffering, and wrestled for the first time, face to face, with human misery, the underworld, and injustice. How little did I know about life before I entered that place! Las Marías meant for me discovering a strange world in which unimaginably horrible human behavior that I had not even known to exist, became an inescapable reality.

It had long been my heartfelt desire to return to Las Marías, but there had been no opportunity to do so. When I began to write this book the wish became a necessity. In order for me to gain a clearer perspective of what that experience meant to me personally, it was very important that I return there. Thus with rising hopes, I began to search for a way to turn this dream into a reality. The idea filled me with inexplicable joy.

When I discussed this plan with another pastor who had been in UMAP, he asked, "And why do you want to go back there? It's best to forget that place."

Thinking that she might like the proposition, I invited my wife to accompany me. "I remember that place all too well, and I never want to see it again," she commented.

However, I felt the urgency to return, and off I went! I was able to make the trip thanks to the efforts of Ernesto Ruano, who lived in Camagüey then, and to the kindness of Julio Bajuelo, member of Second Baptist Church in that city, who kindly lent both his jeep and his time, agreeing to take us there.

It was Ernesto's idea to retrace, as much as possible, the same path that we had taken at midnight on November 27, 1965. From Camagüey, we went straight to the train station at the Lugareño Sugar Mill, today named Sierra de Cubitas, and from there, to the baseball stadium where all the recruits had been concentrated.

On the trip, my son David and another member of

Second Baptist Church in Camagüey, brother Sergio Martínez, accompanied us. We left the city at noon, and went directly to the train station in Lugareño, where the long journey from Havana ended on the morning of November 26, 1965.

The station remains the same: the same brick building with a roof made of wood and tiles, a typical railroad station like so many others in the country. It is adjacent to the highway, but about six hundred meters to the left. It is accessed by a dirt road, bordered by small wooden huts on both sides.

Seeing the place again brought back memories of the bewilderment and weariness that we felt after that endless journey, reviving the confusion of our arrival and the rude and hasty orders to board the waiting trucks. It was to once again feel the fear of the unknown and the dreadful sensation of being unjustly dragged, completely against our will, and without the least possibility of escape.

For a short while it seemed as if I were watching a movie, a dramatic spectacle of nearly 2,000 young men[1] who had arrived on a single train, debarked quickly, with expressions of exhaustion, panic, and curiosity written on their faces. I am not embarrassed to say that knowing all that was to occur afterwards, I felt enormous compassion for myself and for all the rest.

What kind of game did life have in store for us? How little we knew then of what was awaiting us! Which of us could have imagined the magnitude of the experiences that we would have? All of our bewilderment and fear at the events of that day, as we debarked the train at midnight, was a genuine naivety, even a childish ignorance, if you will. We were forcibly transported, without knowing where or what we were going to do. Everything was cloaked in an atmosphere of violence,

---

[1] This number is an approximation, based in the number and capacity of the train cars. This was not the only train, nor the only station where recruits in arrived Camagüey that week of November, 1965.

urgency, and mystery, but we were never able to sense the diabolical magnitude of what had come upon us. We initially thought that it had been some kind of mistake, and that it would be corrected shortly. Exhausted as we were then, we did not yet realize that we were experiencing only the beginning of the ordeal, and that the worst was yet to come. The curiosity of so many new things, after all, clouded our feelings.

My son was interested in knowing if seeing the area again brought back memories. When Ernesto and I began to explore the train station, he approached two old men and a woman who were sitting on the platform. They looked at us with interest as we took pictures and looked over the place.

David greeted them and gestured toward us as he explained, "They were here thirty years ago when UMAP was here. Do you know what that was?"

"UMAP!" said the woman as she opened her eyes and tightened her lips.

"Do you remember that?" David insisted.

One of the old men said, "Why, of course we do. I worked carrying meat to the camps. Look, I remember him," pointing to Ruano. He walked over and asked Ernesto, "Weren't you in La Reforma Camp?" Ernesto had been there after he left Las Marías and was separated from us. It is a small world and the old man had a remarkable memory.

"All of them came this way," the woman said signaling to the railroad, "and they sent them to the camps. There were many camps around here: La Reforma, Laguna Grande, Las Marías, and many more. Some of those boys got married and remained. Not all of them were the delinquents they were said to be." The woman kept squinting her eyes and moving about restlessly.

"Some criminals came, but so did many good people," said the old man.

"I'm forty-three years old; I was just a girl at that time,

but I remember perfectly well that it was a horrible thing. In those camps many people were mistreated," added the woman.

"The truth is that there are some things in the past..." said the old man who was sitting next to them, speaking very slowly, as if he was choosing his words carefully, "that seem unbelievable—but which were true."

We stayed for a few minutes chatting with the strangers and verifying that even after three decades, the memory of the events and their subsequent interpretation had remained. It was comforting to note that the truth always wins out and reveals itself in the end. Who can say that oral tradition is unreliable? The provincial newspaper, back then, published a number of articles that spoke positively of UMAP. My own father traveled from Cárdenas to Las Marías with a copy of *Granma* in his hands, to show me the good intentions that the organization had.

"It's a shame that you give more credit to the newspaper than to your son," I told him, hurt and heartbroken. I began to tell him of my experiences, very different from what was expressed by the reporter. But my father did not believe me. At that time, nobody dared to talk about the atrocities committed in the camps. Only the reporter Luis Báez commented, in passing, on April 14, 1966, that some officers gave vent to their frustration and rage. He said that the first groups were no good and that some of the officers did not have the patience or the experience required.

The press, especially the provincial press, reflected the positive development of the millionaire brigades in the cutting of the cane, and published interviews to raise awareness of the many Jehovah Witnesses who said that they had abandoned their faith, as evidence of UMAP's successful re-educative efforts. They also wrote, on a few occasions, marvelous things about UMAP. However if you delve into the consciousness of the people, there you will find the invincible and powerful truth. Nobody remembers what the press published.

A woman, who was an adolescent at that time, had no problem thirty years later telling strangers that, *"in those camps many people were mistreated."* Where did she get that knowledge? Did she read it from some newspaper? Did she learn it in school, or in a history class? No. The UMAP experience has remained being an ugly stain for many years and it is still very difficult to talk about.

The stories of what happened in the camps were neither written about nor exposed. Events that took place thirty years ago may well have been totally forgotten and unknown, but for the conscientious efforts of those who remember and publish them. However, at the slightest opportunity, memories emerge. The woman had grown up hearing comments that, due to her tender age, had made a great impression upon her and had been fixed in her memory forever. She also said *"not all of them were the delinquents they were said to be,"* which implies that she had mastered *all* of the details of the story. The old man who was listening to the conversation in silence, paused thoughtfully and chose his words carefully to recount past events that *"seem unbelievable, but which were true,"* demonstrated that he remembered those unpleasant events as a shameful reality.

The meeting with these people was crucial for me. It convinced me that I was doing nothing wrong by writing about the memories of my experiences in UMAP. A short time after having published the first articles in *La Voz Bautista* (*The Baptist Voice*), certain groups of people objected to my historical venture into the topic. "Why after so many years do you want to write about that?" they protested.

History is usually written some years after the events occur, when people begin to realize their significance. It is written, because just as there is individual memory, so also is there collective, social memory, which preserves and records the events. For an event to be recalled properly it must be mentally captured so that what has been said by word of mouth can be confirmed, and to make its accuracy indisputable. The accounts of eyewitnesses are indispensible for unraveling the tangled web of human commentary, where contemporary imaginations or evil intentions often can wreak havoc on the recorded truth of history. Without these testimonies, it would be easy for us to lose the reality of human events altogether. When individual eyewitnesses have the same memories about an event, while the official account differs, it becomes clear that the truth has broken out of the bonds created by the official narrative.

The comments from the old man about, *"things in the past that seem unbelievable, but which were true,"* and of the woman, *"not all of them were the delinquents they were said to be,"* convinced me that I had to write this book, and even take the risk of being misinterpreted. I wanted to record the certainty of the events and at the same time show that human mistakes are not only possible, but also common; therefore, it is essential that we address them rather than conceal them. It is necessary to point out that in every historical event there are all sorts of nuances, as well as all kinds of people. In life, no event is absolutely bad or absolutely good. Wherever there are human beings, there will be range of qualities and virtues, defects and contradictions. It is as irrational to think that we do everything well, as it is to believe that everything we do is wrong. That is why it is necessary to preserve the record of the events and to allow freedom, so that they may be interpreted from different points of view. It is the only way to get close the factual reality, especially as time marches on and there are fewer and fewer eyewitnesses that remain.

When we finished talking with the people that we met at the station, we walked toward the baseball stadium where as recruits we had been concentrated. When we arrived, I immediately recognized the same steps, the same fence, and the same pine trees that were at my back when we got off the trucks and had to file in at the center of the field. Everything was amazingly the same, although it had deteriorated after so many years. It was drizzling when we visited the stadium, which did not keep Ruano and me from walking and being in the same place where we had waited to be accounted for and transferred. The human mind is phenomenal. Again, I was able to see the military men who received us and those who were surrounding the stadium. I felt the terror that I had experienced that night as they read the lists, horrified by the fact that we were being separated. Since they were organized in alphabetical order, one could hear his own name, but did not know if the other brothers would go to the same place until they were called out. So, in that way we were divided into groups to be put on the trucks.

It was incredible. I could remember the voices that shouted our names. I felt once again like the twenty-two year old man who had incredulously witnessed the collapse of his dreams, turned by decrees into social scum, into prison meat, like some of the others who were there. I was one of the multitude whom they pretended to re-educate and return as people useful to society. When I placed my feet in the same place where I had stood—terrified—at midnight on Saturday, November 27, 1965, I was instantaneously flooded with the emotions I had experienced there years before. However, I did not feel the same anguish, but in its place, an enormous sense of satisfaction. From the first moment, the experience of returning to those places was liberating.

Before we left Lugareño for the last time, we visited a woman who had married a UMAP recruit and had lived her entire life there. She recounted the story of her experience that same night:

> *The night of November 26, 1965, the young people in town were very excited because on Los Pinos Street the famous Roberto Faz orchestra was going to play. All the dancers were waiting for the night with joy. Suddenly, without any explanation, some soldiers came and confiscated the amplification equipment. To everyone's disgust, they began to hear rumors that the equipment had been taken to the stadium.*

Some of the young people decided to investigate. Everyone was very angry because the activity which had been planned and eagerly awaited was suddenly interrupted. Without much thought they went to the stadium.

In fact, there was a mobilization. Military officials and soldiers surrounded the place. In the field, some browsed through and prepared lists. It was a secret operation. The young people asked questions, but the response they received was that they had to leave immediately. Someone heard a rumor that spread quickly: "In Havana they picked up all the tramps, the junkies, the delinquents, and religious people. They are here because they are going to be forced to work in the country."

But the majority of the people in the Central Sugar Mill knew nothing about what was about to take place, and many wondered in the early morning hours what was happening when they felt the incessant movement of trucks transferring the personnel after the arrival of the train.

When we left the woman's house, we started the trip to Las Marías. In order to save time and fuel, we used a new road that goes through the northern part of Camagüey that links the city of Morón with Victoria de las Tunas. We drove on that road until we turned onto the dirt road that links the Senado Sugar Mill to La Gabriela. From there we were on exactly the same route used on November 27, 1965. I recognized La Gabriela from a distance. It is located on a hill and I could see the same old water tank far above the coconut trees. To the left of the road, half a kilometer before we reached the town, I recognized the cane field where I had been working on that last day in UMAP, June 29, 1968.

The camp, which was the last place I had been assigned before I was demobilized, was located at the entrance to La Gabriela, to the right. It no longer existed! We discovered that the chief who was in charge of the farm, in whose house Miriam and I met the first time, thanks to the arrangement that Lieutenant Concepción had made, no longer lives there either. The settlement is less lively now. I could no longer recognize the farm office where I went almost daily when I worked as an accountant. We took the road from La Gabriela to Jagüeycito where the headquarters of the battalion had been, the two kilometers that I had walked so many times.

In Jagüeycito we saw the ruins of the second company of the battalion. The barracks that were made of masonry walls still were standing but the roofs were gone. Behind them, we saw the ruins of what was once the office of the battalion. That was the place that I had to pass secretly when Lieutenant Marrero gave me the fake passes to go on leave. From there I had quickly gone on my way when I was given the leave after my grandmother's death. It was also the scene of my concocted story about my sister's letter, which enabled me to go on leave in the middle of the harvest. The many trees, especially the coconut trees that I knew so well, were all still there. We turned right and took the road to Las Marías.

The dirt road was now in poor condition. Everything was gloomier, more obscure, and abandoned than before. Since it had rained recently and it was very cloudy, the landscape seemed even bleaker. I do not remember who at that moment said to David, very impressed by the remoteness of the place, "Can you believe this is where your father ended up when he was about your age?"

David glanced over to him as he said, "Even imagining it is terrible."

Then Brother Sergio added, "Not only that, but your mom came here too to visit with him."

While listening to him, I saw Miriam once again, young, thin, twenty-one years old, blond, and very pretty. She would carry bags full of food, traveling the same road every month, getting on trucks, carts, tractors, while taking as many things as she could to Las Marías, where she had always arrived with the same smile, managing to be the first one to show up. I felt my chest tighten and had to breathe deeply several times. I praised the Lord because He had taken care of her.

We continued on the dirt road and crossed the river, still lined with bamboos. Because the road curves, it crosses the river twice over bridges that sink almost to the level of the current. For that reason, the unit had been inaccessible when the river was high. We passed by the place where Lieutenant Rosabal allowed us to sleep all afternoon during that first harvest, when we had worked eighteen hours every day. We continued ahead on the dirt road, crossing the river a second time. The height of the grass and the canes obstructed our view, but I could tell that Las Marías was near, because of, among other things, the beating of my heart. "If memories don't deceive me," I commented, "that grove that you see in the distance is Las Marías."

"You're right; look at the house in front of the unit!" said Ernesto, after we had advanced about 500 meters.

Above the bushes overgrown with grass, we saw in the distance the upper floor of the masonry house that had always been painted white, located across from the camp. How many times had I seen that house on my walks after passing the s-shaped curve after the last river crossing? Because it sat on a slightly higher elevation and was white, it could be clearly seen from afar, even on moonlit nights.

Incredibly, I was extremely happy and eager to arrive. If, while I was fenced in at Las Marías, someone had told me that I would come back one day with an immense sense of nostalgia, I would never have believed it. There was about a kilometer still to go. The dirt road was worse in this part and it was full of large puddles of stagnant water. Although nothing would keep us from reaching the camp since we could have walked from there, I was concerned that the jeep would get stuck.

I was approaching, at last, an inescapable rendezvous with my youth and my past. It was inevitable, although I did not anticipate witnessing a miracle that day. I was about to bury my pain and my UMAP experience forever. The jeep moved ahead very carefully until we arrived at the border of the grove where we had received the visitors.

We turned left to shortcut the remaining distance that separated the dirt road from the camp. I knew that it would be impossible to find the same antiquated, wood barracks that had existed years before in Las Marías. I expected to find a newer prefabricated shelter like so many others in Cuba that were used to move schools or volunteer groups to the country. I planned to ask permission to enter it to search for traces of the old camp.

The overgrown vegetation prevented us from seeing where the unit must have been. As we walked on, I looked at the masonry house, slightly transformed and a little impoverished. I looked for the wooden grocery store that had been across from the camp where, from the porch, one could see the entire unit, but it had disappeared. I searched in vain for the huts that had been behind the grocery store, where Tiempo had lived, the old man who had approached the fence in the early days of our stay there. I looked for the huts that had been on the other side of the house, but they had also disappeared.

The jeep stopped near the house, just in front of the Military Unit 2237 Oscar Lucero, of the Military Units for the Aid of Production. The driver, without knowing it, in one of those inexplicable and wonderful coincidences that life sometimes gives us, stopped the vehicle in exactly the same place that the trucks did when we were taken there in the early morning hours of November 27, 1965. But this time there was no yelling, nor soldiers to push us so that we would get off.

All of us fell silent.

Silence is the language of the human soul for its

transcendent moments. I got off and walked around the jeep looking for the camp. But it was to no avail. The place was now a large field of grass.

Las Marías simply no longer exists.

I cannot deny the emotional impact. It was as if a vital part of my life had been erased. I stopped to look at the fields with grief. The grass, almost two meters high, occupied the entire area where the camp had been, mixing in the distance with the cane fields and the bamboos near the river. Two partially built houses were now in the place where the barracks had been. For some time, I was unwilling and unable to break the silence that had encompassed us all. It was the final tribute to all the pain experienced in that place.

When I could finally open my mouth, I could only say, "My God!"

I closed my eyes trying to reconstruct from my memory the place where I had suffered so much.

"There must be some remnants of the camp somewhere," said David. "Let's hunt for it!" He and Ernesto began to track through the thicket. Standing motionless, I could not take my eyes off the high grass that covered the fields before me. My mind insisted on reconstructing the landscape that I, at times, had hated so much, and now had disappeared forever.

"Here is the floor of the barracks!" shouted Ernesto. They had found the concrete floor of the place where we had slept, easily recognizable in spite of the invasion of the grass. We ran there and began to find the holes of the wooden posts that had supported the roof, around which we had tied our hammocks. I was sure that when we were coming down the dirt road, I had seen something that reminded me of the bathrooms. We began to walk along what remained of the floor of the barracks. We groped our way through the bushes with our hands, felt where the center aisle between the bunk beds had been, and searched for the back door where we entered the barracks.

Then we saw through the grass, two meters from the end of the concrete floor, the ruins of the old latrines that had been used as a jail for the unit, and where we were once forced to store our wooden boxes with our belongings. The walls were still standing, and we were able to climb on top of them so we could see the surrounding area better. From there we discovered that a section of one of the barrack walls that divided the officers' room from the dining hall was still standing.

"Was it here that people were kept, and an officer would throw water on them in the middle of the night?" asked Sergio, referring to the ruins over which we had climbed, because he had read an article in *La Voz Bautista* in which I had written about the episode.

"Can you believe that?" I remembered the expression on the man's face. He always showed a cruel but satisfied expression when the water tank next to the jail was filled bucket by bucket. He enjoyed mistreating those unfortunate ones by throwing water on them as they slept naked on the floor. I wondered what had become of him. What kind of life had he lived afterwards? Was it not himself whom he most harmed by destroying any semblance of goodness that had been in his soul, while torturing helpless kids who had not committed any crime?

Since every person bears the consequences of the things he does and thinks, I suspect that sergeant has lived a dismal, joyless life. If he had to struggle his entire life with a mind that was capable of actively inventing such evil schemes, it must have been hellish. The young victims of his abuse eventually walked away and never saw him again, and it is likely that their lives were more blessed and worthwhile than his was.

My son went back to climb on top of the house that was being built in order to take a picture of us from there.

"Aren't you disappointed to see the house in ruins?"

asked Sergio.

Gradually, I had gotten over the frustration of having found everything destroyed. I realized that God had taken me there after thirty years, exactly for that reason, so that I could see it like that. "Quite the opposite!" I said as I looked over the area where the unit had been, and as the specific memories, conversations, and feelings that remained from three decades ago came rushing back to me. I could even remember the voices of the recruits and the officers in Las Marías, which came back through time. "Finding the place in ruins is fantastic!" I insisted.

Deeply moved, I could not speak; an annoying lump had formed in my throat. The place that I had once considered an evil fortress had completely collapsed. Its miserable ruins, abandoned, invaded by weeds and now completely worthless, were irrefutable proof of God's love for me and of the victory of faith, hope and love.

I wanted to cry.

As I contemplated the destruction of what had been a cruel place of torment, many things became clear to me. Some convictions that I have always held were affirmed like never before. There, standing over the jail of Las Marías, I thanked the Lord that evil and injustice will never triumph. Although they seem to have temporary power, in the end they destroy themselves. It is just a matter of time.

I remembered the words of Lieutenant Marrero when I paid him a visit shortly before the trip to Las Marías. "That was barbaric!" he declared.

Someone had given to me his address in Madruga, and I went see him one afternoon. I parked my car in front of his house. From a rocking chair on his porch, Marrero watched with much interest as I approached him. "Lieutenant Marrero, you are looking very good! I'm so glad to see you."

"And you are...?" he asked me as he got up, trying to

recall me from his memories.

"Many years have passed," I answered, "but you and I were together somewhere thirty years ago."

"Albertico! You can't imagine how many times throughout my life I've thought about you. I thought you had left the country." Visibly excited, he added, "If you have come to visit me, then it's because I wasn't so bad." Marrero told me that when he was chief of the unit he had done his best to lead the company well, but he realized that the entire methodology was wrong. Then he wrote desperate letters to his wife, in which he expressed his decision to get himself discharged, which he did as soon as he was able. Who would have known that he was suffering, and that even the chief of the unit hated what was going on, just as the recruits did? He suffered also, having to live a considerable distance from his family, and he had hoped that it all would come to an end. Thirty years later, as I visited him, I better understood the reasons for his concerns for me when I was in Las Marías and the joyful hope that he always had each time that he announced to the troops any upcoming change in the conditions at UMAP.

He was greatly pleased with my visit, and we talked for a long time like two good friends who had become reacquainted after a long separation. While we were able to talk and remember past experiences, both of us were happy because they were behind us. In this world created by God, evil can have power for a time, but it never can have a future. The final victory does not belong to it.

After thirty years, I returned to the place that could have destroyed my life, and I found it devastated. So, I began to feel love for those ruins, which for me had become a grand symbol of the justice and mercy of God. They were also a reminder that all the bad things of life are fleeting. When somebody is involved in a critical situation it seems that time stops, that there is no strength, and that the future has escaped and abandoned him. So many times, there in Las Marías, I had thought that everything was finished for me! I remembered the night when I wished to die and asked the Lord with all my heart to take me while sleeping! What a tremendous mistake it is to allow our circumstances to rule our lives!

Everything passes. If God had listened to me that night, and acted according to my wishes, how many blessings I would have missed during the rest of my life! Wishing to die, I was dismissing a multitude of happy experiences that would come later. I returned to Las Marías with a completely different perspective from what I had then. In 1965, I thought that my dreams and the best days of my youth had been ripped away.

In sharp contrast to the young man who believed that he was living through his greatest tragedy, the man who stood over the ruins of the jail in Las Marías has seen many of his greatest desires fulfilled many times over. He has lived an immensely happy life. He has traveled the world. God has granted him so many satisfying experiences that sometimes he doubts that there could be any more. How foolish I had been when, locked up in Las Marías, I believed that that experience would greatly limit the opportunities for my life!

How could I have known that night, when we discovered the broadcast from Trans World Radio during the harvest of 1966 and the officer prohibited us from listening to it, that today I would be one of the preachers on that radio station? God's plans are certainly surprising. My radio program, also broadcasted from Bonaire, the Netherlands Antilles, but recorded entirely in Cuba, is entitled *"Messages of Faith and Hope,"* precisely because of what it meant to us to have heard a Christian program then in that place. Today I receive letters from people all over the country and abroad thanking me for the encouragement and the teachings that they receive through this program. The most precious thing to me is to receive such letters from that same area of Camagüey, where we first heard Trans World Radio ourselves.

After seeing what God has done in my life, I recognize that the confinement was not of great consequence, nor did it hinder any of the His plans. It was actually a necessary digression at the beginning of our life journey, a mere unexpected inconvenience that the Lord used to prepare, strengthen, and solidify both Miriam and me for the life and ministry that awaited us.

I returned to Las Marías with the closest friend from my youth, just as we had traveled side by side on June 27, 1965. Together, we encouraged each other in the early days, until both of us were separated from the group and our lives took different paths. I could never explain to myself how this brother had abandoned the faith. I always hoped and prayed that someday he would return to the Lord. It was a long wait, and it was not fruitless. Life had given him many turns, and after three decades of living in different worlds, his life took another turn, a positive one, and we were reunited. We went together to explore the ruins of the place of our early misfortune.

There we rejoiced together, because even though his life had been a mere shadow of what it might have been had he fixed his eyes on Jesus during that time, the trial had not destroyed him nor his faith entirely. Seeing him standing on the wall of the jail was for me a very moving testament that the Lord will always be faithful to His promises and that His Word is true. Without Ernesto's presence on this trip to Las Marías, my memories of him would have been very painful. But instead, his company was a source of indescribable joy.

Ernesto's presence also had another lesson for my life. He had turned away from the ways of the Lord, while I had continued in spite of my doubts and bewilderment. UMAP had become a turning point for both of us, and the contrasting ways we dealt with the difficulties caused our paths to diverge. As a result, our lives have been completely different. He was faced with problems and situations that were completely absent from my life. I experienced blessings and opportunities that never managed to reach him. He had been given the requisite qualities and gifts for successful ministry for God's glory and for the extension of His work, but everything was cut short by a wrong decision. While it is true that the Lord forgives us when we are unfaithful, it is also true that our unfaithfulness can ruin our greatest opportunities. That is a fact that we must never forget.

We got down from there and found the ruins of the newer bathrooms that we had built in the unit, buried by the grass like everything else. As silent witnesses, a couple of avocado trees, now much less leafy, had stood the test of time. Then we walked to the grove where we had always received the visitors, the place of so many conflicting emotions. Although they were overrun by grass and neglect, I recognized the mango trees that had provided us with shade, under which Miriam and I had sung and cried so many times. There also, was the dilapidated and abandoned scale to which the cut cane had been carried on carts for weighing, before being moved to the train cars.

Pushing aside the tall grass with my hands, I arrived at a tree with which I had had a prior meeting. I recognized it, even though the years and neglect of the place had affected it. The afternoon that I had left Las Marías, I had talked to it as if it could hear me and I had said, "I will return some day, and I will bring my children to tell them the story."

I managed to get to it with some difficulty, caressed its bark and…it may seem foolish! I began to talk to it in the same way I had done almost three decades before. "You know? I have told the story in great detail. I have written a book. My son is here with me."

I caressed its bark again in the same way that one treats an old friend; it took some effort to control my emotions. Because of the thicket I could not sit against it as before. Under that tree, during the visits, Miriam and I knit together our plans and dreams. Together with that tree, I wrote letters and poems. Many intimate emotions were covered by its friendly shade. There it stood, still planted firmly in its place, although weaker, older, carrying far fewer leaves. That tree knows more about me and about my feelings than many people who know me. I would like to come back and sit under its shadow, for Las Marías has ceased to be a horrible memory for me.

We started the trip back by taking the new dirt road south. We went to the highway from Morón to Las Tunas, which is about a kilometer from there. If I ever go back again, it will be much easier to use the main highway. While traveling back, I looked for the huts of the Haitians who sold homemade candies in the cane fields, but they no longer exist either. The sugar mill of Las Marías had absolutely disappeared, as if God had wiped it off the map. Praise the name of the Lord!

We traveled to the city of Camagüey almost without talking. I was meditating about everything that I had just seen in Las Marías and the emotions that I experienced as I began to think about this final chapter. The further I moved from Las Marías the more solid became my conviction that my experiences in that place thirty years ago, rather than destroying me, had deepened my Christian faith and the ethical values that have sustained my life. It has required a great deal of effort for me to realize that! The man who writes these lines has been blessed by the changes that he had to undergo and the lessons, some of them bitter, that he learned at UMAP. Should I thank those who classified me as social scum and sent me there?

Still, after so many years, I do believe that UMAP was a tremendous injustice. It should never have existed.

Joseph told his brothers, *"As for you, you meant evil against me, but God meant it for good."* [2] In the same way, I also can thank the Lord for my trips to Las Marías. The first one was difficult and confusing, but it set in motion a process by which I came to better understand life, myself, and my relationship with God. The last trip was illuminating because I recognized that

---

[2] Genesis 50:20

He had instead destroyed the things that might have ruined me. This realization became a consolation, a blessing, and a source of spiritual and emotional growth. I realized, on the way back, that this was really not a new discovery. Paul had written about it thousands of years earlier: *"And we know that for those who love God all things work together for good, for those who are called according to his purpose."*[3] But people are proud and we do not learn well from other people's experiences. It is our own life adventure that causes us to realize that the great tragedies in life can either destroy us or lift us up, depending exclusively on the attitude that we take. Nothing and nobody can do more harm to us than we do to ourselves by allowing bitterness to gain a grip on our hearts. It does not matter what causes us to suffer; there will be victory, as long as we manage to maintain the purity of our souls, kindness, and hope.

Why did God put in my heart this irresistible desire to go back there after so much time? I needed to find the answer to many questions, some of them very foolish, which I had asked myself then. In Las Marías, standing over the ruins of the jail, even though I did not hear Him audibly, I can say that I heard the voice of God speaking to my heart very clearly. *"You see? Do you see what became of this entire place where both you and I suffered? Think of all the things that you have enjoyed since then. Count, if you can, all the blessings that you have received. Do you want a better response to the desperate questions that you asked then? Do you think that I was unfair, and that I abandoned you by allowing such a difficult ordeal?"*

I returned to Las Marías to conclusively deal with the source of my grief, my self-pity, and my despair. There I laid to rest, once and for all, the awkward obsession of a victim who had undergone a bitter test, which in the end was only that: a test. The suffering I experienced at UMAP, far from detracting from my life, actually conferred great benefits to it. The greatest of all was increasing my knowledge of God and deepening my relationship with Him. After all, He was always

---

[3] Romans 8:28

by my side, even during the times when I tried to elude Him.

Today I recognize that God was in UMAP and that He was with us in our suffering, and not just in mine. He suffered with us, who are Christians, but also with the homosexuals, with the drug addicts, the delinquents, and all those that were considered social scum who were uprooted from their homes and sent to Camaguey. Maybe there were good intentions, but it was a failed, mistaken, and cruel attempt to re-educate.

Today I can also see how God was working through some of those who were part of the officer corps. Even without professing a belief in Him, they showed empathy, compassion, and kindness to the recruits. Many tried to be fair, humane, and positive amid the negative circumstances that surrounded them. The experiences with Rosabal, Concepción, Marrero, Zapata, Rojas, and many others, besides mitigating my anguish in UMAP, taught me lessons that I badly needed: lessons that added a new dimension to my life.

Thanks to them, I learned to recognize and form my view of men not by their uniforms, but by their hearts. Is that not what God is looking for in all of us? We can find many traces of the divine image in every human being, as long as we look at them with the love of Christ. If we, who say that we know Him and serve Him, are also full of contradictions, then we of all people should be generous and understanding when considering others, even though they may be in a different place than we are due to the circumstances of life.

While searching the Internet for historical material on UMAP, I found an article titled, *UMAP: Where There was Never a Humane Gesture*. I respect the author's opinion, who like everyone else, certainly suffered greatly. My experience was different. Having been a victim of abuse did not keep me from seeing that not everyone was the same there. I met decent officers who, from their points of view, tried to do the best job they could. They were open, when the opportunity arose, to relationships of genuine friendship, and to helping the recruits whenever possible. I also met others whose lives, customs, and attitudes were truly inhumane.

With respect to those who made UMAP and sometimes my life into a living hell, I hope that they have found, or will someday find and receive God's forgiveness. In the end, we all need that same eternal forgiveness, and He is generously willing to grant it.

Although it may seem incredible, I now remember that time of my life nostalgically, for God used it for my good. It was a very difficult time but...why not? It was also a blessing.

And a blessing from God is the best gift that a person can receive.

Epilogue
What Can't Happen?

In November 1998, my wife and I lived in an apartment on General Lee Street in the Santos Suarez district of Havana. One morning, as she was busy doing her daily housecleaning, there came a loud and insistent knock at the door. Two weeks earlier, I had left for Germany to attend a congress in Berlin, and afterward to take a trip to Spain.

Miriam opened the door to find an elderly man, with a very nice appearance, who looked at her amiably as if to suggest that he knew her. But, at first, she did not recognize him.

"Do you know who I am? Take a good look and see if you recognize me."

The man's eyes glistened with tears showing genuine emotion. Miriam looked at him closely, desperately trying to recognize him from her memories. Although she could not remember his name, she did perceive from studying his face that he was not a complete stranger. The man was dressed in sports clothes and came accompanied by a younger woman.

"Are you sure you don't know me...? Think about Las Marías," the visitor suggested to her.

She shuddered and breathed deeply as she began to

remember the details of her first encounter with this man, thirty-three years earlier in La Gabriela, in the northern part of the province of Camagüey. At that time, he wore a military uniform and was the second in command of what she considered a concentration camp. Recognizing him, she felt once again like the naive and frightened girl who came with her mother to visit her fiancé. The visit had been arranged quietly since it violated military rules. The officers had prevented, for two months, the slightest contact of the young recruits with their families. Miriam had traveled all night long, and still had not known how the meeting would come about. She was exhausted, nervous, and fearful that an unforeseen problem would ruin her plans after traveling to such a remote place.

Now, this man, who seemed like a ghost from the past, was standing in the doorway of her house. Dressed as a civilian, he asked for me excitedly, with tears in his eyes. What was happening?

"Yes, I know you. You are Lieutenant Concepción," she said as she tried to hide her shock.

"I've already been told that Alberto is traveling in Spain. I have been looking for him for a long time! I've always remembered him. I can't wait to see him and give him a hug."

Miriam could not shake the feeling of utter astonishment. It took her a few moments to deal with what she was feeling, considering what he had once represented. She had had very little contact with him, only seeing him for a few minutes the first time, and on a few other visits that she made to Las Marías before he was transferred. Although she knew that he had been agreeable and friendly to me, still he personified everything that UMAP had taken from our lives. Before the lieutenant knocked on our door, he had been to the seminary asking about me, and they directed him to our house. Some distant relatives of his had visited our church in Pinar del Río, and after they spoke to him about me, he decided that he would like to see me again. He was retired from the army and was living in Havana. He spoke with Miriam and then, before leaving, left his address and telephone number, repeatedly begging her to have me call him when I returned, and for us to come and visit him.

Miriam was moved by the amazing affection that the lieutenant demonstrated for me. More than thirty years had passed. He was one of the chiefs and I was a single recruit among the thousands that were under his command among all the units he served. She knew that we had had a good relationship during the seven months that he was in Las Marías; his affectionate interest in finding me was nevertheless surprising.

When I returned from Spain, I was stunned to hear about the surprising visit of Lieutenant Concepción to our home. Immediately, I called him back and we went to visit him that same night. The warm embrace, and the kiss that he gave me, along with his tears and the happiness that he showed when he saw me, broke my heart and confirmed my conviction that God's ways are truly unfathomable. The richness of feelings and emotions that we experience when we allow God's love to control our lives is boundless.

Only now will I confess what I had preferred to hide when I initially published *God Doesn't Come in My Office*. For that purpose, I will repeat a short section from the beginning of the book:

The 120 men who would become that company were gathered, and the "welcome" was overwhelming; an officer shouted with disdain at the whole troop, "You are here for engaging in socially unacceptable behavior within our society." And threateningly he added, "Today you have entered this unit, but nobody knows if you will ever get out!"

There we were told about the honorable duty of serving the homeland in the Obligatory Military Service. They insisted that it was our own deviated behavior that led to our being unworthy of enlistment in the regular units. We were threatened repeatedly with indefinite extension of our internment unless we amended our behavior by hard work and military discipline. The officer added that they could give us neither the name nor the address of our location because it was a military secret. He stated that from that moment on we would not have any communication with our families.[1]

Earlier in the book, I deliberately omitted the officer's name. In spite of all that he said and all the terror that I felt then when I heard him, this same officer offered me his friendship a short time later and allowed me, against specific military orders, to communicate with my family. Is there any greater proof that God can change a man's heart? Concepción understood and strongly agreed that, both for me personally and for many others who, by the circumstances of life, fell under his command, it was a mistake to have sent us to UMAP. That is why I did not want to reveal the name that by now my readers have surely guessed.

What do I do now?

When we came together after so many years, he was able to remember even the smallest details of the experiences that we had shared in Las Marías, including our conversations and discussions. He revealed to me his personal beliefs and experiences, those things that we only share with those who hold a special place in our lives and whom we hold in high esteem. He wanted to hear about the things that had happened to me during all the past years, as well as my tenure as a pastor. In the moving and unforgettable conversation that we had that night, he confessed that, although he had not considered himself a Christian at that time, he was now a believer. I met his family and he proudly introduced his son to me, who occasionally visits a Baptist church. Like a close relative, he showed me every part of his house. He handed me a document that he kept all these years that proved to be of great value to me.

I could not have even imagined that I would ever experience something like this after having heard his welcoming speech that night in Las Marías. God is great! What

---

[1] See Chapter 1

can't happen? Any casual observer of our emotional meeting thirty years later who didn't know about our life's stories, would be unable to guess the origin of our relationship and the enormous distance that separated us then. Nor could such an observer imagine the transformation that we both experienced. Just like the huge gap between the young man who arrived at Las Marías and the lieutenant that received him on November 27, 1965, it looked as if this unbridgeable chasm would seal our destinies. But the God of the Bible is always pleased to give us some surprises.

Those of us who have devoted our lives to the preaching of the Gospel can never lose sight of some truths that I have tried to highlight throughout this book. We must hold on to these truths even when it is controversial or when we have strained relationships with other people. If we want to be consistent with what we preach, our convictions must guide our performance with whatever or whomever we meet.

The first conviction, if we believe in the God revealed in the Bible as loving, omnipotent, omniscient, and sovereign, we must assume that His redemptive purpose will be available to every person. His love for humanity includes everyone, even the most renegade and estranged from Him. *"For God so loved the world, that he gave his only Son, that whoever believes in him should not perish but have eternal life."* [2]

God may despise the habits, attitudes, feelings, or even a person's ideology, but He loves and desires a relationship with every person. He desires it so much that He did not spare the life of his only Son in order to achieve it. Regardless of a man's previous attitude and personal history, God is available to him the moment that he seeks for Him, because that is what God desired from eternity past. If as Christians we believe in the goodness of God, and we have happily come to experience infinite mercy, we cannot lose that perspective when relating to others. Any person who crosses our path is the object of the same mercy and redeeming love of God. Wherever we find

---
[2] John 3:16.

ourselves, we are surrounded by people whom God loves with an everlasting love. He may abhor a man's behavior, but He loves and wants to transform his heart.

There is not a single place on earth where there is a human being who is without hope of redemption by God. If we are conscious of that, the people we find all around us should be seen and received with good will. If only we were to do this, we would prevent a great many problems and mistakes.

I do not understand how some Christians live as if God were interested only in those who believe in Him. They seem to support a bewildering and harmful idea that God loves us exclusively and despises all others who think and act differently. Such attitudes seem to suggest that God despises and is eager to condemn the world; those who hold them perhaps forget that He does not *"wish that any should perish, but that all should reach repentance."*[3]

The second conviction, if we believe in the God revealed in the Bible as loving, omnipotent, omniscient, and sovereign, is that we must assume that his redemptive purpose encompasses every human circumstance, even those that seem most contrary to His will and character. A situation like UMAP can be used by God to build in us stronger, Christ-like character, although from our human point of view, it might be full of painful injustices.

This is a concept that brings about lively disagreement. In the opinion of some, such overwhelming events can have only a negative effect. The consequences are far-reaching; the trauma induced can last a lifetime, in individuals and in society. Such trauma prevents forgetfulness, and transfers to future generations an incomplete, sometimes distorted and incomprehensible memory, which is always a negative memory. This opinion is correct, but only partially; even the worst events can have positive effects.

---

[3] 2 Peter 3:9.

It is true that the men recruited to UMAP came from widely divergent social backgrounds, and were simply thrown together without any attention to the disparity of their needs, abilities, customs and problems. Because these distinctions were ignored, the re-educative mission of the organization, which was the official purpose of its existence, was impossible to achieve. Had human dignity and respect been an integral component of the re-educative program, and individual differences taken into account, UMAP would have been a different story. There would have been no need for unconvincing explanations of its necessity, which never managed to satisfy those who were involved in the program as recruits or family members.

It is also true that the atrocities that occurred are inexcusable. The eventual dissolution of UMAP was tacit admission of its contradictory purposes and procedures, as well as its inherent malevolence. Even the changes implemented in the first few months, which were significant enough that the second group of recruits had a completely different experience, were not enough to redeem the organization. UMAP disappeared completely, as if it had simply been erased, with even the name having been deemed unsalvageable. It was decided to impose the *borrón y cuenta nueva*[4] because this was the only logical conclusion. Within the larger society, the shameful memories were such that the psychological process of memory suppression took place, to the extent that eventually, the slightest mention of the UMAP affair was considered an indication of malice or anger. As a result, those who had been involved in UMAP were denied access to the healing process that occurs in a context of discussion, transparency and accountability.

These truths do not preclude the possible redemptive value of the UMAP experience to those who lived through it. Human suffering invariably puts life into perspective, realigning our value system. As we search for the ability to

---

[4] Spanish idiom for "making a fresh start"

survive adversity, we are often strengthened spiritually, and grow closer to God.

The recruits were not the only people learning difficult lessons brought on by the sufferings of UMAP. Many of the officers were also challenged to make adjustments in their convictions and beliefs. Some grew even more callous by committing the very acts and atrocities that brought UMAP to an end, but others matured and faced those challenges positively. As a result, they began to exhibit consideration and kindness toward the recruits under their command, which eventually benefitted the officers themselves, because they outgrew their prejudices. It is no wonder that when a person holds pleasure, ease, and a lack of responsibilities as his highest goals, his moral principles, his intelligence, and his spirituality actually deteriorate. However, when life takes us through difficult experiences, it can also cause us to become kinder, stronger, and more mature people. Paul taught, *"For this slight momentary affliction is producing for us an eternal weight of glory beyond all comparison."* [5]

Because these officers were brought into close contact with so many Christians, surely the message of the Gospel left its mark on some of them. When Lieutenant Rosabal helped to save our Bibles before a search was made, he was communicating to us something more than his disagreement of an injustice. What did his gesture (incomprehensible to us at the time) mean, when he signaled toward the sky as he was saying goodbye to us?

Not everyone manages to turn bitter experiences into opportunities for spiritual and emotional growth. Sadly, some become resentful, bitter, and hard. They are unable to rid themselves from the burden of anguishing memories. While unaware of its happening, they allow the past to keep them unhappy and frustrated for years. The bleeding wound can affect them for their entire lives; the past inserts itself into the

---

[5] 2 Corinthians 4:17.

present, and becomes an uncomfortable and constant companion. This is a tendency to be recognized and overcome.

And this is the third conviction: we must certainly believe that in the midst of affliction, a person can change for the better, gain a different vision, and learn the most magnificent and essential lessons for life. If we believe in a God Who is loving, omnipotent, omniscient, and sovereign, then we will hold that everything that happens to us is a part of His redeeming purpose. If we believe this, then nothing can surprise us. We will not be astonished even by the arrival of a person who may one day seem to ruin our lives, and then later reappear as a completely different person, bringing out the warmest feelings from our hearts. God is great. He is good. He transforms people's hearts. With some, He does it quickly. Only He knows why He takes more time for others, or never does it at all. Undoubtedly, men and women can be changed. We must believe it and expect it, and be open to surprises that only God can give us. On the path of life, we will likely see amazing events in which the grace of God is obviously being showered on us and on many lives around us. Since that is so, let us be warm, generous, and inclusive. As the Apostle Peter said in the house of the centurion Cornelius, *"God shows no partiality."* [6]

If our lives on earth are full of surprises, what will we encounter when we cross the threshold into eternity? The spiritual realm is invisible to our eyes now, but it will be our reality for all of eternity; even then, we will surely never cease to be amazed at the incredible ways in which God carries out His purposes. Therefore, we should face even the most perplexing events of our lives now with faith and patience.

Life is so very brief! It is past time for us to learn how we can discover the hidden meaning of events and circumstances, which in the past have made no sense to us. We need only to practice those truths and principles that we hold. God will take care of the rest. Can we even begin to

---
[6] Acts 10:34.

imagine the surprises that God has in store for us in eternity?

Absolutely not!

"What no eye has seen, nor ear heard, nor the heart of man imagined, what God has prepared for those who love him." [7]

THE END

---

[7] I Corinthians 2:9.

Afterword 2010

From the daily newspaper "Granma", official periodical of the Communist Party of Cuba, the following was published on Wednesday, September 1, 2010, on page 4. Carmen Lira Saade, director of the daily newspaper, La Jornada, in Mexico, during the second part of her interview with Dr. Fidel Castro was published under the title: *"The World of the future must be common to everyone."*

HAVANA. Although there is nothing that suggests that he is uncomfortable, I think that Fidel is not going to like what I am going to tell him:

"Commander, all the charm of the Cuban Revolution, the recognition, the solidarity of a large part of the world's intellectual elite, the great achievements of the people against the blockade, in short, everything went down the drain because of the persecution of the homosexuals in Cuba."

Fidel does not shy away from the subject. He neither denied nor rejected the assertion. He only asked for time to remember, he said, how and when the prejudice was unleashed in the revolutionary ranks. Five decades ago, due to homophobia, homosexuals were marginalized in Cuba, and many were sent to labor camps for military-agricultural work, charging them at the time with being counterrevolutionaries.

"Yes", he remembers, *"they were times of great injustice,*

great injustice! He repeats emphatically, "Whoever did it. If we did it, we...I'm trying to remember my responsibility in all this because, of course I don't have these type of prejudices."

It is known that among his best and oldest friends there are homosexuals.

"But then, how did it happen that such hatred was unleashed on those who are 'different?'"

He thinks that it all began occur as a spontaneous reaction in the revolutionary ranks, which came from traditions. In the past, Cuba did not only discriminate against Negroes, but also women, and of course, the homosexuals...

"Yes, yes. But not in the Cuba of the "new morality", of which the revolutionaries were so proud from the inside and out. Then, who was directly or indirectly responsible, for not putting a stop to what was happening in Cuban society? The Party? Because this was the time when the Communist Party of Cuba was not explicit in its statutes to ban discrimination based on sexual orientation."

"No," said Fidel. "If there was somebody responsible, it was I...It's true that at that time, I couldn't look after this issue...I was immersed in the October Crisis, in the war, in political matters..."

"But this became a serious political problem, Commander."

"I understand. I understand. I repeat, we didn't know how to deal with it...systematic sabotage, armed attacks, were happening all the time: we had so many terrible problems of life and death, you know?, We didn't pay enough attention."

"After all, it became very difficult to defend the revolution abroad...The image had deteriorated forever in some sectors, particularly in Europe."

> "*I understand. I understand.*" He repeats again, "*it was just....*"
>
> "*The persecution of homosexuals could have taken place almost anywhere, but not in revolutionary Cuba!*" I said to him.
>
> "*I understand. It's like when a saint sins, right? ... It's not the same as when the sinner sins, right?*" Fidel gives a hint of a smile, and then he gets serious again.

The interview went on, but with respect to the subject of this book, the above portion of the transcript will suffice. Although he did not mention the inclusion of drug addicts, young men hostile to the revolution, religious people, and others who were sent also with the homosexuals to the fields for military-agricultural work, it is obvious that he is referring to UMAP. Why did the journalist overlook the rest of the recruits who were sent to those labor camps? It was probably because of the importance that sexual diversity now has, or perhaps she was referring to the units within UMAP that had been created exclusively for homosexuals. The reality is that more than just a few people believed that all of us who were in the units were homosexuals. That Granma published Dr. Castro's comments recognizing that "*there were moments of great injustice, great injustice!*" is, undoubtedly, a historic and a meritorious action. For me, it is meaningful and I am thankful for it. The rare times on previous occasions when there was any mention of the units, nothing was expressed like that. They only argued that the units created an opportunity for those people who were unfit to serve in the military an opportunity to serve their country. Thus the huge discriminatory and oppressive connotation of UMAP was avoided.

As I read the rationalizations in the interview, I grant that, although the October Crisis occurred three years before the creation of UMAP, there can always be extenuating circumstances that sometimes promote, or prevent us, unfortunately, from acting with more foresight and basic justice.

Nothing is more reassuring than to live long enough to see how the truth, always present but frequently hidden in a complicated loop of events and human decisions, manages to finally come to light. Those of us who suffered understood immediately that those units were a great injustice, but it is good, very good, to listen to the official recognition of this reality.

It is never too late, and it will always be commendable, to own up to the responsibility for the mistakes committed. Such declarations cannot change the past, but they do permit those who were injured to experience the recognition that every victim of injustice deserves. Therefore, the recognition was welcome.

Afterword 2010